Manchester, UK

Amsterdam, Netherlands
The Hague, Netherlands
Stuttgart, Germany

Middelburg, Netherlands

BRITISH INDIA

Uttar Pradesh

Faizabad
Calcutta

GUINEA

Gold Coast

Ascension Island

Indian Ocean

Cape of Good Hope

N
W E
S

WHAT *the* OCEANS REMEMBER

Life Writing Series

WILFRID LAURIER UNIVERSITY PRESS' Life Writing series celebrates life writing as both genre and critical practice. As a home for innovative scholarship in theory and critical practice, the series embraces a range of theoretical and methodological approaches, from literary criticism and theory to autoethnography and beyond, and encourages intersectional approaches attentive to the complex interrelationships between gender, class, race, ethnicity, sexuality, ability, and more. In its commitment to life writing as genre, the series incorporates a range of life writing practices and welcomes creative scholarship and hybrid forms. The Life Writing series recognizes the diversity of languages, and the effects of such languages on life writing practices within the Canadian context, including the languages of migration and translation. As such, the series invites contributions from voices and communities who have been under- or misrepresented in scholarly work.

Series editors:
Marlene Kadar, York University; Sonja Boon, Memorial University

WHAT
the OCEANS
REMEMBER

SEARCHING *for* BELONGING *and* HOME

SONJA BOON

WILFRID LAURIER
UNIVERSITY PRESS

This book has been published with the help of a grant from the Canadian Federation for the Humanities and Social Sciences, through the Awards to Scholarly Publications Program, using funds provided by the Social Sciences and Humanities Research Council of Canada. Wilfrid Laurier University Press acknowledges the support of the Canada Council for the Arts for our publishing program. We acknowledge the financial support of the Government of Canada. This work was supported by the Research Support Fund.

Funded by the Government of Canada

Canada Council   Conseil des arts
for the Arts   du Canada

ONTARIO ARTS COUNCIL
CONSEIL DES ARTS DE L'ONTARIO
an Ontario government agency
un organisme du gouvernement de l'Ontario

Library and Archives Canada Cataloguing in Publication

Title: What the oceans remember : searching for belonging and home / Sonja Boon.

Names: Boon, Sonja, author.

Series: Life writing series.

Description: Series statement: Life writing | Includes bibliographical references and index.

Identifiers: Canadiana (print) 20190073012 | Canadiana (ebook) 20190073179 | ISBN 9781771124232 (hardcover) | ISBN 9781771124256 (EPUB) | ISBN 9781771124249 (PDF)

Subjects: LCSH: Boon, Sonja. | LCSH: Boon, Sonja—Family. | LCSH: Identity (Psychology) | LCSH: Home—Psychological aspects. | LCSH: Belonging (Social psychology)

Classification: LCC CT310.B66 A3 2019 | DDC 971.07092—dc23

Cover and text design by Lime Design Inc. Front-cover image: "De plantages 'Nijd en Spijt' en 'Alkmaar' aan de Commewijne Rivier" (ca. 1860), Nationaal Museum van Wereldculturen, inventory number TM-3348-17. Page viii image: "Het hospitaal op plantage Sarah," Nationaal Museum van Wereldculturen, inventory number TM-H-3357.

The epigraph, "The past is remembered and told by desire," is copyright © 2015 by Lauret Edith Savoy, from *Trace: Memory, History, Race, and the American Landscape.* Reprinted by permission of Counterpoint Press.

This book is printed on FSC® - certified paper. It contains recycled materials, and other controlled sources, is processed chlorine free, and is manufactured using biogas energy.

MIX
Paper from
responsible sources
FSC® C103567
www.fsc.org

Printed in Canada

TO OMA,

for bequeathing your stubbornness to me

(and for teaching me how to make pastei*),*

AND TO OPA,

for the music.

"THE PAST *is* REMEMBERED

and TOLD *by* DESIRE."

—LAURET EDITH SAVOY

CONTENTS

List of Figures x
Author's Note xi

	Timeline	*xii*
	Prologue	*1*
1.	Tumbling Stones	*5*
2.	The Facts	*15*
3.	Van Gogh's Nose	*29*
4.	La Vie en Rose	*39*
5.	Opa's Books	*59*
6.	Lineage	*75*
7.	Due South	*99*
8.	Disruptions	*125*
9.	Roosje	*131*
10.	Slavenregisters	*147*
11.	Broko Pranasi	*169*
12.	Joorayee	*195*
13.	Oceans	*215*
14.	Unfoldings	*241*
	Epilogue	*259*

Acknowledgements 263
Notes 269
Bibliography 291
Index 307

List of Figures

1. Gezicht op de Oostkerk te Middelburg, 1743   43

2. Leonard Frederik Adolf Heinemann as a young man   72

3. Accounting declaration (first page), Sarah plantation   83

4. Accounting declaration (third page), Sarah plantation   84

5. Nieuwe Waag aan de Waterkant te Paramaribo, 1829–1830   139

6. Plantation map, de Resolutie, ca. 1871   199

7. Baba and Mai monument, Paramaribo   234

8. Henriette Mathilde U-A-Sai as a toddler   239

Author's Note

This book is based on archival research undertaken
in the Netherlands, Suriname, England, and Canada.
All conversations have been reconstructed.

TIMELINE

1621	Geoctroyeerde Westindische Compagnie (Dutch West India Company) established.
1667	The Dutch capture Suriname, formalizing their claim later that year as part of the Treaty of Breda.
1720	Middelburgsche Commercie Compagnie established.
1798	*Presumed birth of Frederik Noa. Parents unknown. Place of birth unknown. The family name, Redout, was given in 1863, when slavery was abolished.*
1801	J.H. Dietzel is granted Lots 212 and 213 along the coast in the Coronie district, Suriname. These lots would later become Sarah plantation.
1814	Willem I outlaws Dutch slave trade; law comes into full effect in 1818.
1816	*Birth of Philip Elias, son of Frederik Noa. Place of birth unknown.*
1818	*Birth of Edward, son of Frederik Noa. Place of birth unknown.*
1821	Sarah plantation established by John Bent.

		1827	*Birth of Eva Albertina and Frederika, presumably daughters of Frederik Noa, at Sarah plantation, Suriname.*
		1849	*Likely birth of Joorayee Radha, in Uttar Pradesh, British India.*
		1853	*Manumission of Marlon 2e, son of Eva Albertina, under the name Jacob Schove.*
		1855	*Birth of Madleentje Paulina, daughter of Frederika, at Sarah plantation.*
		1862	*Manumission of Annette, eldest daughter of Frederika, under the name Annette Juliane Jurgon.*
1852	Publication of *Uncle Tom's Cabin*.		
1856	Anthony Dessé purchases Sarah plantation.		
1863	Abolition of slavery in all Dutch colonies; beginning of a ten-year apprenticeship period.		
		1866	*Arrival of a Chinese contract labourer named U Asai in Georgetown, British Guiana.*
1867	Surinamese Immigration Society established in Amsterdam, with goal to bring Chinese labourers to work on Surinamese plantations.		

	1868	*Arrival of Chinese contract labourer named U Asai in Suriname.*
	1872	*Birth of Sahatoo, son of Joorayee Radha, in Uttar Pradesh, British India.*
1873		Arrival of the *Lalla Rookh*, the first ship of indentured labourers from British India.
	1874	*Joorayee Radha and her son, Sahatoo, arrive in Suriname aboard the Kate Kellock, the sixth ship of indentured labourers to arrive on Surinamese shores.*
	1880	*Joorayee Radha and Sahatoo granted leave to stay in Suriname. Joorayee listed as being in a relationship with a man named U-A-Sai. Sahatoo formally becomes Sahatoo U-A-Sai.*
	1885	*Birth of Adolphina Margaretha Redout, daughter of Madleentje Paulina.*
	1900	*Death of Joorayee Radha, followed by U-A-Sai's departure from Suriname.*
	1902	*Adolphina Redout in a relationship with Theodor Wilhelm Heinemann. Heinemann was born in Stuttgart, Germany.*
	1905	*Birth of Leonard Frederik Adolf Heinemann, son of Adolphina Margaretha Redout and Theodor Wilhelm Heinemann in Albina, Suriname.*

		Birth of Henriette Mathilde U–A–Sai, daughter of Sahatoo U–A–Sai and Maria Mathilda Ameerbie, in Paramaribo, Suriname.
	1911	
1916	End of British Indian indentured labour immigration to Suriname.	
	1935	*Marriage of Henriette Mathilde U–A–Sai and Leonard Frederik Adolf Heinemann. Birth of their first child, Deryck Heinemann, later that year.*
	1949	*Leonard Heinemann travels to the Netherlands for a year of musical study at the Royal Conservatory of Music, The Hague.*
1954	Suriname granted home rule within the Kingdom of the Netherlands.	
	1969	*Birth of Sonja Boon, granddaughter of Leonard Frederik Heinemann and Henriette Mathilde U–A–Sai, in Manchester, United Kingdom*
1975	Suriname gains full independence, becoming the Republic of Suriname.	
	1975	*The Boon family immigrates to Canada from Venezuela.*
1980	Military coup orchestrated by Dési Bouterse, followed by several years of political unrest in Suriname.	

PROLOGUE

~~~~~~

Middelburg, the Netherlands, 2014

ARCHIVES ARE SEDUCTIVE SPACES. In their vaults, they hold the dreams and longings of those who have come before us. Their reading rooms, meanwhile, gather the hopes of all the researchers who have ever come through their doors in search of the fleeting truths of the past. Archives are places where a seeker's dreams can come true, but also where they can be shattered. You would think that after almost twenty-five years of poring over manuscripts, I would have learned to heed these warnings.

Middelburg, the capital of the Dutch province of Zeeland, had captivated me; I was fully in its thrall. *Omgeschakeld*, I'd written as a social media status update. Switched over. It's a word that implies a mechanical change of direction. I'd thought I was writing about language; the transition from English to Dutch had been almost seamless. But really, it was sensual. Within just a day of my arrival, Middelburg had overwhelmed my senses. I wanted to consume the city, and I wanted it to consume me. And so, perhaps, I was particularly susceptible to seduction.

I wasn't in Middelburg as a tourist. Although I could easily lose myself in this Dutch city's winding streets, I hadn't come to check out the town. Not primarily, anyway. My destination was much more specific. I had come to visit the Zeeuws Archief, the archives of the province of Zeeland. On a grey Monday morning, I arrived at ten on the dot. A sign on the front door indicated that they were doing roof work. Apologies for the disturbance.

Archives are usually quiet, bright, peaceful places to work. This one was no different. The man at the front desk took my identification, handed me a registration card, and pointed me in the direction of the lockers. Downstairs, in the study room, another staff member showed me how to use the computers. Natural light streamed in from above, and the work tables were large. Materials arrived with quiet efficiency. There was some drilling on the roof, and dust fluttered to the floor at regular intervals, sparkling in the light. A broom and dustpan stood at the ready, and every now and then a staff member swept up the debris.

I'd come to survey the records of the Middelburgsche Commercie Compagnie, a powerful trading company established in Middelburg in 1720. Company journals. Account books. Surgeons' diaries. Employment records. Invoices. Receipts. This collection is so complete that it's been included in UNESCO's Memory of the World Register, and I couldn't wait to explore it.

Among other activities, the Middelburgsche Commercie Compagnie had plied the waters of the Atlantic, engaging in the slave trade between Africa and the West Indies. Over a seventy-year period between 1732 and 1803, the company transported 31,095 enslaved Africans across the Atlantic, and by the late eighteenth century, Middelburg had become the centre of the Dutch slave trade.

The Dutch transported some 550,000 enslaved Africans to the Americas between the sixteenth and nineteenth centuries.

Approximately 300,000 of them ended up in Dutch Guyana, now Suriname. Some were my ancestors, and it's their stories I was looking for.

~~~~~

My relatives weren't quite sure what I was doing back in the Netherlands. To be fair, I wasn't sure yet either.

"Oh, you're doing a genealogy project," some of them said, after I emailed them to let them know I was coming. This they understood. But as our conversations continued, I found myself growing frustrated with their responses.

"It's not genealogy," I insisted. Genealogy is about family trees. About embedding the self into a logical history organized by marriages and legitimate offspring. Our family has a messy history, and we don't fit these moulds. They know this too. But perhaps this didn't matter to them as much as it now seemed to matter to me. When they pressed, I couldn't explain.

"It's more," I said.

That was as far as I got. Inside, I was irritable. Sullen. Uncomfortable in my skin. I couldn't explain what it was that beckoned me. I could only say what it wasn't.

The last time my relatives had seen me, almost fifteen years earlier, I was a musician, a flute player on the brink of a professional career. There was so much to catch up on. They were interested in my work. They wanted to understand. They wanted to bridge this space that had opened up between us.

In my resistance, though, I didn't really want to talk. I wasn't yet ready to bring them into my world. I wasn't even sure I wanted them to understand. I wanted to be on my own. Alone with my thoughts. Alone with the dead.

Be quiet, I wanted to say. *How can I hear anything with all your gabbling?* That wasn't fair, and I knew it. But I needed the silence of the archives, so the ancestors could speak.

~~~~~

Where does a story like this begin? Does it begin in the narrow, cobbled streets of Middelburg's city centre? Or in the salt waters that brought my ancestors to the Americas? Does it begin in stilted conversations and uncomfortable silences?

Or does it begin with a question?

For me, the question—if not the whole story—emerged in another seductive place an ocean away: on the wild, untameable island of Newfoundland.

I

Tumbling STONES

~~~~~~

WE DISCOVERED MIDDLE COVE BEACH within days of our arrival in Newfoundland in 2008, and over the years, this small beach just outside St. John's has become one of my favourite places to hang out. There's nothing much to it; on that even locals would agree. It's just a sheltered inlet between craggy cliffs, one of thousands along the coast of Newfoundland. It's not sandy, but then, so few beaches here are. Rather, it's covered in thousands of small beach stones that form hills and valleys according to the ocean's moods.

Some are round, others egg-shaped. Some are perfect for skipping across the water. In the summer, the stones are warm, almost alive with the sun's energy. In the winter, when ice waterfalls cling to the cliff's edge creating ethereal curtains of bluish white, the cold bites into your skin and the stones are best left alone. A few years ago, a storm rushed in and the ocean took them all away, leaving behind a stark, barren landscape. But months later, the beach stones were back, once again shifting with the tides.

Officially, you're not supposed to collect them, but somehow, over the years, at least a dozen have found their way into our home. I can't help myself. The beach stones are smooth and soft, sharp edges worn away by their constant tumbling in the ocean's waves.

At home they lie cool and heavy, each a comfortable weight in the palm of my hand. One has a thick quartz vein running right across it. Another, round like a perfect pumpernickel loaf, is purple, tiny bands of grey circling its balanced shape.

When they are wet, each one is a jewel, glowing rich and warm. But when dry, they almost fade into one another. Indistinct, their meaning is collective, rather than singular. As a group, these stones hold the rhythm of the sea; together, they make water music: a serenade of waves rising and crashing against the shore, and then, as if in response, a clattering rush of stones spilling over each other at the water's edge. As they bump and roll against one another, they tell each other's stories, too, shaping and polishing that smoothness that I cup in my hands every summer. In them is the story of this place called Newfoundland. In them, too, I have discovered, is the story of my family, a collection of tumbling stones worn smooth by oceanic migrations, each one a fragment, together an always moving landscape of histories, memories, longings, and dreams.

~~~~~

I have no roots here. There is nothing that binds me to this windy rock in the North Atlantic, no family history that clings to the cliffs or washes up from the seas. But it is here, among the polished stones of Middle Cove Beach, that I first began to grapple with questions of origin, here that I started thinking about the meaning of home, here that I began to work through my own desires for belonging.

Home is important to Newfoundlanders, place central to their identity. Many can pull their family histories across this island, tracing stories that go back centuries. They can picture the saltbox houses where their grandparents lived; they walk the paths of their ancestors; they know the voices of those who have come before them. As a people, they are one with the land, deeply rooted in this place, profoundly shaped by weather, landscape, and the volatile moods of the sea.

"Where are you from?" they would ask during our first year here, and I would struggle to answer.

"Most recently from Vancouver," I eventually said, and it was true.

"You must have married a Newfoundlander," they said confidently, because they couldn't imagine any other possible reason to be here.

But that wasn't true.

I'm a Mainlander, a Come From Away. Someone who doesn't quite fit, whose roots haven't dug themselves into this soil or crawled along these rocks. *Come From Away*. It's a phrase that used to frustrate me. It made me angry. A Come From Away will never belong, will never fit in, this phrase suggests. *Mainlanders aren't like us*, it whispers. More than this, a Come From Away is an interloper, someone who doesn't really have the right to be here. The boundaries were drawn well before we arrived, and none of us had a say in where we were placed.

"No," I'd shoot back, "I'm an NBC—Newfoundlander by Choice." But that term isn't quite right either.

I'd always thought that home was wherever I happened to be at any given time. I'd thought that community was something people built together, regardless of their origins. But maybe there's more to it. Living in Newfoundland, with the ocean lapping at my toes, has brought all of this into high relief.

~~~~~

I've spent much of my life on the outside, looking in. I've never lived in a place that I could fully call "home." I am rootless, my selves spreading across three continents, my histories spanning five. Belonging is fragile, fragmented, multiple. Home is impossible. I am an outsider within, a chameleon who can take on the guise of the local, but who will never be fully recognized as one, and, perhaps more to the point, will never truly feel like one. But here at Middle Cove Beach, where the capelin come to play, I wonder.

Middle Cove Beach is where my children learned to skip rocks. It's where they sailed the wooden boat that their great-grandfather built, some forty years ago, for their father. It's where they've fallen, shivering, into icy water, and where they've stood, laughing, watching as their dad poured a cold salt waterfall out of his boots. Middle Cove Beach is where they almost got caught behind a rogue wave, where they've clambered around like mountain goats, moving higher and higher along the slate cliff ledges. It's where we've watched winter storms, awed by the power of the heaving ocean, and where we touched our first capelin. Middle Cove Beach has taught us about weather, about water. It has taught us about fish and community. It has taught us about Newfoundland—the place and its peoples. It has shown us, too, the possibilities and the limits of belonging.

~~~~~

It was the prospect of a job that first lured me to St. John's in February 2008. I was almost finished my doctorate in women's studies. My research funding had ended the previous December, and we were living on air, a family of four scrabbling on almost nothing in Vancouver, one of the most expensive cities in Canada. The academic job market was miserable. There were only six possibilities in the entire country, and even then, I felt like I was stretching my expertise very thin.

"Do you ever wonder what will happen after we finish our degrees?" my friend Heather, a fellow doctoral student, had asked me a few months earlier. "Do you worry about getting a job?"

"Always," I said.

The abyss yawned before me. I'd been staring at it since the day I started classes, watching it come ever closer as I progressed through my degree. By this point in my program, it was only steps away and just as impenetrable as ever.

I'd scored two interviews, one in Lethbridge and the other in St. John's. Both windy cities, I said to my husband, thinking about our toddler, a tiny, fine-boned kid who was afraid of the wind's volatile moods. But that's where the similarities between those cities ended.

My sister was living in Lethbridge at the time. I knew the prairies from my childhood. It was an obvious choice. But I had no desire to move back to Alberta. And after over a decade of living along a coast, I wasn't sure I could handle a landlocked province again. St. John's, option number two, pulled at me: I liked the idea of the city. I loved its colours. My husband, Búi, meanwhile, born and raised in the Faroe Islands, wanted the rock, the fog, the wind, and the rain. He wanted an island. And our west coast ocean didn't quite cut it.

"The Pacific is beautiful," he said, "but it's not the Atlantic."

As the plane turned back over the ocean on its final descent into St. John's that February in 2008, I reflected on the journey that had brought me to this point. Research hadn't always been my passion. I had started out as a musician, a flute player who found wonder in sound, rhythm, and harmony. As a teenager, I had developed a relationship with myself through music. Music allowed me to speak when all other avenues had failed, to say things I would never otherwise have said, to move forward even when everything was confused. Music became my voice; it was how I could tell my own stories. For a long while, it was the *only* way I could tell my stories. For the more than two decades that followed, music had been much more than a job; it had been my heart, my body, my soul.

My decision, in 2005, to leave my musical career had initiated a long process of grieving, a mourning for everything that had been and could possibly be. The truth was that I hadn't managed to find a way to balance my musical life with my growing interest in research and my young family. As I watched the city appear below me, part of me wondered what I was doing. I was a flute player, not a scholar. But here's the thing. The interview in St. John's—and everything that came along with it—was the right step. It was the right time.

Sometimes there are no easy choices.

~~~~

I knew exactly two people in St. John's, neither of them Newfoundlanders. Like me they were Come From Aways who had somehow managed to find their way to the island. Like me, too, they were musicians. One, an Australian baroque oboist turned management type, had married a piano-playing Newfoundlander and followed her from Amsterdam to St. John's. The other was a flute player, Michelle. She and I had studied together at Indiana University, two of a group of five Canadians among a batch of almost forty flute students.

When I emailed her to let her know I'd be in town, she responded with an enthusiastic request: "Awesome! Do you think you'd have time to do a masterclass for the flute students?"

On the surface, it was a stupid idea. I had a full two-day itinerary that included not only a long interview with the search committee but also a public research talk, meetings with fancy people with fancy titles, and a series of meals where even my eating habits would be on display. But from another perspective, Michelle's invitation was a perfect opportunity for both of us. She would be able to introduce her students to a new teacher and new ideas. I would get to settle into the interview environment by doing what I did best—teaching and playing the flute. I could meet some students, get a feel for the university, and relax before the big event.

And so, hyped up on adrenalin and lack of sleep, I spent my first afternoon in St. John's listening to Telemann and Bach.

The weather had shifted by the next day, the crisp winter sun giving way to winds that roared around the hotel. Talking to my husband, I held the phone up to the window.

"Can you hear it?" I'd never experienced anything like it.

Outside, the rain was horizontal. In fact, I could have sworn that sometimes, it was completely upside down. Everything about me was wet, before I'd even managed to set foot outside.

I was nervous but also excited, in that state of hyper-awareness that can be either completely destructive or deeply generative. Pushed the wrong way, I would topple into that gaping chasm of absolute terror. But if I nurtured that awareness carefully, I could give the performance of a lifetime. I knew this sensation intimately. It was what sizzled in the background every time I put my flute to my mouth in front of an audience, and over the years, I had come to rely on this magic elixir. I not only enjoyed it, I depended on it.

In many ways, this interview was another performance, another show. But at two full days, it was going to be the longest performance of my career. And the stakes were high: there was a permanent, full-time job at the end of this rainbow. I had to shine. There was so much on the line.

~~~~~

I wasn't thinking about origins or histories during those three days in February 2008. I wasn't thinking about home, or memory, or belonging. I wasn't thinking about beach stones or about cobbled Dutch streets. No. I was looking forward, my eyes directed firmly towards a future horizon. With the possibility of a permanent job, everything was about pragmatics and practicalities. Búi and I had already spent countless hours discussing the various options. We'd played out possible scenarios in our heads. What were the schools like? Could we afford a house? Was there decent public transportation? Would we need a car? Would there be job opportunities for him, a trumpet player who had just finished retraining in mediation and negotiation? And what about groceries, extracurricular activities, parks, hikes? Was this a place where we could live and thrive?

But the past makes its presence felt in the most curious ways. The search committee had booked dinner at Red Oak, a restaurant on the top floor of The Rooms, a bold architectural statement of a building designed to pay homage to the fishing heritage of the province's outport communities. Outside, the wind and rain lashed against the windows. Inside, we were cozy. It was Valentine's Day, and the candlelight cast an intimate, wavery glow. All around us were couples celebrating romance.

"The view is incredible here when the weather's good," one of my future colleagues offered.

"Honestly, it is," another chimed in.

But equally honestly, we couldn't see a thing. It was dark outside, as dark as a messy, blustery evening in February can get. This was weather having a tantrum; like the toddler I'd left at home, it was yelling, screaming, and roaring. We couldn't see the harbour, or the ships, or the colourful houses. We couldn't see Cabot Tower standing sentinel on Signal Hill. We couldn't even see the city lights glistening against the snow because the heavy rain had washed all the snow away, leaving a slushy mess and deep, mucky puddles in its wake.

After a full day together, our conversations came easily, slipping and sliding across a range of topics both professional and personal. Travel. Food. Drinks. Research. Friends. Colleagues. Books.

"You should read my friend Gloria's book," one of the committee members said. "It's perfect for teaching. It's really amazing. And it just won an award."

I nodded and smiled at her effusiveness.

"It's all about women's sexual cultures in Suriname," she continued. "It's fantastic. Ethnography ..."

She kept talking, but my brain had snagged on something.

"Did you say Suriname?" I finally managed to ask.

"Yes. Do you know it?" She sounded surprised.

"My mom is from Suriname."

"No way! Do you think she knows Gloria?"

My mom, it later transpired, did indeed know Gloria. In fact, she'd dated Gloria's brother when they were teenagers growing up in Paramaribo. Apparently one of my second cousins was studying with Gloria in the Netherlands.

St. John's and Suriname, 4,600 kilometres apart. Just like that, my past and my future collided.

~~~~~

Like the water-worn beach stones that tumble along these shores, boundaries have softened in the years since we arrived in Newfoundland. I have learned some local ways, and silently, without any words at all, bonds of tenuous trust have formed.

"Boon," people will sometimes ask. "The Boons from [name your outport community]?"

I shake my head. No. Not those Boons. At heart, I'm still a Mainlander. And things divide along those lines here. Mainlanders hang with Mainlanders, or, if they're lucky, with Newfoundlanders who have spent so much time on the mainland that they've almost lost their own claims to belonging.

~~~~~

Where are you from?
I thought I knew.

The FACTS

~~~~~~

THE FACTS ARE STRAIGHTFORWARD. I was born in Manchester, England, to a Dutch father and a Surinamese mother. It was midnight on the cusp between Scorpio and Sagittarius, and because it was Manchester, it was probably raining. My parents got me a Dutch passport to match their own, and we criss-crossed the English Channel visiting family and friends. Hull, Dover, Calais, the stamps announce.

Two years later, we moved to Cumaná, Venezuela, and then, because I'd passed the larval stage, it was time for a new passport and photo. Look at me, serious and brown with uneven pigtails! My mom sent a copy to her parents.

"Look," she said, "we adopted an Indian child!"

A few years after that, on 16 March 1975, we immigrated to Canada and moved into a house with a curvy, creaking staircase on Sunset Avenue in Windsor. I went to Prince of Wales Elementary, where every morning we had to sing "O Canada" and "God Save the Queen." Less than a year later, we were on the move again, this time to Alberta and our little town on the prairie. A new passport, but no new photo. I wouldn't be rid of the old one until 1981, when I exchanged it for a curious picture where I'm sporting jagged bangs and, thanks to a peculiarity of Dutch passport guidelines, an exposed left ear. Canada and I formalized our relationship at citizenship court in 1984. And then we all lived happily ever after.

~~~~~

I could have pulled most of these details out of the public record. Birth. Death. Marital status. Nationality. Migration patterns. Governments love this kind of data. They hoard it. Bureaucracy exists for it. I should know; these are the materials I've spent the last few years sifting through in search of my histories. The problem is that they can't even begin to tell the stories of lives lived, of experiences, relationships, emotions.

They can't reveal that I was born a year too early for my parents' liking. Or that my father apparently danced and sang on the night of my birth, crashing out unrecognizable tunes on his accordion. They can't capture the snippets of memories that remain from our lives in South America: the smell of a fresh loaf of bread next to me on the back seat of our car, so tempting that I nibbled off a corner before we even got home. The pleasure of throwing a dead snake down a cliff, illicit but satisfying. The magnified horror of an Argentinian family friend, at her birthday party, falling, hands first, into a cactus. My fascination as each thorn released a single drop of blood. Government documents can't show me teaching a neighbour what happens when you run a piece of broken glass against your thumb. They can't capture my panicked flailings in the ocean waves while my mom was teaching me to swim, can't record the rhythmic slap slap slap of my flip-flops swatting at cockroaches.

Dry data can't tell me about my first encounters with winter: the spiky chill of fresh snow melting on my cheeks, the heavy weight of damp mittens hanging from crocheted strings, the smell of a warm, wet dog chewing ice pellets from his fur. They can't show the sled my dad made out of scraps of wood and painted a glossy forest green, or the hammock we hung across our front porch, or our trip to the Detroit Zoo, or my toes, straining and stretching so I could keep my head just barely above water in my friend Scott's backyard pool. They can't capture the fumbling feel of English syllables garbling in my mouth after three years of Spanish and a much longer family history of Dutch.

They don't show us getting stuck in a freak snowstorm somewhere in Minnesota or North Dakota, along a lonely rural route my dad had chosen because it would save us a few kilometres on the journey from Ontario to Alberta. Or my eyes blinking and squinting as we emerged in the bright sun a few days later, astonished to see a snowdrift in the car parked next to ours, its window left open.

And what about the fear, loneliness, and trepidation as I started school over and over again? The cool darkness in the Venezuelan classroom, where I discovered that my uniform, with its buttons running down the back rather than the front, was all wrong. The bright space with big windows way up on the third floor of Prince of Wales Elementary in Windsor. In Alberta, bearded Mr. Shapiro with his hippie guitar. A few months later and another school, young and beautiful Miss Horne, fresh out of university, her thick, dark hair parted exactly in the middle.

They don't record the envy I felt towards friends with relatives who lived next door, down the road, a couple of hours' drive away. Frustration at parents who wouldn't allow me to use colloquialisms. *Gross is a measure of weight.* Baffled ignorance about the game of hockey in a small town that, even today, continues to produce NHL players. Official government documents can't capture that sense of peace I still experience when I encounter low horizons and the endless prairie sky.

～～～

My passports tell me that I travelled to France, the Netherlands, Italy, Suriname, Chile, Bolivia, Peru, Ecuador, Curaçao, Colombia, the United States, Argentina, and Trinidad and Tobago, all before the age of six. By sixteen, I'd added Barbados, Belgium, Germany, Korea, and Japan, every entry and every departure meticulously noted. Another decade later, and I held a Canadian passport issued in The Hague and a Dutch passport issued in Vancouver. Short hair by now. Dangly earrings. Those big glasses so popular in days gone by. Today, there are even more stamps in my collection: New Zealand. Ireland. Denmark. The Faroe Islands. Switzerland. Guyana.

These are the facts. And facts matter. But they can't tell anyone why I travelled. They can't tell anyone why I had Dutch passports and Canadian passports, and why I've never held a passport from the country of my birth. They can't reveal why I looked like a little Indian child. Or why I love tasting the sounds of different languages. Nor can they explain how a family like ours came to be, each one of us born in a different country, on a different continent. They can't tell why I long for home even as I simultaneously seem to have resisted it.

~~~~~

Where is home? What does it feel like, smell like? Whose voices do I hear? Which sounds and flavours belong there? Unlike my students, always quick with responses, I have no answers to these questions. Home, as a concept with weight and memory, has no real meaning to me.

"Where are you from?" people ask. In Newfoundland. In Alberta. In BC. In Ontario. In Indiana. In Quebec. In Manchester. In The Hague.

"Where do you belong?" I hear. "Who do you belong to?"

"I'm a child of the world." An easy answer. And true. I've lived in many places.

But a child of the world is also a child without origins. A child of the world has nowhere to hang her hat. No place to call home, no place where she can ground herself. A child of the world is not uprooted, but unrooted. A chameleon constantly changing her colours, she becomes a mystery even to herself, a cipher that nobody understands.

Those of us who have moved around a lot leave traces of ourselves in various places. Home is a collage of scattered experiences and memories. More than this, it's a mirage, something intangible and inscrutable that we can never quite touch, always just out of reach.

~~~~~

When I became a Canadian citizen at the age of fourteen, we were there as a family: my father, my mother, my sister, and me. I remember only one aspect of the actual ceremony. After his speech, the judge called up each family, welcoming us into Canadian citizenship. Picture a process that went something like this:

"The Abidi family—Tariq, Ayesha, Zainab, and Noor—from Pakistan."

"The Lemieux family—François, Marianne, Jean-Marie, and Christine—from France."

"The Schroeder family—Max, Martina, Ulrich, Eric, and Daniel—from Germany."

Each family proceeded to the front of the room as a unit, a self-contained package of names united in a single history.

And then it was our turn.

"The Boon family—Johannes from the Netherlands, Hedda from Suriname, and Sonja from Great Britain." My sister, born in Canada and, at seven, sitting listlessly through a ceremony that bore no real meaning for her, didn't merit a mention. Even within the category known as Immigrants, we were the odd ones out.

Citizenship courts are strange places. They fix your place of origin in order to map your journey to becoming a Canadian. But I have no connection to Great Britain. It's where I was born, but it feels foreign. British English doesn't fit inside my mouth. The people don't feel right. The country smells wrong. When people ask me where I'm from, what should I say?

~~~~~~

We arrived in Canada in 1975, in the early years of the great Canadian experiment in multiculturalism. At school, I learned about the Canadian mosaic and the American melting pot. I was told we were a patchwork of individual identities, all gathered under the umbrella of Canada.

For me, multiculturalism was a celebration. It was the Scottish sword dance at a school assembly, and eating samosas and Greek salad during the early August Heritage Days in Edmonton's Hawrelak Park. It was intricate *pysanka*—Ukrainian Easter eggs—at the craft fair, and perogies and borscht from neighbours.

In Fort Saskatchewan, that prairie town near Edmonton that I called home for eleven years, there was nobody else who looked like me, nobody else who had that strange, indefinable, chameleon-like brown. I found multiculturalism a refuge. It was something that said I could belong even if I came from away. It said that my multiracial family and its complex histories—many of which I didn't yet understand—made sense. At school, I happily glued postage stamps from around the world onto a photocopied map of Canada, creating a collage to represent the multicultural mosaic. *Look at how colourful we are!*

What I didn't understand back then was that Canadian multiculturalism is based on the idea of *two*. Home, it says, can be in two places. After all, that's how a hyphenated self works: I could pledge allegiance to a hybrid identity. In Canada, I could be Japanese-Canadian. Greek-Canadian. Or that double barrel that I eventually claimed as my own: Dutch-Canadian.

What about the other bits of me? The problem is that multiculturalism can't acknowledge the complexity of multiple belonging. The mosaic assumes a singular origin story.

"Sonja," it says, "from Great Britain."

~~~~~

My kids, born in Vancouver and raised in St. John's, couldn't care less about family histories, identity, or belonging. Stefan, the almost-adult, is entirely future-oriented. Linear and logical, he's interested in computers, robotics, self-driving cars, and a world founded on efficiency. Historical museums are merely curiosities that reveal how much we've progressed and how much further we still need to go. He sees his future in aerospace engineering, flight, and the possibilities of interplanetary travel.

"History is boring," he says. "Why does it matter, anyway?"

Tóbin, the new teenager, much more of a romantic, is quite happy to traipse through abandoned cemeteries with me—at least until his attention wanders. He loves the fact that his ancestors include not only a knight, a goldsmith, and a prime minister, but also slaves and indentured labourers. He loves that his family history stretches across several continents, reaching from north to south and all around the globe. But even he, while driven much more by passion than his older brother, is nevertheless located in the here and now. He's lived in St. John's since just after his third birthday, so he's never felt a need to question the past. Newfoundland is the only home he's ever known.

For my husband, things are different. Growing up in the Faroe Islands, a small, insular country that in some ways bears a striking resemblance to Newfoundland, he's long felt stifled by traditions, and has spent his life trying to escape the weight of his heritage. His grandfather could place his friends by their resemblance to their forebears. "You," he would say, peering at a boy, "belong to the Olsen family." And then he'd nod, satisfied, rattling off some names, as he situated each new face in the family tree. Together, Búi's father and grandfather had followed the family back four hundred years. Apart from a branch in Iceland and a small offshoot somehow linked to France, they'd all stayed in the Faroe Islands. And that, in fact, is what my husband's name—Búi—means: one who stays close to home. How ironic, then, that Búi is the only one of his siblings who has chosen to live so far from where he was born.

~~~~~

I've never felt like I belonged anywhere. Maybe it's because we moved so often when I was a young child. Maybe it's because I'm brown—that not-quite-white that obscures what might otherwise be seen as an apparently unambiguous ethnic heritage. Or maybe it's because, since childhood, nobody else has seemed to think I belonged either.

"Exotic creature," I've been told.

"Vietnamese?" people have asked.

"What's your treaty number?" queried a salesclerk in Saskatchewan.

Maltese?

Maybe Pakistani?

Middle Eastern?

Chinese?

Japanese?

East Indian?

"A dark woman," my husband's good friend said, way back when we were still dating.

"Dutch," I'd reply. And it was true. It wasn't the whole story, however.

Moving to Newfoundland brought all these questions about family, heritage, and belonging into high relief. The kids brought home family tree projects and heritage assignments, and among locals, the questioning seemed to grow ever more insistent.

"We're just interested," people said, when my responses got snippy.

The thing is that I was interested too. I just hadn't quite figured out what to do about it. I had a busy job and an equally busy family. There were chess tournaments, soccer games, band practices, piano lessons. There were student loans, RRSPs, electricity bills. There was a mortgage. And car payments. Every day, it seemed, there was laundry. There was no time. There was no space. And so I put my questions—and everything that accompanied them—away.

Then, in February 2012, everything changed. A new message from my cousin Elvira appeared in my inbox. "*Sonja-Maria,*" it read, referencing the full, hyphenated name that I had ditched soon after arriving in Canada, "*laten we samen onze stamboom maken.*" Let's make our family tree together.

Elvira is my eldest cousin. More than nine years older than me, she's always occupied a shadowy space between generations. In some ways, she belonged more to my mother's generation than to mine, and it was only as I moved into adulthood that this started to change. For better or worse, this in-between position as the eldest child of my eldest uncle means that Elvira has been cast as the bearer of stories, as a confidante and go-between entrusted with a range of family narratives, not just nostalgic rose-tinted snippets from years gone by but also those long-simmering jealousies that can erupt unexpectedly in the present. She didn't have much choice in that role as family mediator, so perhaps it stands to reason that she was behind this collaborative venture that could see stories shared more broadly. But there are still disputes burbling under the surface. At least one family member wanted nothing to do with the project. Another mistrusted everyone's motives. As the invitations were received, however, many chose to participate. And slowly, over the years, our online family tree has grown, both wider and taller. An uncle has been piecing together German histories in Stuttgart. An aunt, meanwhile, has been perusing Moravian records from Suriname. Bit by bit, details have moved from the probable to the certain, from the invisible to the visible.

By the time Elvira sent out the invite in 2012, she'd already amassed a large body of material. I logged in and clicked through the photos she'd uploaded. My grandfather, a choir director whose footsteps I'd followed into the classical music profession, dapper in a white suit and slicked-back hair. My grandmother as a small child with ringlets and tiny earrings, gold bangles circling chubby brown arms, and later, as a young woman, petite and stylish with her sisters in downtown Paramaribo. A great-grandmother wearing traditional Creole dress. An imposing great-grandfather with a florid face and a puffed-out chest.

Another click, and I found myself as a toddler in my grandparents' back garden in Zutphen, the Netherlands, together with Elvira and another cousin. My grandmother's seventy-fifth birthday in 1986. Wedding photos. New babies. Each click brought back memories. My grandmother had passed away fifteen years earlier, but I could hear her voice and her laughter, smell the *kippenpastei*—Surinamese chicken pie—that she taught me to make, feel the firm foam of the bed that I slept in whenever we visited.

With another click, I found myself in uncharted territory. Here, suddenly, I encountered digitized transcriptions of emancipation records. I'd always known, of course. There were slaves in the family. I'd even written about Ghana for an eighth-grade social studies project. But that was vague, distant. Now there were names. I felt my mental landscape shift.

For me, as a teenager in small-town Alberta, a slave history wasn't about individual people. It was about finding a way to explain why I didn't quite look like everyone else. That history didn't seem *real* to me at the time, but it gave meaning to my brown skin and my mixed-race family. It helped make sense of why one of my parents got stopped at the airport and the other one never did. Why an adult cousin who'd immigrated to Canada was told to "go home," and why some of my classmates felt compelled to say the same thing to me. A slave past was a way of claiming my place, a way for me to value my differences.

I sense this same flirtation with the exotic in my younger son. He's fascinated by these elements of our shared family history, seeing in these stories a uniqueness, something that allows him to stand out from the crowd. But he's one of the lucky ones; these are adventures that he can play around with in his mind without ever having to live the consequences. My children look completely white. There's no hint, on their skin at least, that some of their ancestors were enslaved Africans and indentured labourers from what was then known as British India. My sons don't have to go through life in a world where they are seen as threats and where threats to their own physical safety are premised on the colour of their skin. They can try this history on for size; they can own it, because they are not tasked with living its effects every day.

<hr>

We'd been living in St. John's for almost four years by this point. Elvira's invitation brought all my questions about home and belonging to the fore again. The family tree reminded me of missing origins, and of deep-seated longings. But it also reminded me that I wanted more than places, dates, and names. A family tree was only the beginning. I wanted passion, desire, longing, grief, rage, sorrow, joy. I wanted it all, and with my background in music, I thought I knew how I could get it.

It was through music that I had first discovered archives—and the wonder of intimately touching the past. In 1993, soon after trading the brilliance of my silver modern flute for the intimate, chocolatey velvet of boxwood and ebony historical flutes, I set foot in the reading room of the Gemeentemuseum in The Hague for the first time. I was immediately enthralled. My classmates and I crowded into the heart of the collection—the basement storage vaults—our necks craning to see the treasures unearthed for us. It was cool and shadowed, temperature- and light-controlled to ensure that these documents could live on for as long as possible. The archivist showed us a medieval manuscript, pointing to the thickness of the paper, the richness of the colour. We passed it among ourselves.

"Wait," said one of my fellow students, "this is *eight hundred* years old?"

She couldn't even comprehend it. And to tell the truth, nor could the rest of us. Eight hundred years. In our hands. Right. There.

That day, I learned that medieval manuscripts, while fragile, are much less fragile than nineteenth-century ones. Pulp and paper mills may have revolutionized paper production, but they haven't made for lasting products. As I would later experience during the search for my histories, nineteenth-century paper can crumble at a touch, the past turning to dust before your eyes. I also discovered how much I loved to burrow into the past and to follow a story, finding pieces and trying to figure out how they fit together. Archives are my childhood dreams of locked trunks and dusty attics realized. They are the mysteries that filled both my imagination and the books I devoured. That day in The Hague was my first experience with the tactility of the archives, with the idea that the work I was touching was created by hand, and that hands, present and past, could somehow touch one another through time.

Later, my doctoral research would take me to other archives. In Lausanne, Switzerland, I read the personal letters of an eighteenth-century salon woman named Suzanne Necker, following her thoughts as she sought to reconcile her Calvinist belief with her glittering life in Paris. Over the two years that I worked with her letters, I got to know Madame Necker intimately through her words, her ideas, her turns of phrase. She came to life through her letters, her voice speaking to me across the centuries.

I thought I could do the same thing with my ancestors. I wanted to get to know them better. I wanted them to come alive for me in ways that a family tree, on its own, never would. But there was so much more at stake. I realize now that I should never have expected this family history project to unfold just like the early projects I'd undertaken. Archives are filled with promise and possibility, but they can also be deceptive. If researchers aren't careful, they'll find themselves telling the stories they *want* to see, and not the stories that are actually there. They'll look into the gaps and the silences, and they'll imagine all the possible riches there, because that's where the story lives.

"No position is neutral," a colleague reminds his students every year. This is true. Archival puzzles can fit together in a number of ways. How we see the patterns that emerge, and how we miss some other patterns entirely, is shaped by a range of factors—political, personal, ethical, moral, historical. We shore up our findings, but our results are inevitably coloured by our passions, our desires, our longings, our histories.

In those heady days in 2012, I somehow thought that I could remain neutral. I thought I could keep my distance. I thought I could take on the guise of the objective researcher. I didn't know that this work would pull me in and wouldn't let go. I didn't know that this would be the hardest archival work I'd ever done, that it would demand more from me—ethically, personally, and emotionally—than any work in which I'd previously engaged. More than this, I didn't realize that in telling the stories of my pasts, I would need to do to myself what I had done to so many others. I would have to excavate my heart.

I had no idea that this research, rather than anchoring me, might unmoor me.

Van Gogh's NOSE

I FOUND MY NOSE in the Van Gogh Museum.

One minute I was admiring *Wheatfield with Crows*, and the next, I was looking at my nose. Four of them, actually. Four bulbous protrusions on four dark faces illuminated by the glow of a small oil lamp. Hunched over the table, rough-hewn clothes against their skin, the painted family was sharing a pot of coffee and a single platter of lumpy potatoes whose contours matched the noses on their faces. *The Potato Eaters* was like looking in a funhouse mirror, everything slightly distorted but still recognizably me. I wanted to touch the painting, to feel those contours, which were so familiar, and yet, so strange.

I think I loved Vincent van Gogh's paintings before I had ever seen them in real life. The thick layers and textures, the richness of his colours, the sheer power of his artistic vision. In grade eight, I'd written a cheeky rhyme about van Gogh for an English-class assignment. *Vincent van Gogh*, I wrote, *did not know, that he could not hear, with a cut-off ear.* Looking back, I realize it was cruel, a cheap shot. But there I was, years later, at the museum with Vincent, his ear, his extensive oeuvre. The living blue of his sky. The vibrant gold of his wheatfields. The lumpiness of his noses.

The Potato Eaters is van Gogh's homage to a simple peasant existence—not the romantic vision promoted by political thinkers like Jean-Jacques Rousseau, a century before him, but a starker approach. The features are rough, shadows highlighting every angle, with tired eyes looking out of gaunt faces. The colours are dirty and, in van Gogh's words, "something like the colour of a really dusty potato, unpeeled of course."

There is something dark and ugly about *The Potato Eaters*. Van Gogh may have wanted to style himself the painter of the honest, simple, rural life, but there's a harshness to this work. This isn't a generous representation; it's the brush of an outsider looking in and not quite comfortable with what he's seeing. The paint is slathered on in thick strokes. The colours are dreary and heavy. Maybe *The Potato Eaters* is more about van Gogh himself than it is about his subjects. Maybe it is about an artist who hadn't yet found his style, hadn't yet worked out his vision. After all, it's an early painting, dating from the period when he was still seeking to establish himself as a professional artist.

Perhaps the painting is also about me and about my own discomforts. Who were these people who looked so much like me? Who were all these Dutch peasant folk who lived and toiled in small towns and villages: the farmers, the fishermen, the wooden-shoe makers, the tulip growers, the men who skated on canals and put their fingers in dikes? The potato eaters, I realized, were my history. These were my ancestors on my father's side. The faithful Catholics who named their children with Latin names and took religious orders. The men who snuck out of Mass early because the pubs opened at noon.

It was December 1992. I was twenty-three years old and visiting my extended family in the Netherlands for the Christmas break. My aunt Sheila and uncle Sonny lived within walking distance of the Van Gogh Museum, their tall nineteenth-century rowhouse nestled in the shadows of Amsterdam's famous Concertgebouw. And so it was that my aunt and I walked to the museum together, the two of us falling into an easy conversation on the way.

My aunt had found a nose in the museum too.

"It was a profile I recognized," Sheila said. "I'd seen it before. And I almost went over to say hello ..." Her voice trailed off.

"But?" I prompted.

"Then I realized why it looked so familiar. It was the Queen, visiting the museum with her bodyguards."

I would have recognized that profile too. An avid stamp collector as a child, I had endless Dutch stamps featuring Queen Beatrix's pixelated face in a range of colours and denominations, all carefully steamed from the packages and letters that family sent from the Netherlands.

The queen wasn't there when we visited, but the noses were, and as I gazed at them, I resisted the urge to feel my own nose on the landscape of my face.

I would visit the Van Gogh Museum again twenty-four years later, during the summer of 2016—this time, with my children. I told my sons that they would find their Opa's nose there. But they weren't impressed with *The Potato Eaters*, turning away from the dark and dreary browns towards the richer hues of van Gogh's self-portraits and bedroom. They weren't interested in my nose. Or in my father's nose. Or his mother's nose. They didn't care about the several generations of noses that preceded them, Dutch noses on Dutch faces.

On the generations of Catholics who had made their lives—for almost two hundred years—within a twenty-kilometre radius of the southern Dutch town of Dongen, in the province of Noord Brabant, where my father was born.

I've learned over the years that it's easy to make fun of Dutch people who come from Brabant. There's something unsophisticated about them. They laugh too loud. Drink too much. Party too hard. Their hands are too wide. Their accents too strong. They are too Catholic, so the commentaries go, and there are way too many nuns. Their noses are too big, too round, too bulbous. This is the Dutch side of my family. This is my inheritance. It's in the shape of my body. The sound of my name. Even my Dutch pronunciation has been inflected by the sound of Noord Brabant, hints of dialect that have marked my history on my tongue.

My dad's family tree is easy to piece together. One afternoon a couple of years ago, armed with a bit of information about naming traditions, I went searching through church and civic records online. Forty-five minutes later, I'd tracked the family history back to 1750. It was so easy, in fact, that I almost felt cheated. Through the generations of Latin names, I traced a path from my grandfather Quirinus past David to another Curinus and then to Petrus and, finally, to a David Boon, born in Doesburg, a fortified city in the eastern Dutch province of Gelderland. At that point, the trail grew murky, as the names began to bleed into one another. I'd already discovered that one ancestor was a hat maker, another a carpet maker. A few others were *dienstmeisjes*—maids in service. I learned that from about 1810 onwards, the majority of them had lived close to Dongen, the central town where this branch of the Boon family eventually settled. Most of the records didn't reveal their positions, but it's clear these were simple folk, those whose ghosts haunt van Gogh's paintings.

My Boon ancestors didn't travel far. Their bodies moved to the rhythms of rural life; their perspective was coloured by the green Dutch landscape, and their worldview by their deep and abiding Catholicism—and their resistance to Protestantism—which ostracized them from the more prosperous northern parts of the Netherlands. To this day, most of my father's family has stayed in the region. While none live in Dongen anymore, they have clustered nearby, in Eindhoven, Breda, Tilburg, Oisterwijk. Brabant is home, and they still feel it in their core.

~~~~~

I don't know if van Gogh, himself Brabant-born, was trying to paint Noord Brabant in particular. He nevertheless captured my father's family's nose, its slightly uneven shape. Its prominence. Its presence. There is nothing aristocratic about this nose. It doesn't project poise or grace. Nor does it project erudition. Mine is just a series of round lumps in the middle of my face.

This history of noses, farms, pubs, and potato eaters is what allowed me to claim a Dutch identity. This is the Netherlands of farms and windmills, of rural charm, wooden shoes, and cobbled streets swept clean every Saturday morning.

My skin, though, just a hair too dark to be Dutch, tells a different story.

"From the colonies," a visiting flute professor once pronounced, looking at me closely after learning I was Dutch.

According to my mother, that's what people in my dad's town would have said too.

"Wasn't there that Boon who married a black woman?"

~~~~~

"Why don't you tell people you're from Suriname?" my aunt Sheila had asked me during that same visit when we'd walked so companionably to the Van Gogh Museum. Her voice was curious and troubled. Why was I ignoring half of my heritage, half of my history?

It was a good question and one I'd already struggled with for a long time. It felt like I had already spent a lifetime trying to explain my history.

"Where are you from?"

"Well ... I was born in England, and my dad is from the Netherlands, and my mom is from Suriname."

"Suri-*what*? Where's *that*?"

"It's on the northeast coast of South America."

"Never heard of it."

"It's between Guyana and French Guiana."

"Huh. I never look at that part of South America."

"It used to be Dutch Guyana."

"Oh."

The process was complicated, took too long. And even after my explanations, people were confused. Over time, I had perfected my spiel, so that country name, geography, and history came out in one blurp: "I was born in England and my dad is from the Netherlands and my mom is from Suriname, which used to be Dutch Guyana, and it's a country on the north coast of South America between Guyana and French Guiana." It was a mouthful and it was still confusing. My audience wanted a simple response. A single country that they'd know and recognize. They wanted something that would accord easily and neatly with what they thought they saw when they looked at me. Maltese. Vietnamese. First Nations. Italian. East Indian. Pakistani. Chinese. Japanese. But I couldn't give them what they wanted.

If I'm being honest with myself, I know that I, too, wanted that easy answer. Something with a brand that people would recognize. Something that would allow me to fit in. When it came right down to it, I wanted to be just like everyone else; I wanted to be *normal*. In rural central Alberta, with its Ukrainian and German immigration histories, Suriname was definitely not normal. So I gave up. And what *was* Suriname, anyway? I'd never lived there; I'd only ever visited. And the last time I'd been there was in 1974, when I was four years old. For me, it was a country of shadowy stories, a space informed by the alternately passionate and ambivalent responses of my mother and her siblings. It was a place of mysteries, whispers, and silences. A place that they alternately joked about, worried over, dismissed, and longed for. It was a place I couldn't begin to understand, even though my heritage and history were fundamentally influenced by it.

Over time, I had begun to piece fragments of family stories together. Some of these came from my mom. Others came in hints from aunts and uncles. My cousin's collaborative family tree project had unlocked other stories. There were slaves—fourteen of them emancipated in 1863—and there was an indentured labourer, a young mother who travelled somehow from a tiny village in northern India with her toddler son. There was a Chinese man who worked magic with watches and gold, and a Catholic branch likely from Pondicherry, with French names. There was a German mining company representative and his Creole concubine, a freemason later knighted by the Dutch queen, and, in 1980, a coup that scattered one branch of the family to the wind. A cousin came to live with us in Canada. Another fled to the Netherlands. And an aunt and uncle began an itinerant existence that saw them move through Barbados, Antigua, Washington, New York, London, and the Netherlands before finally returning to Suriname.

At home in Alberta, there were books with stories about independence and books about the coup. Photos of bloodied bodies, barbed wire, and tanks contrasted with others of glowing white buildings and the brightest tropical flowers—bougainvillea and *faya lobi*—and smiling Surinamese women. But I was too young to really understand what any of this meant. I couldn't share any of these stories with people who asked about my background. I could barely make sense of them myself. And really, those people weren't that interested. So I took the path of least resistance.

"I'm Dutch," I'd say, when anyone asked. And just like that, one long, complicated paragraph was reduced to a short, simple phrase. Dutch was neat and tidy. It was perfect, a simple brand that conjured up recognizable images: clogs, wooden shoes, tulips, windmills, and perhaps, for the prurient—and the teenagers—sex shops. I didn't need to explain anything. It wasn't like I was lying. Not exactly, anyway. My dad is Dutch to the marrow. Almost all my relatives live in the Netherlands. Most of my cousins have never lived anywhere else. One, in fact, has never even left Amsterdam. My grandmother had lived on the Sloetstraat, a small cobbled street in the eastern Dutch town of Zutphen, since before I was born. Besides, I had a Dutch passport, didn't I?

In Alberta, Dutch was the language of our intimate thoughts, critiques, and commentaries. It was what we spoke when we didn't want anyone to know what we were saying or thinking—*Can you believe those polyester pants she's wearing?* Or *Did you buy that birthday present?*—or when we wanted to express ideas that just didn't work in English. *Gezellig. Lekker.* Cozy and tasty, the Dutch–English dictionary tells me. But that's not quite right, and we all know it. We even ate Dutch food. There was a Dutch bakery in Edmonton, and sometimes we'd get Gouda from the butcher, a sheet of wax paper between thick slices. Oma would bring treats when she visited: *speculaas, ontbijtkoek, marsepein, kaas.*

The more I told the story, the more Dutch I became. Dutch-ness seeped into my senses and oozed out of my pores. This is who I was. Slowly, Suriname and the Surinamese part of my identity fell by the wayside, victims of circumstance and confusion, details I trotted out only when asked to explain my "exotic" features.

~~~~~

I couldn't articulate any of this to my aunt when she asked. I couldn't talk about longings and belongings. About my need to fit in, to be recognized. It's possible that she understood all of this, and perhaps that's why she asked the question in the first place. All I could say was, "It's too complicated. And really, nobody is that interested." I knew that wasn't a satisfactory response, but it was all I could come up with.

There was a much more complicated story waiting to be told, and that story was always within me. It's a story written on my skin, moulded in the shape of my face. It's in the range of bodies and voices and colours and flavours that make up my family. It's also in the many and varied identities that others have ascribed to me, in the reasons why so many people continue to feel compelled to ask me where I am from, even though I have called Canada home since 1975. It's a story that could explain who I was and how I came to be me.

Elvira's invitation to collaborate on our family tree gave me permission. All I needed to do, I convinced myself, was go to the archives. The archives would show me the way.

4

LA VIE *en* ROSE

~~~~~~

T HE WOMAN AT THE COUNTER handed me three blue folders, each carefully tied with string. Anticipation threaded itself through my blood, my nerves. I was allowed only three files of archival material at a time. It doesn't sound like much, but each one would be rich with data. I knew this. I was holding my breath. I couldn't wait to learn what was inside.

Back at my desk, I laid out the first folder and reached for the string. It was stiff. Starchy, almost. It stuck and wouldn't slide easily. I untied the bow and carefully opened the file. Inside lay a leather-bound book. The leather was worn, aged, the paper inside thick and linen-rich. This was the journal, or ship's log. There were short, precise entries for almost every day of the ship's journey, and next to them, in the margins, small notes and images, all rendered in a beautiful copperplate.

As I turned the pages, I wondered what it was like to write in a book like this. To dip quills into ink. To form letters on this rough paper. I wondered how the captain managed to write so beautifully while sitting on board a rocking ship, when I couldn't even manage it on the solid ground of my island home. I stroked the paper, revelling in its tactile qualities: its knobbly texture that reminded me almost of weaving, its substance, its weight. Already stories vibrated under my fingers.

<center>~~~~~~</center>

I arrived in Middelburg, a small city in the deep southwest corner of the Dutch province of Zeeland, in late September 2014, alighting from my train after three hours trundling past farms and tidy villages in rural Netherlands. *It's so flat,* I thought. Somehow I'd forgotten this detail of geography. It had been thirteen years since I last visited the Netherlands, seventeen since I lived there. I'd landed at Schiphol Airport in Amsterdam on a Saturday. My friend Jelma, a guitarist I first met in Manchester, picked me up at the airport, and I slipped effortlessly into Dutch. This surprised me; after so many years away, I hadn't been sure what to expect.

We spent the afternoon at the seaside in Zandvoort with her partner, drinking coffee, eating *broodjes*—sandwiches—and catching up on a decade of life. The breeze felt cool but familiar here on the other side of the Atlantic.

On Sunday, I woke up thinking in Dutch. *Omgeschakeld.* Switched over. Only later would I realize just how mistaken I was.

<center>~~~~~~</center>

Middelburg is one of those ideal European historic towns, the kind of town that tourists—particularly North Americans unaccustomed to long built histories—fawn over, a place where time appears to have stood still. Tall rowhouses lean against one another. Painstakingly renovated, they don't sag under the weight of their history. Instead, they wear their histories on their gables, their proud reflections traced in the still waters of the canals: *Anno 1715. Anno 1652. Anno 1597. Anno 1761.*

Narrow streets, like bicycle spokes, lead to a central square. On that Sunday afternoon, the square was busy. The cafés were full and the shops bustling. I breathed in the twinned smells of *gebak*—pastries—and coffee. At the far end, near the town hall, a queue of chattering people balanced odd-shaped packages and boxes. *Tussen kunst en kitsch*, the Dutch version of *Antiques Roadshow*, was filming. I edged closer but couldn't go in. Admission only to those who received invitations, I read on a sign.

At the grocery store, I went a bit mad, buying far more than I could eat. There was *vla*, *Beemsterkaas*, *candijkoek*, *krentebollen*, *speculaas*. There were *stroopwafels* and *chocolade hagel*. Custard, cheese, raisin buns, breakfast treats, and baked goods: the flavours of my Dutch heritage. Later, in my room, I stowed my treasures near the open window, hoping for cool night temperatures. Except for the *krentebollen*, that is, which were *op*, as they say in Dutch—quickly finished—and nestled in my warm stomach.

I realized that I had been starving. For flavour. For welcome. For the familiarity of tastes I hadn't enjoyed in such a long time. I had been yearning for the tangy bite of a sharp Dutch cheese, the crunch of chocolate sprinkles on bread, the thick, milky comfort of cold custard poured from a milk carton. I can buy some Dutch foods in the international aisle at my local grocery store in St. John's. *Koek. Stroopwafels. Chocoladehagel.* All just a fifteen-minute walk from my house. I can even buy *Beemsterkaas* at the big-box supermarket on the edge of town; it's really expensive, a special treat. But none of it tastes the same in St. John's.

Middelburg's cobbled stones massaged my feet, and warmed blood flowed up and through my body. Each cobbled pattern is different, my body remembered. Each has its own voice, its own rhythm. Some are noisy, insistent when you walk over them. Some rumble. Others murmur gently. As I walked, they awakened my memories.

I could taste the sounds of Dutch rolling around in my mouth and floating in the air. My body digested familiar words, feelings, smells. Dutch entered my body with every word that I spoke, finding its former lodgings. My jaw adjusted itself, warming into movements it had almost forgotten. Every sound affected my imagination, shifted my perspective. I felt myself changing, generating new flesh.

Walking the narrow streets of Middelburg, I was fully aware of my histories, which allowed me unique entry into Dutch culture while simultaneously leaving me on the sidelines. In some ways, I was born into this place, this identity; in others, I didn't know it at all.

"How can you possibly be Dutch," my cousins have teased me, "when you don't even like coffee, licorice, or beer?"

I thought about my cousins, smiling as I snacked my way through yet another *krentebol*. As rich as all these memories were, I hadn't come to Middelburg to revel in the senses. This trip wasn't meant to be about nostalgia. I'd come for the archives, and the archives of the Middelburgsche Commercie Compagnie in particular.

~~~~~

I'm never sure what to expect when I first encounter a new collection of materials. Archival stories don't reveal themselves in a predictable, linear fashion; rather, they emerge in fits and starts. Sometimes the archives tantalize, offering hints but no clear evidence. And in this space of dead-end alleys, mirrored passageways, and treasure-filled vistas, I'm a detective, an archeologist, an adventurer. I hold the fragments to the light. I inspect them from all angles. I arrange them. I rearrange them. And over time, patterns begin to emerge. Voices begin to speak. And then we work together, the voices and I, finding routes to further understanding. It's a dialogue.

I'm not sure anymore why I went to Middelburg first, why I chose those particular archival materials as my starting point. I don't know if I was actually certain of what I was looking for. But every journey, real or archival, must start somewhere.

~~~~~~

The Middelburgsche Commercie Compagnie was founded in 1720. A Zeeland-based upstart that sought to nose its way into Dutch West India Company business in the eighteenth century, this trading company wasn't initially focused on the slave trade. But in 1732, after the West India Company lost its trade monopoly, the Middelburgsche Commercie Compagnie sent its first slaving ship down to the coast of Africa. In early December of that same year, the first enslaved African—a man traded for a range of European dry goods—was brought on board. After four months of trading, the ship was full, with 318 enslaved Africans on board, all of them numbered and recorded in the ship's log.

I began my research with the *Vigilantie*, a ship that sailed from Middelburg to the Guinea Coast and then on to Suriname between August 1778 and September 1779. It took time to figure out the handwriting, to sort out the shorthand. Each entry in the journal gave a brief overview of the weather conditions and a summary of the day's events. *Wind northwest. Stormy.* The marginalia gave more detail. *Saw flying fish. Saw two French ships. Many birds.* After the ship laid anchor near African shores, the annotations changed. *Good weather bought 7 slaves 2 men 2 women 2 boys 1 girl.* The summary told me that negotiations were conducted on board, the local trader making his way to the ship via canoe. *Bought 5 men slaves and 8 elephant tusks.*

The journal told me that it took a few months to fill a slave ship, and before it even left the coast of Africa, some of the enslaved had already died. *No. 7, No. 9, and No. 2*, the captain had written, his annotations embellished with a skull and crossbones. The journal recorded the next few months of the journey. *Fed the slaves salt meat and fish. Saw flying fish.* At Paramaribo, along the coast of Suriname, they dropped anchor and readied themselves for the trade. *Took 50 slaves to shore to walk them. Returned to the ship in the evening. Sold 70 heads.* Each statement succinct and precise.

The second file returned me to Dutch shores. Inside, in a neat stack, lay hundreds of invoices, orders, and receipts. Bakers contracted to make hard tack. Merchants providing pots, glasses, plates, cutlery, jugs. Orders for beer, whiskey, and other alcoholic drinks. Fabrics. Dried foods. Weapons. Ammunition. And here, further in, contracts for carpentry. Wood, nails, and other building supplies. There were hundreds and hundreds of single sheets. I was amazed by how much it took to provision a slaving ship. Was the whole province of Zeeland employed by this company in some way?

By the time I reached for the third file, my thoughts were jumbling together. What right did I have to page through these documents? Were these materials—and the stories carried within them—mine to comb through, to read, to share? Was it fair to my ancestors to tell my story through their lives? To live through their dying, to speak through their silence?

In the course of a previous research project, I'd encountered a haunting letter written by a young man so ashamed of his sexual activities that he'd begged his doctor to destroy the letter so that nobody else would be privy to his immoral behaviours. He hadn't signed it; all that remained was an anonymous account of sexual excess. But what did it mean that I could still read his words over two centuries later? And what were my ethical responsibilities to this man's story and to his request for privacy? The man's words forced me to pause; they were a reminder that I needed to tread lightly, to be as generous with the dead whose voices I encountered in the documents as I am with the voices of those with whom I live in the present.

This time around, nothing was anonymous; everything was personal.

I reminded myself, amid the fog that was descending, that these were nothing more than accounts tallying up expenditures and income, profits and losses. In these documents, I could trace the inner workings of the slave trade. I could measure its economic impact with breathtaking clarity. I told myself that I would remain objective, that I would take notes on exactly what I saw before me.

I knew that not all stories were joyous. I'd followed stories of suffering. I'd witnessed birth, death, and mourning.

But I can see the captain purchase slaves, I protested silently. I was there when the ship's crew fed them salt fish, cleaned out their quarters, walked them on the decks. I was sitting right there in that canoe, and I joined the negotiations. I traded weapons and beer for black bodies and ivory. I took my slaves to market, and I sold them. I numbered them, and then I tallied up the profits. And there, in the margins, I watched them die.

None of this matters, I instructed myself. *Draw on your background. Record what you see. Stay objective.*

Over the years, I'd developed a rhythm for working in the archives. I'd created endless spreadsheets. I'd taken thousands of photos. I'd written pages and pages of careful field notes.

You're ready for this.

I thought I was.

But I hadn't read stories like these before. I couldn't have anticipated my shock of recognition, horror, and grief. These records traced history with unseemly impartiality. There was a disembodiment that made the ugliness of the slave trade even more visceral. I found myself consumed with insurmountable sorrow. In this space, I was soon lost.

～～～

That afternoon, I followed the stories across oceans, from continent to continent to continent, and the journey tore me to shreds. These documents were dark. There was almost no light here. This archival silence wasn't welcoming; it was unearthly. This was the silence of violence. I reached out to touch the skull and crossbones in the margins of the page. *No. 5. Woman.*

As the day progressed, the light shifted. I moved my body and camera to get a better angle. There was a shadow on the page—my shadow—and this frustrated me. I moved again, but it was no use. The shadow remained. My hands, my camera, my body, all blocking out light. My shadow on the overly bright accountings of history. My shadow communing with the shadows of my past. Outside, one of the roofing guys burst into an enthusiastic if tuneless rendition of "Waltzing Matilda," only to stop abruptly before the end of the first verse. Perhaps he, too, could sense something?

I couldn't know if my family was here. I would never know. That branch of my genealogy was lost among the numbers and accounts, lost in the vast randomness of the African continent.

~~~~~

"We'll be closing in fifteen minutes."

The archivist's voice interrupted my thinking, returning me to the concrete materiality of the reading room. Time to go.

I packed up my computer, pencils, passport, and camera. On autopilot, I smiled at the staff and thanked them, assuring them that I'd be back. But really, I hadn't yet returned to the land of the living.

The next thing I knew, I was back outside again. Middelburg's clock tower chimed the half hour, sounding Edith Piaf's classic "La vie en rose."

> *Quand il me prend dans ses bras*
> *Il me parle tout bas*
> *Je vois la vie en rose.*

~~~~~

On the way back to the hotel, the cobblestones seemed to dig into me, bruising my soles. I stumbled, imagining bleeding black feet marching under a hot sun. I couldn't have known, this morning, that my world would be turned upside down from touching linen paper. That I would read and read, desperate for something that was impossible to recover. That I would begin to count each numbered body.

Genealogy couldn't tell me where I come from. It couldn't tell me why my skin felt chafed. Raw. Why words now tangled themselves on my tongue. Genealogy could only put names and dates on a chart. But who was I, when those names were missing? Who was I, when the stories were gone?

My genealogy is told in beer and wine, cutlery and weapons, fabrics and pots, in the price of a slave. It is told in skull and crossbones. In the branding of the slave market. My story is told in the provisions that stocked a well-prepared ship. In the marginalia of a trading company journal.

~~~~~

What were you looking for? I asked myself. I was using my mother's voice. It's the voice that says that I should have known better. I could hear her exasperation, her irritation. *What on earth did you think you would find?*

What do you think I was looking for? My own voice now, equally exasperated. *A transoceanic cruise?* How could I make sense of the Middelburg slaving journeys? How could I understand them? Maybe the seamen aboard joined up for a spot of adventure, an opportunity to see the world on someone else's dime. Or maybe it was a way of life, the only way they could make a living and support families back home. I wanted to ask the sailors how they could live with themselves, when they knew what was going on, when they became full participants in the trafficking of humans. I knew the answer, of course. Most of us do what we can to survive and turn a blind eye to that which we cannot change. We pretend. We tell ourselves it's not as bad as it looks. And, disturbingly, some of us don't even think it's bad at all. It's how the Holocaust happened, how it lasted as long as it did. The traffic in enslaved Africans lasted for centuries. And slavery, as an institution, continues today.

I wanted to throw things, scream, curl up into a ball. I wanted to cry. I wanted to do all these things, but in the quiet of my hotel room, I could do nothing.

~~~~~

In 1788, a former slave trader named John Newton wrote a forty-page pamphlet decrying the atrocities of the slave trade. I'd first read *Thoughts upon the African Slave Trade* well before my trip to the archives, before my cousin had invited me to the family tree. Near the end of the pamphlet, Newton describes the process of loading enslaved Africans onto ships and folding them under the decks into chambers where they are lined up, in his words, "in two rows, one above the other, on each side of the ship, close to each other, like books upon a shelf…"

Like books upon a shelf. It was an arresting image, and I'd had to stop there. I read it again. And then once more. Even now, several years later, it feels intentionally provocative. It's an analogy I never would have considered. Books, to me, are rich treasures filled with delight, imaginings, and wonder. Even John Newton's *Thoughts upon the African Slave Trade*, an ugly, tawdry tale of greed, corruption, and profound inhumanity, has much to offer. How could something so precious, so rich—a bookcase filled with words, ideas, voices—be linked with the atrocities of the slave trade?

I have no doubt that Newton chose his words carefully. Linking the cramped, disease-laden misery of the slave quarters with the cozy romance of an overfilled bookcase brought horrors that might otherwise be ignored—easily bypassed as happening far away to foreign people with foreign beliefs, in foreign climes, on foreign shores—into the sanctity of comfortable, educated, elite

British homes. And from there, these words also entered my own comfortable Canadian home.

In Newton's critique, I learned about the extent of human depravity. I learned of insurrections, violence, death. I learned that one-quarter of transported slaves and one-fifth of crew members perished during these journeys. And I learned about the case of the *Zong*, whose human cargo was tossed overboard, alive, in a time of water scarcity—so that the cost of lost slaves could be picked up by the underwriters rather than by the ship's owners. Imagine a ship so full of slaves that it belched them out of its sides, 132 in total, at thirty pounds sterling per head.

Maybe I should have let the ghosts sleep.

~~~~~

What did you expect? My mother's voice again. *I don't know*, I answered. I don't know what I expected. It was as simple as that. And whatever it was that I thought I was looking for, it wasn't what I found. What I found were the records of a business enterprise. There was no room for moral questions here. The only thing that mattered was balancing the books. I hadn't expected to see it all written out with such impersonal clarity. John Newton had warned me. But I hadn't been paying attention.

In my room, I sat with my grief, my words spilling onto the pages of my notebook. The stories I was listening for were lost. Where could I go from here? What was I supposed to do, when I couldn't account for my genealogy, or when the accounting couldn't account for me? What was I supposed to do with my fractured, splintered self?

Day turned to dusk and then to night. The numbers on the clock tower glowed. The bells rang their last chorus. I shut the curtain, changed into my pyjamas, and settled into bed, the echo of Edith Piaf's gravelly, smoke-stained voice singing me to sleep.

The next morning was hazy, the tower of the Oostkerk nothing more than a shadowy bulb. There's a quiet to fog, a stillness; even the pigeons, normally scrabbling across the roof tiles by this point, were silent. The town was a dreamspace, eerily quiet and not quite in focus. The church bells rang on the quarter hour. I listened to their echoes, just out of sync but still remarkably resonant.

My host, it transpired, had run a touring company.

"We've been to Newfoundland," he told me after breakfast. "First St. John's and then we took a boat to … Lewisporte?" He looked over at me, questioningly.

I nodded.

"And from there along the Labrador coast. Battle Harbour. Rigolet. Makkovik. Nain."

Over a decade in Newfoundland and I haven't yet managed to visit Labrador, and here was my host, a man who had travelled the globe but still lived in the city of his birth, listing off the names I heard every day on the radio.

The day looked promising. Behind the mists, the sun was already warming the sky. After breakfast, I grabbed my camera and headed out the door. A short train ride later, I was in Vlissingen. If Middelburg is the middle of nowhere, then Vlissingen, its close cousin, is at the end of the line. I was here for the same reason that I had gone to Middelburg.

For a long time, Vlissingen's role in the Dutch slave trade was thought to be minimal. Middelburg, so the story went, was the heart of this industry. But in 2014, a historian named Ruud Paezie published a new study on the Middelburgsche Commercie Compagnie. Drawing on newly recovered archival materials, he claimed two things. First, he said, Vlissingen was a centre for the slave trade. Second, he argued, the workings of the slave trade affected the whole island of Walcheren, the westernmost part of the province of Zeeland. Predictably, many responses to the newspaper articles were incredulous. Some were outright hostile.

"What nonsense," wrote one commentator, who went by the moniker "A True Vlissinger." Vlissingers, he said, were hardworking people who had built up everything with their own hands. This was probably true, but Vlissingen's role in the transatlantic slave trade was also true. Just the act of provisioning a ship involved the participation of hundreds of small-business owners from across the island of Walcheren. I'd seen the evidence for myself. And even without all the archival evidence, it stood to reason that Vlissingen, a town that overlooked the ocean, must have played an important role in the maritime economy. Indeed, recent economic research only confirms this: during the second half of the eighteenth century, fully one-third of Vlissingen's local economy was based on the trade in enslaved Africans.

Vlissingen's fortunes and misfortunes have been determined by the sea. The town lies nestled behind a dike at the mouth of the Schelde River, where fresh water meets the sea. The whole region, fully exposed to the wild storms of the North Atlantic, is vulnerable. But it's an ideal location for those who have made their living from the water: fishermen, privateers, and slavers. It's also a politically strategic location; whoever controlled the mouth of the river controlled Antwerp, the trading city at the other end. The lowlanders, who lived there from about 600 CE, knew this. Others figured it out soon enough. Spain tried to invade in the sixteenth century. In 1795, Napoleon captured Vlissingen. During the almost twenty-year occupation that followed, he built up the town's military defences in preparation for an assault on Britain. A century and a half later, on New Year's Day 1940, the Germans moved in. Protected by the dikes, they settled in for the long haul and wouldn't be driven out till November 1944, by a month of decisive—and devastating—Allied military action.

The Germans thought they were safe. And they were. It was only the Allied decision to blast the dikes themselves that drew them out. Such a military decision could not have been made lightly. Breaching the dikes caused extensive flooding throughout Vlissingen and the island of Walcheren, and nearly 200 civilians lost their lives. Before the war, Vlissingen had been a thriving community of some 20,000 people. But the war had taken its toll. By the time the Allies moved in, only 3,000 remained. Some 1,200 had perished as a direct result of the war. Others had fled.

I pondered this history as I walked the dike from the train station to the heart of the city. The fog had melted away, leaving a glorious blue sky. Across the waves, in a hazy distance, I could make out another shore, the last bit of the Netherlands before it shifted, imperceptibly, into Belgium. This channel of water, which leads from the Belgian city of Antwerp right out to the ocean, was essential to World War II. It was also vital to the slave trade, an ideal trade route that linked the fortunes of Vlissingen not only to Antwerp and other major European centres, but also to the Dutch colonial world.

That morning, I saw only a few sailboats floating lazily on the water, and a single container ship moving silently past. At the shore, men had set up for a day of fishing. The paved dike trail was busy with locals enjoying their morning constitutional. Some stopped to chat, their dogs straining at their leashes. Others, more focused, pushed on. It still felt rural here; I could hear only the quiet bleating of sheep and the gulls calling out to one another. But after I'd walked about a kilometre, the town appeared, opening up below me behind the dike.

Unlike Middelburg, Vlissingen doesn't wear its architectural history on its sleeve. Rather, it is mostly newly built. Vlissingen's townscape has been profoundly influenced by war. Fully 20 percent of its houses were destroyed as a result of the 1944 flooding; all but one of those that remained needed substantial renovation. Perhaps as a result, there's a certain grittiness to Vlissingen's facade that appears to be born of adversity. We survived, the town says, despite it all.

Today, Vlissingen's waterfront has the feel of a tired resort town. Next to the white sand beach, still quiet at this time of morning, stand rows of faded condos, their bleary windows turned to the sea, many for sale or rent. The beach was almost empty when I was there. But the early morning brought out the parents with their eager toddlers and preschoolers, and, somewhat incongruously, a cluster of Eastern European men deep in conversation and cigarette smoke.

~~~~~

Near the town centre, I met up with the statue of the Fisherman's Wife. I don't often see statues of women. In St. John's, most statues honour the lives of famous men whose stories have indelibly shaped that city's understanding of itself. Gaspar Corte-Real, the Portuguese explorer who arrived in Terra Nova in the fifteenth century, stands firm, legs apart, arms crossed, and facing the Confederation Building, his strong jawline evoking the mythical stoicism of the seaman ready to face any challenge. Across the road, in a field of dandelions, stands Sir Wilfred Grenfell, the legendary medical missionary who tended to the needs of rural fisherfolk along the northern coast of Newfoundland and Labrador. John Cabot takes pride of place at the Confederation Building, his dour face surveying territory he may or may not ever have seen. And downtown, at the harbourfront, stands another statue, a young man poised as if to start his run. This is Terry Fox, who dipped his prosthetic limb into the cold St. John's harbour on 12 April 1980 when he began the Marathon of Hope.

But here, in Vlissingen, stands the statue of an anonymous woman. *De Vissersvrouw*, as she is called in Dutch, has her arms wrapped around her body, shawl and skirts blowing out behind her, her face raised to the sky. There's nothing special about her. She's not an explorer, a merchant, or a ship's captain. She's not a political or religious leader, a famous doctor, or a cancer survivor whose determination made her a national hero. Rather, her presence on the dike points towards the everyday, to the lives of all those hard-working Vlissingers who have made their lives from the sea.

It's as if she'd climbed up the dike that very morning, as if she'd paused to catch sun and sea breeze on her face. Behind her, somewhere in the narrow streets of this walled town, was the busyness of her daily life. A small house, dark and damp. A gaggle of children ranging in age from fourteen right down to the baby. Endless washing. Whites flapping in a salt-infused breeze. Potatoes to peel. And a husband who was out on the water day after day after day.

How many women walked this way in search of their husbands, looking for ships on the horizon? How many spent hours here on this widow's walk of a dike, scanning the seas? How many sought the solace of wind and sun?

But the Fisherman's Wife wasn't looking out at the ocean. She didn't appear to be looking for her husband at all. Her head was angled toward the heavens.

My friend Jelma was prosaic.

"She's praying," she said. "They're very religious in that part of the country."

Maybe that's what the Fisherman's Wife was doing. As we stood there together in silence, our eyes raised, I wondered what life was like for her. I wondered how she imagined the world beyond these shores. And I wondered how I, whose horizons have been so very different from hers, might see differently.

~~~~~

As a child on the prairies, my worldview was shaped entirely by land. But like coastal dwellers, I came to understand myself through a low horizon with an endless sky. Unlike coastal dwellers, who imagine themselves through the swells of the ocean waves and the emptiness of an ocean that seems to go on forever, my landscape is solid, firm, flat.

"The prairies are boring," everyone says. "There's nothing to see."

But that's because they're looking at the land. To orient yourself to the prairie, you must orient yourself towards the sky. Like the Fisherman's Wife, prairie folk look up, basking in stories of clouds and wind.

"There's a thunderstorm over there," my dad would say, pointing to a swathe of deep grey, far in the distance.

"How far?" I wanted to know.

But he couldn't tell me. Twenty kilometres? Thirty? Fifty? Distance is meaningless on the prairies. Time stands still. As a child, I learned to follow clouds that sometimes raced across the sky, to hike through grassy open spaces, to watch for the aurora borealis shaping and reshaping the night sky. And because the prairies stretched out before me in every direction, land, for me, is something that is meant to reach forever. Like the sea, it undulates gently. Vast and deceptively empty, it reminds me just how small I am, even as it tells me that I can be the centre of my own universe.

Such vastness can, however, be disconcerting. A friend travelling through the prairies for the first time was completely overwhelmed. He couldn't even begin to orient himself in all the space.

I didn't understand how much the prairie horizon had influenced me until I began to feel claustrophobic in the treed neighbourhoods of Vancouver, where I lived for a decade before moving to St. John's. Vancouver's natural beauty is stunning, enthusiastic Vancouverites say. And on that point my Faroe Islands–born husband and I would agree. Snow-capped mountains. Rich foliage. Whales in the Georgia Strait. None of this beauty should ever be taken for granted. But these natural wonders can get in the way. The mountains and the trees restricted our views. We couldn't quite see far enough. My husband's psyche was attuned to the ocean and mine to the land. Both of us wanted to see forever.

~~~~~

In the late-afternoon sun, the bronze fisherwoman and I stood together contemplating our lives, our places in the world. The Fisherman's Wife turned her eyes to the sky, her face bathing in the warm sun. My eyes turned to the west, to the opening that led slave ships, and the seamen who sailed them, out onto the ocean.

5

Opa's BOOKS

~~~~~~
===

A FEW DAYS LATER, I boarded the train again, heading north towards the country's capital, The Hague. The Hague is a gracious city. The seat of government, it has a certain formality to it, a reserved and somewhat distant personality.

"It's a snobbish place," Amsterdammers sniff, without irony. And to be fair, The Hague is very different from the colourful chaos of Amsterdam; it doesn't have the same rambunctious flair, that flouting of social convention that is so central to Amsterdam's psyche. Instead, it is serious and proper; it bears the weight of its political responsibilities.

But for me, The Hague had once been home. It was the first city Búi and I lived in after we were married in 1995. We were both students, and our studio apartment was almost like a Parisian garret. It took up the top floor of a tall late-nineteenth-century rowhouse and featured hand-cast original windows that offered a rosy, if somewhat distorted, view of the street. We furnished our apartment with odds and ends scavenged from family and the street, bought our first pieces of furniture, hung our laundry out the kitchen window, and grew a basil jungle on our windowsill.

Our street was magical. Narrow, with rowhouses rising along either side, the 2de de Riemerstraat is just a few minutes' walk in one

===
~~~~~~

direction from Paleis Noordeinde—one of the Dutch royal family's three palaces—and in the other, about ten minutes from the city's downtown core. It has a cobbled street worn uneven by a century of traffic and a history that includes the photographer Adolphe Zimmerman, known as the first person in the Netherlands to own a car. The neighbours took good care of the street too. Monthly community street sweeping—a tradition dating back to the 1970s—and community-adopted square planters meant that everything was neat, clean, and quintessentially Dutch. Everything, that is, except for our house. In principle, it was like all the others. Tall and brick, with three storeys. But ours was a rental property. And so where the other houses were bright and shiny, ours had a dull patina. The brick walls weren't quite as crisp. The door was flat, drab, and peeling. And because each floor was a separate apartment, there was no pleasing uniformity to the windows.

"Doesn't matter," my friend Jelma said. "You don't have to look at your house when you're inside; you get to look at all the other houses." And she was right. Peering through the warped distortions of century-old glass, we could almost imagine ourselves back in the nineteenth century, when the street was new.

~~~~~

It was music that had first brought me to The Hague. I'd been accepted into the early music program at the Royal Conservatory of Music, following in the footsteps of a musical grandfather, my Opa Heinemann, who had studied at the very same school almost fifty years earlier. I was a flute player; he was a choral conductor. But music somehow united us across generations. I suppose I was chasing a legacy, even then.

I don't remember Opa Heinemann. He died of cancer when I was still young. We had just immigrated to Canada from South America. It was, I gather, a difficult time. Money was tight, and my parents had had to scrape together all their careful savings to send my mom to her father's sick bed one last time.

I know Opa only through his books. In the early 1990s, just after I finished my undergraduate degree, two boxes arrived on my parents' doorstep. My grandmother had packaged up all of her husband's remaining music books and sent them to the only grandchild who had gone on to study music. Through these books, I could imagine his musical spirit, his creative energy captured in the fragmentary marginalia he left behind. In the spaces between the printed words, I caught glimpses of our shared genetics, and I wonder how it might have been had our musical paths been able to cross.

Opa and Oma lived in the eastern Dutch town of Zutphen, in a cobblestoned neighbourhood filled with identical squat rowhouses. They had arrived in the Netherlands in the 1960s. It was a big move, from subtropical Suriname, on the north coast of South America, a colony whose plantations had sustained and supported the Dutch economy for centuries, to a compact home in small-town Netherlands. The Netherlands wouldn't have been completely foreign to them, of course. Growing up in a Dutch colony, they had learned the Dutch language, imbibed Dutch history, and sampled Dutch culture. My mother, for example, has told me that she learned to knit woollen underwear in grade one. That skill might have been useful in the damp cold of Dutch winters but would have been practically useless in the face of tropical heat. And so, I imagine that Zutphen, with its beautifully preserved medieval town centre, might have seemed oddly and eerily familiar.

It was that same sense of odd familiarity that I'd been looking for when I'd first moved to Europe to continue my musical studies. The Hague wasn't my first European port of call. Before moving there, I had previously studied and worked for two years in Manchester, the city where I was born. But I'd felt discombobulated in England, something I hadn't expected. How could the country of my birth feel so very strange? We shared the same queen. Our histories were deeply linked. But Manchester felt more foreign to me than any other place I'd lived. English coins were too heavy. I couldn't get a handle on social dynamics. And it was dreary. Manchester's suburban streets looked tired, worn down. The buildings were grimy, coated with a century of industrialization, smog, and class politics.

I thought we spoke the same language, but words made no sense.

"Do you have laundry detergent?" I asked a Manchester store clerk.

"Laundry *what*?" she replied.

"Laundry detergent."

She looked perplexed.

"You know, stuff to wash clothes with."

"Ohhhh. Washing powder."

It was the first time I realized the power of language to define social relationships. At the music school, opera students took elocution lessons to rid themselves of colonial accents, shaping their Irish, New Zealand, Australian, American, and Canadian mouths and vowels into something resembling the Queen's English. In everyday conversations, we were ranked by our accents, our words marking us by class and place. With my Canadian accent, I was inevitably "from the colonies," a somewhat boorish misfit who could be tolerated even though I lacked the requisite history. The Irish were always at the bottom.

I'd hoped for something very different. Manchester had been a beacon of sorts. I'd thought I could make a go of living in the United Kingdom, of making a home and a professional career for myself. I'd thought the accident of birth would make Manchester feel like home. But it didn't. And the longer I was there, the less comfortable it became. I was born in Manchester. I met Búi there. We were married there. But I didn't recognize Manchester. And it, in turn, didn't recognize me.

I transferred those same longings onto The Hague. My red passport—the European Union one—granted me entry. It said I was Dutch, and that I could stay as long as I liked. But just because a government document said I had a right to belong, that didn't necessarily make it so.

I imagine that my grandparents, who arrived in the Netherlands with their Dutch colonial passports, might have experienced something similar. How did they go about making a home for themselves in the Netherlands, the country that had exploited the labour of their ancestors, a country that, even now, is not fully willing to accept slavery's descendants into its midst? What was it like for Oma and Opa, members of two very different ethnic communities, to find a common space together, though their individual backgrounds should otherwise have divided them? And perhaps more important, what was it like for Opa—the son of a German father and a Creole mother—to find his passion in the history of European art music?

~~~~~

We didn't listen to much classical music when I was a child. My parents had bought me a record with Mozart's *Eine Kleine Nachtmusik* on one side and the famous Toy Symphony, possibly by Haydn or Leopold Mozart, on the other. Of the two, it was the Toy Symphony with its peeping nightingale, twittering cuckoo, rattles, drums, and trumpets that captured my imagination. But even that recording couldn't compete with my album of Venezuelan children's music or the storybook records that I got as birthday presents. My sister, seven years younger than I, had a collection of Raffi records, and my mother always had the radio tuned to an easy-listening station. My father, meanwhile, nurtured a love for folk music, particularly the boisterous energy of Greek music. My mother wasn't a fan, so he'd wait until she was out, and then he'd turn the stereo up loud and dance around the room, his chin jutting out and a big smile on his face. Classical music had a place in his life, but not a central one.

"Why would Canadians need to learn classical music?" he once asked me. "Classical music is European music; there's nothing Canadian about it." Why did it matter in the Americas? he wondered. What was the point, when there were already so many local traditions?

But European music and a European family were precisely what I was looking for. Apart from one aunt and uncle in Suriname and a cousin in Canada, all my relatives lived in the Netherlands. Most had lived there since before I was born. On my father's side, they'd lived there for centuries. Europe was an inheritance that I had come to claim. This was where I would belong. This was where I was meant to be. Dutch-Canadian flutist, my bio read, and that's who I was determined to become.

~~~~~

As a student, I learned The Hague by foot. Fifteen minutes took me to the central square, where we bought our first Christmas tree, half price, on Christmas Eve. Down the road stands the Historical Museum of The Hague, where I discovered not only an early photo of that magical dream street we called home, but also a tiny wood and glass case containing the salted and petrified tongue and toe of the de Witt brothers, Johan and Cornelis, Dutch republican politicians executed by a lynch mob in 1672. After their murders, their bodies were desecrated and pillaged by locals, who not only sought souvenirs—relics that then became part of their family lore and, in their material form, legacies that they could bestow on subsequent generations—but apparently also, in gruesome fashion, consumed body parts.

I remember gazing on these curiosities with morbid fascination. It was certainly, as the historian Robert Darnton would have said, one of those "areas of opacity," moments when one is confronted by a past that is completely unfathomable. But looking back on that encounter with the past, I wonder if it was actually as unimaginable as it first seemed. I, too, am fascinated by the past, by its stories, and by the bits and pieces that have been bequeathed to me over the years. My grandmother's gold bracelet. A commemorative headscarf from my mother. My grandfather's books. Would I have kept bodily relics, too, if they'd been given to me?

~~~~~

Opa's books recalled my own musical training. Harmony. Theory. Orchestration. History. I knew all these stories; I'd read them too. A well-worn theory book, published in 1947. A biography of Mozart from 1949 and purchased in Amsterdam: Alsbach & Doyer, Kalverstraat 176. A two-volume *Geïllustreerd Muzieklexicon*, 1949 edition. Another theory book, wrapped in brown paper. *Algemeene Muziekleer* by Sem Dresden, seventh edition, 1949. And then, *De instrumenten van het orkest* signed L. Heinemann 10-5-50 and bearing the deep blue sticker of Muziekhandel Albersen, Groot Hertoginnelaan 182, the very same store that I would regularly visit almost half a century later.

As I paged through these books, I found myself back in a sun-filled room with high ceilings, revelling in the comfortable clutter of manuscripts and musty second-hand books. Volumes of music history. Scores for esoteric and obscure compositions. Antiquaria. Sometimes it was enough just to smell the paper. *I was there too, Opa.* Provenance, I thought, holding Opa's book in my hand, my finger stroking the blue sticker.

I'd smuggled the first books from Opa's collection in 1986. We'd been in Zutphen, celebrating Oma's seventy-fifth birthday with the whole extended family. I was sixteen, and as a keen flutist, I'd spotted the books on her bookshelf mixed in with other works of nonfiction, among them some books on Anne Frank and, strangely, a book of spells. It's possible that I asked permission to take Opa's books, but I prefer the idea of smuggling, of a furtive encounter with the grandfather I barely knew, but who, my aunts have told me, would have been so happy to know that someone was finally taking up his musical legacy.

Two music books came home with me that year, a two-volume general music reference set. A year later, my books and I took a Greyhound bus from Edmonton to Victoria to begin university, and that fall, I referenced them in my first-year music history paper. It felt good to read in Dutch, to pass over the same words that my grandfather had read before me, to turn the same pages, to trace my fingers over his signature, to consider our shared musical identities. It didn't occur to me that books dating from 1932 might be out of date.

The rest of Opa's books arrived just after I started graduate school. I'd just spent the summer in my first full-time—if underpaid—professional orchestral gig. Eighteen different concert programs in eight short weeks. Bach. Mozart. Prokofieff. Beethoven. And truly terrible arrangements of Anne Murray's greatest hits. It was trial by fire. Maybe I'd finally come to earn my birthright; maybe I was finally ready to celebrate my genetic claim to Opa's musical legacy. It's much more likely that Oma had finally decided her late husband's books took up too much room. Whatever the case, that summer the books began their ocean voyage from the Netherlands to Canada.

As for Opa and me, well, I like to think that we met somewhere in the mid-Atlantic, our spirits mingling with those of the great masters of centuries past.

~~~~~

At the conservatory in The Hague, I was the odd one out. The Dutch student with a Canadian passport and relatives who came to every recital. The Canadian student with a Dutch passport who could pronounce Scheveningseweg and lived on Dutch student funding. In daily conversations in the cafeteria, I regularly switched among English, Dutch, and French, my personality lodging itself in the comfortable spaces between languages. French locates itself high in my tonal register; it's precise, polite, and fast. English, the language of my Canadian everyday, is at the bottom, relaxed and loose. Dutch finds itself somewhere in the middle. A language that I learned orally but only ever intuited in written form, it feels both familiar and foreign at the same time. It's the language of family get-togethers, a language of intimacy and love, but I still sometimes miss some of the subtleties. In each language, I'm a slightly different person, voice, words, and inflections highlighting different aspects of my personality. Together, they complement one another, telling different stories. That should have been a sign.

I learned Dutch at the breast, as they say, imbibing it from my parents. But while my Dutch was functional, it was dated. My parents had left the Netherlands in the 1960s; much had changed in the intervening decades. During those early months in The Hague, my husband and I used free trial newspaper subscriptions to work on our reading skills, progressing upwards from a month with the easy Dutch of the *Algemeen Dagblad* and *De Telegraaf* towards *De Volkskrant* and, finally, to the serious and formal *NRC Handelsblad*.

Everything was going well until we encountered a baffling word in the *NRC Handelsblad*. In those pre-Internet days, there was no online translator to help us out, so I phoned my parents.

"We can't figure out this word in the paper."

"Tell me," said my mom.

"*Geslachtsgemeenschap*," I replied, my tongue tangling on a word I'd never previously spoken aloud.

A peal of laugher from the other end of the phone. When my mom finally composed herself, she replied, "It means sex."

Seriously? A word that long and complicated?

I've never seen the word *geslachtsgemeenschap* in print since. But my daily newspaper habit did prepare me for something else: I became comfortable reading in Dutch, something I'd previously experienced only while reading letters from my grandmother, most of which, I now recognized, were likely carefully crafted for easy second-language learning.

~~~~~

Just as newspapers brought me closer to Dutch language and culture, so too did they bring me closer to my grandfather's life. Family stories can't usually be traced through newspapers; most of us don't live public lives. But performing musicians do. Concert announcements. Reviews. Interviews. The stuff of a musician's professional life is written for public consumption. I turned to my computer and pulled up the Dutch online newspaper archive. If I wanted to know more about Opa's music, I reasoned, this would be the best place to start.

I was in for a surprise. The earliest newspapers gave me only shadowy glimpses of Opa's life, none of them remotely musical. 1927: Assigned to a new school. 1935: Cricket news. L. Heinemann played for the Victoria team. 1936: Information for students interested in being part of a study circle. Opa listed as one of the contacts. Later that same year, the birth of a child, a son—my uncle. January 1939: Another child, a daughter who, I know, was born on Christmas Day. Opa as a young man, a teacher, a lover, a father.

But in 1943, the music began. The online newspaper archive had much to share. Concert announcements. Articles. Previews. Reviews. Opa as choir director. Opa as musician. Is it any surprise, then, that fully eighteen of the books in my collection date from the subsequent decade?

A concert review in the 19 February 1954 edition of *Het Nieuws* revealed that "Leo Heinemann presented, with his CCS Mixed Choir, *Psalm 92, Verse 2*, a composition of the Surinamese composer N. Helstone, only to surpass this exquisite work later with his men's choir, in *Die Almacht* by Franz Schubert, in which both the singers through their interpretation, and the conductor through the breadth of his gestures, rendered the omnipotence almost frighteningly suggestive, climbing the heights and descending into depths which made the hall shake."

How did my grandfather experience music? That, to my great disappointment, is something that I'll never know. Did he feel awe when he listened to Bach's cantatas? Would the transparent crystalline purity of Richard Strauss's *Death and Transfiguration* have reduced him to tears, as it did my husband, when we sat in the Amsterdam Concertgebouw listening to the Netherlands Radio Orchestra one wintry morning? Did Opa feel the agony of music, the way it wrenches you at your core, pulling and tearing at your ligaments and bones? Did he, like me, allow music to sear his flesh? Or was his rapture more cerebral? Did he delight in structure, form, harmony, and cadence? Did he enjoy the rational beauty of a well-formed movement, the delicate balance of a chord that was perfectly in tune? Did he celebrate tonal beauty? Did he value the mathematical precision of perfect intonation?

~~~~~

"Breathe right down to your toes," my flute teacher would tell me during my lessons in the Royal Conservatory. "Imagine your favourite smell—even this banana," he'd say, pointing at his lunch. "Draw it in. Feel the air moving through your body. And then, finish the cycle. Spin it. Release the sound." Air. Breath. Body. Sound. I can feel Bach's flute sonatas deep inside. Even today, when music is no longer such a central part of my everyday life, I know exactly where the sound lies; I know how my body resonates. I can hear the music before I release it into the world. I have no words for any of this; my body alone knows the way. How did my grandfather move through the world? How did his body resonate?

~~~~~

Between the lines of articles and concert reviews, I searched for Opa's musical desires, his politics, his passions. I looked for them in programming choices, in political alliances, in commemorative gestures and activities. "The men's choir, Harmonie, under the direction of Leo Heinemann, will celebrate its twentieth birthday on Thursday, 26 September," I read in the 25 September 1963 issue of *Nieuwe Suriname*. "The choir will begin the day with two wreath-laying ceremonies: at the Musicus-Helstone Monument on Church square around 9 o'clock in the morning and at the gravesite of Daan Samuels (Dario Saavedra) in the Jewish Cemetery on the Kwattaweg."

Opa's musical lineage granted pride of place to the remarkable Surinamese composer-performers Johannes Nicolaas Helstone and Dario Saavedra. Helstone was born in the Moravian mission on Berg en Dal plantation in January 1853 in the last decade before the abolition of slavery. Saavedra, meanwhile, was a celebrated pianist known particularly for his interpretations of Beethoven. But he also regularly performed Caribbean and South American compositions, celebrating, through them, the rhythms, harmonies, and melodies of his youth. Both composers featured on concert programs, their voices jostling, soaring, and dancing with those of the composers whose biographies stand sentinel on my bookshelves. Bach. Brahms. Schubert. Mozart. Bartók. Hindemith. Honegger. Helstone. Saavedra. Opa's musical autobiography was written in their memory; I could have heard it all for less than three guilders per concert.

~~~~~

My cousin Elvira's collaborative family tree includes two photos of Opa as a young man. In one, he's wearing a white suit, his angular face turned directly to the camera. I don't know how old he was when it was taken, but he projects an air of professionalism; there's a stillness, a seriousness of purpose, gravitas. The other is very different. Dressed in a dark suit with his body angled forward and his right hand resting on his thigh, Opa looks younger. Gangly, he hasn't quite grown into his body. There's a mobile energy to this photo, a restlessness. It's almost as if he can't wait to get moving again; he has things to do, places to go.

This was the young man who later paired great German choral masters with the sounds of Suriname, the man who travelled the Atlantic for music, leaving his wife and several children for a year. But who was he? What would he have wanted me to know? As I considered the two photos, I realized that while I'd bonded with my grandfather over music, I'd never really thought about him as a person. And somehow, I'd never even considered questions of race or belonging. Looking back, it seems so obvious. What would it have been like to be a Surinamese man in The Hague in 1950? Did people stop him as he walked the streets of this city? Or was this young brown man in his natty suits such an oddity that they kept their distance? There was a reason that Opa's choir, so firmly embedded in European art music, nevertheless drew its inspiration from Helstone

and Saavedra. There was a reason that choir members laid wreaths at their headstones. Was he, too, looking for a way to fit in?

Because here's the thing. I wasn't entirely sure *I* belonged in The Hague. At the market, near the bank, by the post office, I was regularly stopped by women wearing headscarves and trailing children behind them.

"Turks?" they or their children would ask, hope in their eyes.

"No." I'd shake my head. "I'm sorry."

The women were looking for a translator, someone who could help them navigate the various bumps and encounters of daily living in the Netherlands, and in me, they saw something they recognized. A way of being, perhaps. A skin tone. A relationship with the rest of the Dutch world. Western, but with a certain exotic flair. And something about all of this looked familiar. In that encounter, "Turks" was not just a question; it was an endearment, an intimacy. It was a way of seeking allegiances, a moment of recognition that acknowledged that we were both outsiders here.

Music was what brought me to The Hague. Music was what brought me to my grandfather. But all these years later, as I thought back through our shared history, I realized that there was so much more, so much I hadn't seen, so much I had yet to understand. My two years of study had given me an avenue into a family that I'd only ever known from a distance. Opa had left me a musical inheritance, but that inheritance wasn't only European, and it wasn't only musical. My aunt was right. Whatever purpose "Dutch-Canadian flutist" had served, that hyphenated identity was no longer enough. Europe couldn't tell me the whole story.

What about Suriname?

2.   (Facing page) My grandfather, Leonard Frederik Adolf Heinemann, as a young man. Photographer unknown. *Family photo.*

6

LINEAGE

~~~~~~

I F MY GRANDFATHER'S GHOST accompanied me through my musical studies, it was the ghosts of his ancestors who called to me on my return to The Hague seventeen years later. The National Archives of the Netherlands was a short walk from my budget hotel near the central shopping district. Inside, I headed to the locker room to put my backpack and jacket away and pulled out the archival tools of the trade: pencils, laptop, notebook, camera, and magnifying glass, and placed them in a clear plastic bag. These were the only things I was allowed to bring to the reading room with me. After my bag was thoroughly examined by a security guard, I walked into an open reading room filled with large white tables and generous workspaces that quickly filled with researchers. Within the first hour, over forty of us had scattered ourselves around, our noses buried in documents.

Across the room, I spied a renowned French historian whose work on French women's history had inspired my own early forays into archival research. Well into her eighties, she's still an active researcher, but her interests have shifted to early Jewish history in Suriname. She was scribbling in a notebook, a volume of seventeenth-century letters nestled on a comfortable pillow in front of her. I resisted the urge to ask for her autograph, knowing that on a scale of one to ten, where ten is the worst breach of archival etiquette, that request would count as an eleven. On the other end of the room, a man stood on a raised platform, his camera carefully slotted into a giant tripod, a professional lens pointing straight down at an enormous map laid out on the table below him. Another group of researchers clustered in the centre of the reading room, examining particularly vulnerable or unique documents under the eagle eyes of the archives staff.

Archives have their own cultures. Some are formal. Some are relaxed. But all share similar behavioural expectations. The first person in wins the best seat in the house. Don't take up more than your space. Expect dirty looks if you start to chat with your neighbour. Smile at the archivists, and always say thank you. Trust comes with time. Above all, cultivate your poker face, and keep it on, no matter what you're reading. Archives are no place for emotions.

For many, archives seem dry, impersonal spaces, dusty repositories of long-dead pasts. But for others of us, working with manuscripts can be a surprisingly intimate experience, and the past can touch us in unexpected ways. A number of years ago, several of my undergraduate students were researching women's letters sent to the first premier of Newfoundland and Labrador, Joseph R. Smallwood. Most had never visited archives before. But they were interested in women, and in Newfoundland, and in social justice. Letters to a political leader were a good place to start.

Paging through a file of letters from her hometown, one student was so moved by the discovery of one of her ancestor's signatures on a petition that she burst into tears and had to leave the reading room. Another, in a dogged search for more information about an impoverished family looking for help to support the medical care of their sick child, was brought up short when she learned that the ten-year-old child had died less than a year after his mother's first desperate letter.

"He was a real kid," she said, showing us a photograph of his tombstone. "This was his life, and this was his death."

Over the years, I'd learned archival ways. I knew how to be a proper researcher and how to keep my poker face on. But I was still reeling from my time in Middelburg, and I'd grown wary. I didn't know what stories these materials would reveal, or if I was ready to read them.

~~~~~

Unlike in Middelburg, where I had had to order documents after my arrival, here my files were waiting for me when I arrived. Three heavy boxes of documents from the Algemene Rekenkamer—the General Accounting Chamber—the federal department tasked with managing the nation's finances and accounts. Each box was filled with materials relating to the abolition of slavery in 1863. Somewhere inside them I would find the records for Sarah plantation, where my ancestors had been enslaved.

On the surface, it seems odd to look for plantation histories in accounting records. But plantations were businesses, concerned with profit. And plantation owners, distressed by the Dutch government's decision to abolish slavery, had demanded compensation. The government agreed. Owners—*granmasra* in Sranan Tongo, the local Creole language—would receive a sum of 300 guilders for every slave they owned. But first, they needed to prove it. And so it was that in 1862, plantation owners filled in paperwork declarations to register their human property. A few months later, enumerators travelled around the colony—from plantation to plantation—to confirm these numbers, annotating lists and making notes. They counted and listed all the slaves, noting who was on the plantation, and who was not. They also identified those who were old or infirm, those whom they thought were faking it—listed in the declarations as malingerers—and those who had run away or died.

I pulled the first box towards me. *Plantages P-S.* Plantations P-S. *de Gekroonde Paauw. Perou. Perseverance. Plaisance.* There was a curious playfulness to some of these plantation names that I hadn't expected. The Crowned Peacock. Peru. Perseverance. Pleasure. The names made me think of Sunday teas, cream puffs, and raspberry cordial. They were the stuff of romantic fantasies, frothy dreams, and adventures.

But as I looked more closely at the records, a different sort of playfulness emerged. Here, among the names given to the enslaved, I came face to face with an ugly, malicious sense of humour, a meanness. *Profijt. Onverwacht. Nooitgedacht. Suspicie. Vaderland. Geluk. Nieuwjaar.* Profit. Unexpected. Never thought of. Suspicion. Fatherland. Luck. New Year. These were names designed to humiliate, names specially bestowed to provoke the laughter of other owners and directors. I pictured a plantation owner chuckling at an evening dinner, the flickering candlelight reflected in his eager, feverish eyes, and I despised him.

I moved on, eager to reach the records for Sarah plantation. *Quasibo. Rama. La Rencontre. Resolutie. Ma Retraite. Rust en Werk.* Rest and Work. Another cruel irony. I paused for a closer look. Enumerators made careful lists of owners. In some instances, where plantations were jointly owned by a group of individuals, the calculations were complex. Rust en Werk, a coffee plantation established in 1750 in the Commewijne region of Suriname, had seven owners. Of those, three held a one-quarter share each. The rest shared the final quarter share. La Rencontre had a list that seemed to go on forever, every ownership share carefully accounted for.

I paged farther through the stack. *La Sonnette. Mon Sort. Mon Souci. Spieringshoek.* I'd gone too far. *Spieringshoek. Mon Souci. Mon Sort. La Sonnette. Rust en Werk. Ma Retraite.* Too far again. I went back and forth a few times, before I concluded that Sarah wasn't there.

It wasn't there. Until that moment, I hadn't realized how much this would matter. The words drummed a rhythm against my brain. *Not there. Not there. Not there.* But Sarah was a large plantation. One of the largest in the country at the time. I'd seen digitized transcriptions. Where was Sarah? I grew frantic, looking back and forth, back and forth. *Spieringshoek. Sort. Sonnette. Souci. Sonnette. Sort. Souci. Spieringshoek. Sort. Sonnette. Souci.* Sarah had to be there somewhere. It had to. The reading room receded, and the only thing that mattered was the stack of papers in front of me.

Then, there it was. *Sarah*, at the bottom of the pile, after *Susannasdaal*.

Immediately I retreated, my professional research shell sliding firmly in place. Like the enumerators, I catalogued and organized. I counted pages and laid them out for careful photography. I remained impartial. In my research journal, I wrote: "The list includes a total of 178 men and 146 women. Youngest is 2 months old. Photos taken. This is a much larger plantation in terms of numbers of slaves than the other ones I saw today. An awful lot of young people on this plantation. Many teenagers and children. The oldest appears to be 77 but there are only 2 over 70, one man who is 73 (Glasford) and one woman. 60s: 10 in their sixties, more men than women. ca. 90 between the ages of 10 and 19. That's about 25% of the total. 102 between 0 and 10. Thus, fully half the slaves were below the age of 20 with a large number below 10, even."

I saved my document. Then, after emailing the photos to my cousin, I turned off my computer and shut the manuscript file. Closed it. Tied the ribbon. Put everything back into the box. All around me, a light brown dust from the crumbling edges of nineteenth-century paper. *Ashes to ashes*, I thought, *dust to dust.* I returned the box to the counter, packed up my computer, straightened out my notes, and headed out the door.

Back in my hotel, I logged on to social media and updated my status. "Today I found part of my family tree," I wrote, attaching a photo I took of the first page of the plantation register.

A colleague, looking through this list that included John, Abraham, Riley, Charles, Wilson, and Philip, noticed how anglophone the names were. My sister, Sarah, cut straight to the chase.

"Nice to be named after a plantation," she wrote, with no small amount of sarcasm.

It was only much later that evening—long after a sushi dinner with an old friend from my conservatory days—that I realized I had turned myself off. My professional self had silenced my personal self. Finding my family tree in the archives, in a plantation register, should have been a momentous thing. I should have allowed myself to feel, to savour, reflect, grieve. But instead I'd cocooned myself, retreating behind the safety of the research lens. I hadn't taken time to feel the paper. I hadn't thought about its smell. I hadn't really read the names. I hadn't sounded them out inside my mind, felt them on my tongue. Like the enumerators, I'd just sorted and organized, catalogued and counted. And now that moment—that very first encounter with the materiality of my past—was lost. I would never have it back again.

~~~~~~

In 1862, there were 324 slaves at Sarah plantation: 178 men and boys, and 146 women and girls. Fourteen of them were my ancestors. Frederik Noa. Philip Elias. Edward. Frederika. Eva Albertina. Cornelis. Jack Abraham. Janny Rebecca. Madleentje Paulina. Wilson Boas. Leander. Sultan Timotheus. Joseph Elias. Amsterdam Job.

The next morning, when I returned to the archives, I ran my fingers down the pages, looking for the names I knew would be there. Philip. Male. 41. Field. Moravian. Edward. Male. 43. Field. Frederik. 63. Male. Old. Moravian. Eva. Female. 34. Field. Moravian.

Sultan. Male. 14. Apprentice Carpenter. Moravian. Wilson. Male. 4. Playing. Jeanny. Female. 12. Field.

In between them, hundreds more. Name. Sex. Occupation. Coffie. Male. 46. Field. Cupid. Male. 45. Field. Augustus. Male. 17. Smith. Manchester. Male. 62. Old. Titus. Male. 52. Watchman. Peter. Male. 13. Cattleherder. Mermaid. Female. 52. Caregiver. Catharina. Female. 50. Cook for the ill. Delia. Female. 51. Caregiver for Creole children. Petronella. Female. 15. House Slave.

Page after page after page. This wasn't just my family; this was a whole community. The register transformed itself into a census. Census: an account of a population in a given place at a given time. The names ran together, tumbling one after another through my consciousness, overwhelming me. Peak. Johnson. Isaac. Riley. Simon. Samuel. John. Abraham. Ned. Sandy. John. Audain. Cruden. Theodore. Augustus. Prins. Charles. Elder. Wilson. Phillip. Coffie. Cupid. Sluyce. Edward. Frans. Chance. Yaw. Charley. Sidney. Kitt. London. Thomas 2e. William. Johnny. Pallas. Ajax. Robert. Quamie. Kingsmill. Johannes. JeanBaptist. Jack. Slengarde. Christoffel. Robertson. James. Ben. Bernhard. Gausie. Darby. Marcus. Charles. David. Arthur. Gilbee. Jacob. Vrolyk. Doris. vanThol. Farwel. Anderson. Jacques. Douglas. Demion. Anthony. Henry. Greenfield. Andrew. Ricketts. Whitecomb. Menosabie. Augustinus. Samuel 2e. Dirk. Dick. Harris. Sampson. Heintje. Hendrick. Peter. Frederik. Glasford. Manchester. Hercules. Titus. Alfred. Daniel. Steward. Fortuin. Adrian. Salomon. Cupido. Nooitgedacht. Romeo. James. Ryder. Rozain. Casper. Archy. Vigelant. Ferrier. Frederick. Bathol. Ferdinand. Cornelis. Sutan. Peter. Welcom. Christopher. Richard. Elder 2e. Edward. Toussaint. Blandford. Munroe. Amsterdam. Bethune. Green. Jurgenson. Adam. George 2e. 2e Glasford. Simon 2e. Nelson. Carlisle. Duncan. Jack 2e. Primo. James 3e. Charles 2e. Thomas 2e. Lancaster. Samuel 3e. Francis. Harris 2e. Peter 2e. Simore. Klaas.

Mars 2e. Frederick 3e. Kitt 2e. Isaac 2e. Joseph. Tom 2e. Sluis 2e.
Phillip 2e. Cambden. Abraham 2e. Desse. Brunings. Wilson 2e.
Johnson 2e. Stewart 2e. Christian. Mentor. Ned. Fortuin. Alex-
ander. Maandag. Mingo. Harry. Frits. Edwin. Henry 2e. George
4e. Greenfield 2e. Cicero 2e. Jacob 2e. Bent 2e. Trobie. Lodewijk.
Willie. Bonaparte. Ferdinand. Winst. Tom. Peak 2e. Leander.
Venus. Fanny. Hannah. Caledonia. Clarissa. Sophietje 2e. Sarah.
Dolly. Nancy. Flora. Rosina. Sussanna. Helen. Margareth. Elis-
abeth. Sena. Clara. Diana 2e. Philles. Patience. Meintje. Sophonosbia. Celestina. Eve. Jane 2e. Frederika. Adjuba. Bella. Molly.
Madleentje. Kea. Jetta. Coba. Jeannetta. Dorothea. Sophia. Tru-
itje. Doortje. Lucretia. Marianna. Jane 3e. Lysie. Emma. Victo-
ria. Pandora. Aurora. Constancy. Lotje. Johanna. Jansje. Rebecca.
Daphnij. Wilhelmina. Georgina. Mietje. Betsey. Gratia. Antje.
Minerva. Petronella. Mermaid. Louisa. Sally. Jane 1e. Delia. Flo-
rinda. Laner. Catharina. Bell. Clarinda. Princess. Lucia. Catharina
1e. Kitty. Bell. Saraatje. Cato. Amba. Magie. Christiana. Louisa.
Julia. Peternella. Eliza. Antje. Esther. Vinette. Eva. Charlotte.
Phillippina. Jeanny. Jeanny 3e. Jansje. Grace. Lidia 2e. Sarah 2e.
Rozette. Sophietje. Johanna 2e. Clarinda 2e. Mary 2e. Azia. Harri-
ette 2. Caro. Venus 2e. Martina. Betty 2e. Princess 2e. Catherina 3e.
Mermaid 2e. Elize. Fidella. Cicilia. Cecilia 3e. Caledonia 2e. Fanny

3. (Facing page) The first page of the accounting declaration for Sarah
plantation. This record, which runs to eleven pages, includes not only
the names of the enslaved, but also their age, work title, and faith.
My great-great-great-uncles, Philip and Edward, are both listed here
as *veld*—or field—slaves. National Archives of the Netherlands,
Algemene Rekenkamer / Comptabel Beheer, Stukken tot opheffing
der slavernij in West-Indië, 1863–1868, catalogue reference 2.02.09.08,
inventory number 227, Public Domain. *Photo credit: Sonja Boon.*

№ 2199

Borderel van Aangifte.

De Ondergeteekende *Jacobus Barkey*
woonachtig *op Plantagie Sarah*
verklaart dat de Slaven, behoorende aan de Plantaadje *Sarah*
gelegen aan de rivier _____ divisie *Coronie*
waarvan eigenaar is *Anthony Derfe*

woonachtig te *Nickerie, thans in Europa*

op heden bestaan in de navolgende hoofden: *Namelijk*

NAMEN.	GESLACHT.		Ouderdom.	bedrijf of beroep	Godsdienst.	Verkregen regt op Manumissie.	Suspectverklaarden aan de ziekte der Melaatschheid of Elephantiasis.	Aanteekeningen.
	Mann.	Vrouw.						
Peak	1		67 jaar	Veld	M B G	Geen	Geen	
Johnston	1		52	„	„	„ 1		
Isaac	1		60	Sieken oppasser	R C	„		
Kelly	1		50	veld	M B G	„		
Simon	1		53	timmer	R C	„		
Samuel	1		60	Smid	„	„		
John	1		49	veld	M B G	„		
Abraham	1		42	timmer	R C	„	„	
Ned	1		40	„	M B G	„	„	
Sandy	1		38	„	„	„	„	
John	1		35	„	Luther	„	„	
Adain	1		21	„	R C	„	„	
Cruden	1		21	„	M B G	„	„	
Theodore	1		17	„	„	„	„	
Augustus	1		17	Smid	„	„	„	
Prins	1		17	timmer	„	„	„	
Charles	1		61	veld	„	„	„	
Elder	1		51	„	Geen	„	„	
Wilson	1		48	„	M B G	„	„	
Phillip	1		47	„	„	„	„	
Coffie	1		46	„	„	„	„	
Cupid	1		45	„	„	„	„	
Sluyer	1		43	„	„	„	„	
Edward	1		43	„	Geen	„	„	
Frans	1		42	„	M B G	„	„	
Chance	1		42	„	Geen	„	„	
Juren	1		42					
	27							

	Geen	Aanteekeningen.						
"	"							
"	"							

NAMEN.	GESLACHT.		Ouderdom.	Bedrijf of beroep.	Godsdienst.	Verkregen regt op Ramentalie.	Aanteekeningen.	Aanteekenis
	Man.	Vrouw.						
portransport	60							
Anderson	1		19	Veld	R: C	Geen	Geen	
Jacques	1		18	"	M B G	"	"	
Douglas	1		18	"	"	"	"	
Dennison	1		18	"	"	"	"	
Anthony	1		18	"	"	"	"	
Henry	1		18	"	"	"	"	
Greenfield	1		18	"	"	"	"	
Andrew	1		18	"	Geen	"	"	
Ricketts	1		18	"	R: C	"	"	
Whitecomb	1		18	"	M B G	"	"	
Menesabie	1		18	"	R: C	"	"	
Augustinus	1		17	"	M B G	"	"	
Samuell	1		17	"	R: C	"	"	
Dick	1		15	"	M B G	"	"	
Dick	1		13	"	R: C	"	"	
Harris	1		42	"	M B G	"	"	
Simpson	1		43	Vischer	"	"	"	
Heintje	1		20	veld	Geen	"	"	
Hendrick	1		53	"	"	"	"	
Peter	1		42	Timm.	M B G	"	"	
Frederick	1		63	oud	"	"	"	
Glasford	1		73	"	"	"	"	
Manchester	1		62	"	"	"	"	
Hercules	1		62	"	Geen	"	"	
Titus	1		52	Vischman	"	"	"	Malinks arme boe
Alfred	1		36	—	M B G			Malinks Teenn
Daniel	1		25	Ziekin Oppasser				
Steward	1		42	veld	"			
Fortuin	1		63	Geen	"			
Adriaan	1		50	Veld wachter				
Salomon	1		69	"	"			
Cespedo	1		64	oud	Geen			
Nooitgedacht	1		58		"			
	93							

2e. Venus 3e. Carolina. Peggy 3e. Madleentje 2e. Amelia 2e. Josina. Bebe. Betsey 2e. Margareth 2e. Hannah 2e. Princess 2e. Jacquelina. Josephina. Sophia. Florence. Annatje. Clarissa 2e. Sena 2e. Calista. Hendrina. Helena. Lena. Jeannette 2e. Francina. Christina. Betty 3e. Kate. Cathryntje. Clasina. Kitty.

Once I looked, I couldn't look away. This family history of enslavement was real. The pain of knowing was acute. And as if pursuing some ritual form of self-flagellation, I kept coming back for more that day, returning over and over to the records for Sarah plantation. There was a rhythm to the names, and typing them out, one after another, became a meditation. Letters into sounds into words into names into communities. Letters lay under my fingers; names settled on my tongue. Speaking their names brought them into existence, made their lives tangible, material, real. Typing became a way of keeping vigil, bearing witness, honouring the dead.

So many names. So many stories. How did they weave in and through my own family histories? What loves had brought them together? What passions had divided them?

~~~~~

Sarah plantation was located in the west of Suriname, in an area known in the archival records as the Zeekust, or Sea Coast. This region was opened up for development sometime around 1800,

4. (Facing page) The third page of the accounting declaration for Sarah plantation. My great-great-great-great-grandfather Frederick Noa (notated here as Frederick) is listed as *oud*—or old—and therefore not working. National Archives of the Netherlands, Algemene Rekenkamer / Comptabel Beheer, Stukken tot opheffing der slavernij in West-Indië, 1863–1868, catalogue reference 2.02.09.08, inventory number 227, Public Domain. *Photo credit: Sonja Boon.*

while Suriname was temporarily under British control. In contrast to other plantation lands in Suriname, which opened onto rivers and canals, these final plots of land opened out to the Caribbean Sea. These coastal properties were snapped up one by one, most by Scottish and English investors—Tyndal, Rickets, Cruickshank, Walton, Carstairs, Murphy, Cameron, Pickering—and cleared for plantations. Lots 212 and 213, totalling one thousand acres, later became Sarah plantation.

In two watercolour paintings dating from around 1860, Sarah is a fully developed plantation: one painting depicts a wide, fenced avenue leading to a large two-storey wooden plantation house with a covered verandah, the other an idyllic treed road to the plantation hospital. The palette is watery; the landscape looks tame, gentle, quiet. But for the two coconut palms in the first painting, I'd almost think I was looking at an English scene, the Cotswolds, perhaps. There's a timelessness to the paintings; it's as if this is how it always was and how it would always be. There's no hint of the labour required to keep the hungry jungle at bay. In fact, there is no hint of labour—of the hundreds of people enslaved at Sarah—at all.

The survey document from the early part of the century is much simpler. It shows two measured parcels, almost perfect rectangles, opening out to the ocean. These parcels were purchased by a German man, J.H. Dietzel, in 1801. Dietzel wasn't wealthy. A former soldier, he'd established himself along Suriname's west coast, where it's possible that he earned his living from selling alcohol to Indigenous people and capturing escaped slaves from Berbice. He acquired the plots with no real intention or even ability to develop them. Instead, he sold them, using the proceeds to establish himself and his family in Paramaribo.

By 1820, the lots, then named Sarah plantation, were under the ownership of a man named John Bent. Bent was an Englishman whose name has faded into complete obscurity. But he played an active role on the Surinamese plantation stage in the first half of the nineteenth century. Born in 1776 to a relatively lowbrow English family, Bent later served from 1818 and 1820 as a Tory Member of Parliament for Sligo, and then from 1820 to 1826 as MP for Totnes. He was also a prominent slave owner in both Suriname and Guyana. Bent appears to have begun acquiring plantations in Suriname sometime in the early nineteenth century. In the 1820 *Almanac*, he is listed as the owner of a number of plantations in various parts of the colony: Descanzo, Domburg, and Sarah. He also owned a final, as yet undeveloped, parcel of land—Lots 223 and 224—along the Zeekust. It's possible that Frederik Noa, then in his early twenties and already father to two children—sons Philip Elias and Edward—was purchased for the plantation around this time. It's also possible that Bent transferred the family from one of his holdings in Guyana. What is certain is that from a planter's perspective, Frederik, his unnamed partner, and their two sons would have been an ideal investment: three healthy males and one female who could populate the new plantation space.

From Frederik's perspective? I can barely bring myself to imagine it.

Over the next decade, Bent actively engaged in buying. By 1828, he'd added two more plantations to his holdings and had developed his previously unnamed land into Totness plantation, perhaps in honour of his parliamentary role.

I've looked in vain for a painting of John Bent; his is a face I'd like to see. Was he a jowly man whose doughy face reflected the apparently comfortable life of a slave-owning planter? Or was he dour, narrow, and haughty, possessed of a sour face and disposition? Maybe he had the eager, rat-like face of an entrepreneur, twitchy nose raised to the wind, sniffing out the perfect investment opportunity. In the archives, he comes across as an ambitious if somewhat bumbling character, a man who wanted to make a name for himself as a wealthy and successful planter but who wasn't quite as adept at business as some of his colleagues.

How does such a personality inscribe itself onto a face? Onto a body? What did this man who once owned my ancestors look like? I wanted to be able to look him in the eye. It's easier to ask someone questions that way, and there were so many questions I wanted answered. But this was the most significant one: Mr. Bent, where did your slave Frederik Noa, the one listed after Peter and before Glasford, the one born in 1798 to a mother listed as "unknown," come from? Before 1798, the record is silent. *Onbekend*. Unknown.

~~~~~

Frederik Noa's first name was probably bestowed on him by his first owner. His second was likely a gift from the Moravian Church on the date of his baptism. Noa, they said. Noa, from the Hebrew, meaning "rest and comfort." Noa, who led the animals, two by two, away from the flood. Noa, who built an ark so that his family and God's creatures might live.

Noa, the patriarch.
Noa, the leader.
Noa, the ark builder.
Noa, I hoped, the bearer of stories.

~~~~~

I have no idea what my great-great-great-great-grandfather looked like, how he walked, what his voice sounded like. And so I created him in my head, pulling him together from the bodies of Creole men in early photographs. Frederik Noa, I imagined, was a lanky man with a quick smile, bright white teeth in a dark face. I thought I could see tufts of white hair, like the balls of cotton his family spent their days picking, sprouting from his head. The image wobbled, out of focus, then dissolved. I found myself back in the archives, my hand resting on the record for Sarah plantation.

Frederik Noa Redout was born in 1798, at the turn of the century, on the cusp of a period of profound social and political change. And this is precisely why I needed him to be the bearer of histories. He was right on the front lines, a witness to these far-reaching shifts. Frederik was there when the British abolished the slave trade, and later, when they abolished slavery itself. He was there when three runaway slaves were charged with setting fire to the capital city of Paramaribo in 1832. And three years later, when the silence of Tata Colin, a man enslaved on nearby Burnside plantation, inspired a revolt at neighbouring Leasowes plantation. And he was there, too, in 1862, when enumerators came to count the enslaved.

Frederik must have carried these stories in his body. He must have stored them in his memories and shared them with his children, his grandchildren. He must have carried them with him into a life of freedom. But I couldn't see him in the archives; I couldn't hear his voice. All I had was the disintegrating paper on which the few details of his life were recorded.

I don't know where Frederik was born. I don't know where he passed his childhood. What I do know is this: for most of his adult life, Frederik was enslaved at Sarah plantation. The official record says that in 1862, Frederik was owned by a man named Anthony Dessé. It says that two of Dessé's Sarah plantation slaves were away when the count happened: Jurgenson, age eleven, had been sent off to another plantation as part of a Moravian educational experiment. Madleentje Paulina—listed as Madleentje 2e, or Madleentje the second—was somewhere in Paramaribo, possibly a domestic slave or perhaps as a playmate for a young white child. Madleentje 2e was only seven years old when the enumerators came to visit. She was Frederik's granddaughter and my great-great-grandmother.

I wondered what Madleentje Paulina was like as a child, and how she managed this separation from her family. At seven, I was quiet and reserved, a child who spent more time observing the world than interacting with it. I lost myself in books, experiencing life through the various exploits of the fictional heroines who became my closest friends. Like the orphaned Anne of Green Gables, I lived in a story world of my own making, creating adventures in which I was the heroine. The Lake of the Shining Waters, the Haunted Wood, Lover's Lane. Anne, Diana, Gilbert, Moody. But before Anne, I'd latched onto Mary Lennox of *The Secret Garden*. Thrust into a completely foreign world after the deaths of her parents, she had to learn new customs, new behaviours. She had to make new friends. And she wasn't always gracious about it. Like Mary a lonely and sometimes whingy interloper in worlds that were unfamiliar to me, I needed to find my way into new cultures, customs, languages, ways of being. And then there was Laura Ingalls, the rough-and-tumble child whose family left behind the Big Woods, and everything they knew, for a life of homesteading and adventure on the western frontier. Laura wasn't an orphan like Anne and Mary. Rather, her whole family was marooned on a vast prairie that promised adventure even as it seethed with the unknown—deep dark winters, locusts, uncertain relationships with townspeople, and tenuous and often highly problematic encounters with Indigenous people.

Anne, Mary, and Laura. These were the heroines to whom I gravitated as a child, the characters whose stories I returned to, over and over again. All of us were destined to create our own presents in the absence of our pasts. We had no larger context in which to locate ourselves. What it came down to, in the simplest terms, was this: like Anne and Mary and Laura, I didn't fit in. Wherever I was, it was as if I'd been dropped in, falling from the sky.

I sat in the National Archives in The Hague with my great-great-grandmother. Madleentje 2e. Madleentje Paulina. Another marooned young girl.

~~~~~

Sarah plantation wasn't Dessé's only property. A mixed-race planter originally from elsewhere in the Caribbean, Dessé had worked his way up the plantation ladder. In the beginning he managed plantations for others. But by 1854, he owned three cotton plantations in the western region of Suriname, and within three years, he'd purchased Sarah—another cotton plantation—and Paradise, a sugar plantation. By 1857, he owned more than 1,100 slaves and had settled himself into a comfortable existence in the town of New Rotterdam in the far west of Suriname. He was one of the most powerful plantation owners in Suriname.

Abolition only added to Dessé's wealth. For the slaves under his ownership, he received compensation of more than 140,000 guilders. The fourteen members of my family were worth 4,200 guilders. I typed the numbers into an online currency conversion calculator. Today, they'd be worth about 42,000 euros. That's 3,000 euros per person. Almost 4,500 Canadian dollars.

For the value of a slave, I could take a cruise, that transoceanic one with the flying fish, but 4,500 dollars couldn't begin to buy me a professional flute. Depending on the model I decided on, it might not even buy me half of one. What does this mean? How does this kind of accounting even work? I was losing touch with my family, the archives drawing me instead into numbers and accounts. I thought I could see my great-great-great-great-grandfather laughing, as he turned towards me. But when he opened his mouth to speak, no words emerged.

The walk home from the archives took me down the Bezuiden-houtseweg and then onto the Herengracht, one of the main down-town shopping streets. I passed a store selling incense, Buddhas, and bags made of sari silk. Across the street, a giant clog marked the entrance to a tourist shop that offered Delft blue kitsch, *stroop-wafels*, and wooden tulips. In the bike store, I picked up a name plate for my older son. Like me, Stefan can never find anything with his name on it in Canada. But in The Hague, I could buy us both one.

I paused when I reached the Spui. It was a Wednesday. Turn-ing right would take me to the organic market outside the Bin-nenhof. Turning left would take me past the public library. The tram announced its arrival, and I stepped back, my decision made. I turned right, making my way towards the Hofvijver, the large rectangular pond that lies next to the cluster of historic buildings— some dating to the thirteenth century—known as the Binnenhof, or Inner Court. I wasn't ready to go back to my hotel room yet. I needed time and space to think.

~~~~~

What does it mean to live in the shadow of freedom? To hear the word on everyone's lips, to feel it just out of reach? What does it mean to one living a life of slavery?

In my late twenties, I visited Berlin in search of eighteenth-century music from the court of Frederick the Great, the flute-playing monarch who ruled Prussia from 1740 to 1786. I spent my days immersed in the past, revelling in handwritten manuscripts by Carl Philipp Emanuel Bach, Johann Joachim Quantz, and King Frederick himself, and marvelling at the opulent excess of his palace in Potsdam. Because I was in search of the eighteenth cen-tury, the twentieth left barely any impression on me. I didn't pay attention to the crumbling remains of the Berlin Wall, or to the grittiness of East Berlin.

While I had been losing myself in the ridiculous frothiness that is Sans Souci, Frederick the Great's fanciful eighteenth-century palace, one of my roommates, a university student from Coquitlam, British Columbia, had taken the train north to Oranienburg to visit the former Sachsenhausen concentration camp. Sachsenhausen, in operation from 1936 to 1945, was mainly used for political prisoners. Its location also assured that it would become an administrative and training centre. As a museum, Sachsenhausen wasn't yet well known at the time, and my roommate was the only visitor that day.

The site was quiet, a barren wasteland of concrete and barbed wire.

"There was nobody else there," she told me later. "It was just me and the wind."

What the eye can't see, the imagination fills in.

Arbeit macht frei.

"I just sat down on the ground," she said, "and cried."

She told me she was a criminology student and that she volunteered for the John Howard Society, helping incarcerated individuals prepare for life after release. She worked with men at the Mission Institution, a minimum- and medium-security prison in British Columbia's Fraser Valley. She taught them about shopping, transit, housing.

"You're telling me that there's a whole aisle of cookies in the grocery store?" one man had asked her.

She nodded.

"I've been in for ten years," he said, "and I haven't made a single decision for myself. And you're telling me that I have to choose from a whole *aisle* of cookies?"

The man had tears in his eyes. He had no idea what he was going to do, no clue how he'd even begin to live his life as a free man.

"The prison system gives them fifty bucks and sends them off," my roommate said. "There's no way they're ready to enter society again. Things have changed so much while they're in."

When you've spent years dreaming of freedom, what do you do when that dream is finally granted? How do you prepare for a reality you've never known?

I've never lived in a state of captivity. I don't know what it is like to be imprisoned, enslaved, confined. I don't know how it would be for my family to live this way for generations, to be aware that my children, my grandchildren, my great-grandchildren would know nothing different. And so I can't imagine, either, what freedom must have meant. What did the word, the concept mean to those who had never experienced it?

"Man is born free," the eighteenth-century political philosopher Jean-Jacques Rousseau wrote, "and everywhere he is in chains." Two hundred years later, another philosopher, Jean-Paul Sartre, observed that we are "condemned to be free." Both are great starting points for philosophical conversations about the nature of freedom and the essence of being human. But what did either of these men really know of this, at the level of lived experience? What could they write about slavery, about bondage, about unfreedom? Can their comments help me to understand what my ancestors lived through, and how they imagined and understood their lives and their worlds?

~~~~~

By the time Frederik Noa was born, the transatlantic slave trade was already well established. There were some 600 plantations in Suriname, and the slave population was enormous, outnumbering the white population by more than ten to one in the plantation districts.

But things were finally changing. The British formally abolished the slave trade in 1807. The Dutch followed in 1814, two years before the birth of Frederik's first son, Philip, in 1816. While an illicit trade continued after this point, slave owners could no longer, at least in principle, purchase new slaves; instead, they had to breed them. As revolting as this sounds, this was an improvement for many enslaved women, who received better health care, improved working conditions, and increased food rations. A decade later, when Frederik's twins, Eva and Frederika, were born, the British were deep into abolitionist debates. Just a few years after that, in 1834, the British Slavery Abolition Act came into force, freeing hundreds of thousands of slaves in the West Indies, including those in neighbouring British Guyana. In 1852, a year after Frederik's granddaughter, Jeanny, was born, Harriet Beecher Stowe published *Uncle Tom's Cabin*, a book that profoundly influenced the Dutch abolitionist movement. The contours of my family history followed, almost exactly, the contours of the shifting landscape of slavery and abolition.

The enslaved themselves weren't silent either. In 1823, some ten thousand slaves in Demerara staged a two-day rebellion. In 1832, three runaway slaves—Cojo, Mentor, and Present—set fire to a house in Paramaribo. The subsequent inferno burned down over a hundred structures in the heart of the city. Three years later, at Burnside plantation, a slave named Tata Colin emerged as an *obiaman*, a prophet who promised to turn the world upside down: the blacks would turn white, he said, and the whites black. Some slaves committed suicide in their bid for freedom. Others simply walked away from their plantations and disappeared into the rainforest. In 1862, on the eve of abolition, an enslaved woman named her newborn daughter Libertina. Freedom, however it could be achieved, was a promise.

The *Oxford English Dictionary* is frustratingly oblique in defining "freedom":

"The state or fact of being free from servitude, constraint, inhibition, etc."

"Exemption or release from slavery or imprisonment."

"Liberation from bondage."

Freedom, the dictionary says, is the opposite of unfreedom. But how can you know that freedom is what you want, when all you have ever known is its absence?

~~~~~

I settled myself onto a bench near the statue of Haagsche Jantje, a character from a well-known Dutch children's folk song, and looked across the pond at the Mauritshuis, a seventeenth-century aristocratic home that now houses the Royal Cabinet of Paintings, an impressive collection of Dutch art. When we'd lived in The Hague in the 1990s, the Mauritshuis had hosted the largest exhibition of Vermeer paintings ever gathered under one roof. *Girl with a Pearl Earring. The Milkmaid. View of Delft. A Lady Writing a Letter. The Guitar Player. The Lacemaker. The Astronomer. The Geographer. Lady Seated at a Virginal. The Music Lesson. Girl with a Red Hat* ...

Búi and I had booked tickets months in advance, securing a two-hour slot between four and six in the afternoon. The Hague, meanwhile, went Vermeer-mad. You could buy "Vermeer's bread" and posters of the girl with the pearl earring. Even a lingerie shop got in on the fun, remaking Vermeer's milkmaid as a young woman sporting a fashionable bra. *De beha van Vermeer*, the poster proclaimed. Vermeer's bra.

I sat quietly on the bench, remembering, the tune to *Haagsche Jantje* running through my mind. *In Den Haag daar woont een graaf, En zijn zoon heet Jantje. Als je vraagt waar woont je Pa, Dan wijst hij met zijn handje.* . . . In The Hague there lives a count and his son is named Johnny. When you ask, "Where lives your pa?" he points with his tiny hand ...

While Vermeer was painting his richly detailed domestic scenes, the Dutch were building their global empire. The seventeenth century was the Dutch Golden Age. The Dutch East India Company, founded in 1602, had established a powerful trade network that stretched from the Cape of Good Hope to China and Japan. Its slightly younger counterpart, the Dutch West India Company, controlled the Atlantic. Established in 1621, the West India Company engaged in territorial conquest and privateering before turning its hand to the Atlantic slave trade. The Dutch became particularly active during the second half of the century; between 1650 and 1675—the period during which Vermeer painted every single one of his iconic works, from *The Milkmaid* and *Girl with a Pearl Earring* to *Lady Seated at a Virginal*—fully half of all ships transporting enslaved Africans to the New World were Dutch ships.

～～～～

How do those of us who have never known bondage honour these legacies of violence? Some descendants of Holocaust survivors have chosen to tattoo their ancestors' histories onto their bodies, claiming their grandparents' concentration camp numbers as their own. These arm tattoos are acts of remembrance, ways for them to acknowledge, witness, and pass on difficult stories. For some, the tattoos opened up a space to talk about painful experiences, to work through fraught family silences. For others, the tattoos remind them of the ongoingness of injustice and violence, and of their responsibility to live different lives, imagine different futures.

The accounting declarations were like a family tree. They told me who lived and who died. They told me who ran away and who stayed, who worked and who malingered. They could begin my story, but they couldn't end it. Survival, as Indigenous activists and writers have suggested, is an act of profound resilience. It is the story that says, *You tried your best to destroy us. You treated us like the lowest of creatures, and yet we lived. And we still live today.*

Maybe, then, it's enough that Frederik Noa lived. That his children lived. That their children lived. And their children too. Maybe it is enough that I exist. Maybe survival itself is the only form of resistance to the horrors of slavery.

I struggled as I read the declarations. These weren't family bibles, passed down through generations, new names added along the way. I wanted so desperately to understand. How could it be that three generations of my family—and probably more—lived through slavery?

~~~~~~

Tell me a story, Frederik. I'm here, I'm listening.

But that afternoon in The Hague, my great-great-great-great-grandfather remained frustratingly silent.

7

Due SOUTH

"YOU'RE GOING BACK," a friend said to me before my departure for Suriname.

Back? I thought to myself. *Back where?* I wondered what he meant by this. It's hard to claim an identity that is mine only by inheritance. An identity constructed by a land that I barely knew. I wasn't born in Suriname. I'd never lived there. For most of my life, the country had remained on the periphery of my thoughts. *Return. Back.* These are difficult words to make sense of. I shied away from them, uncertain of how to respond.

It was February 2015, forty-one years since I'd last visited Suriname. The stamps in my passport were clear, but my memories were dim. I remembered my great-aunt Hélène—a nurse—piercing my ears in a bright tiled room in the local hospital. I remembered climbing the long flight of stairs into my aunt and uncle's home, and blubbering in a bedroom, my heaving, sweaty body finally giving way to an exhausted sleep, but even that single memory is hazy around the edges. In photos, I saw myself playing with cousins, teasing my grandfather, pointing towards a plane at the airport. I saw a round child with pigtails and an open smile, toes squishing into the sand. How could I call Suriname home? How could I call this going back? How could this be a return?

At the international travel clinic before my departure, the nurse injected me full of vaccines—typhoid, yellow fever, tetanus, hepatitis—and listed all the possible viruses that could infect my soft, northern body.

"It's not only malaria," she said. "You need to watch out for dengue fever and chikungunya too. And you should take an emergency antibiotic. You can't trust the medical care down there."

On my way out the door, she handed me a list of useful items to purchase before travel: anti-diarrhea pills, electrolyte formula, antihistamine, sunscreen, bug spray—"Don't forget: at least 30% DEET!"—After Bite, Polysporin, and condoms.

"Avoid salads and lettuces," another friend warned, while expressing horror at the thought of large insects.

My mom dispensed helpful hints one at a time during weekly phone calls. "Don't forget your flip-flops. It's damp. You don't know what kinds of bacteria there will be in the shower." She also suggested an umbrella against the sun. Later, "Watch out for stray dogs. They're everywhere." I wasn't sure what I was supposed to do with that information.

And then, just before my departure: "Drugs. There will be people trying to smuggle drugs. Make sure you have a lock for your suitcase."

Even my dentist got in on the action. Worried that I was travelling with a temporary crown on my newly root-canalled molar, he asked me to stop by the clinic.

"It's a plaster cast of your upper teeth," the hygienist said, passing me a bubble-wrapped package. "If something happens, you can give this to the dentist, and they'll know what to do."

I bought out the drugstore, purchasing everything but the condoms. I forgot the flip-flops. I couldn't find an umbrella, and honestly, I wasn't expecting to. It's hard enough to find an umbrella in my windy city at the best of times, and essentially impossible in the dark days of winter.

In the end, there were fewer dogs than I was expecting, and most of them, exhausted from the heat, were catatonic, tongues lolling. Those that weren't were vocal in their outrage, but they were behind fences and didn't bother me. The American Transportation Security Administration broke my TSA-approved lock before my flight even left Miami. Fortunately, nobody tried to put drugs in my bags. My stomach was stable. I carried my purse close to my chest, and no bacteria invaded my body in the shower.

~~~~~

My memories of life in South America drifted through one another. Running a film strip in my mind, I couldn't pull the images apart. I wasn't sure where things took place; I didn't know exactly where I was. Venezuela? Barbados? Curaçao? Guyana? Colombia? Ecuador? Argentina? I didn't even know. But I could feel the heat of an equatorial sun. The busyness of a city market. The tang of a tamarind pod on my tongue. I could hear the sound of an ocean, feel warm salt water running against my ankles, a tiny crab scuttling over my toes. I remembered peeling my sticky thighs from a vinyl car seat, the dotted patterns imprinting themselves into my flesh.

My film strip fragmented into grainy snapshots. In a car driving to get honey from a farm, tall trees all around. A party where all the girls were wearing saris. Everyone bigger than me. Piñatas at a celebration. Mighty Sparrow, his voice soaring into the night sky. A rainbow of flickering lights suspended over tables. The rumble of a steel drum band. The vowels of Caribbean English, a sway to hips and bodies. A cool tile floor. Slapping at cockroaches, their shells hard, impenetrable, prehistoric. Guavas. Mangoes. Soursop. Passion fruit. My aunt Hanny at the stove, making lime syrup to pour into tall glasses. Spicy peanut butter. A mosquito coil smoking in a corner. The cool of an evening breeze. Curry from a roadside vendor. Student protests and a flaming bus. Men with ponytails. Water wings, fear, an impatient ocean ...

I reached back into my childhood and came up almost empty. Nothing more than snippets and sounds, fleeting hints of feeling burbling towards the surface, experiences that had lain dormant for decades. The memory box that says "Life Before Canada" was a mess inside, and I couldn't pull the details apart. South America—and Suriname—existed only in my imagination. I remembered almost nothing. These memories felt distant; they weren't inside my body. And yet, I had lived in Venezuela for three years. I had spoken Spanish and Dutch. I had started school. I had travelled, crossing many borders. Stamps filled the pages of my passports. Suriname. Ecuador. Bolivia. Curaçao. Trinidad and Tobago. Chile. Colombia. When I returned to this part of the world that I once knew so well, would anything feel at all familiar?

~~~~~

The trip from St. John's to Paramaribo is almost directly due south. The time difference is only half an hour, but because of the plane routes, it's a long journey that spreads over two days. On the first day, I flew from St. John's to Toronto to Miami, my knees squashed up against the seat in front of me. The next afternoon, Surinam Airways took me from Miami to Paramaribo via Georgetown. The plane, acquired from an Eastern European airline and filled with labels in a language I couldn't work out, had left Miami in the late afternoon, an hour or so behind schedule. Every single seat was occupied, the overhead bins bulging. Just under four hours of flying time took us to Georgetown, Guyana. The plane emptied, and only about thirty of us remained. I looked out into the inky blackness and wondered what would await me.

It was well past midnight and, if possible, even darker by the time we touched down at Johann Adolf Pengel International Airport in Zanderij, about forty kilometres south of Paramaribo. The air was muggy: thick and heavy. I picked up my luggage, paid twenty-five dollars for my tourist visa, cleared customs, and trudged towards the taxi-bus stand, my jeans sticking to my legs. Emerging from the depths of a Newfoundland winter, I was discombobulated.

"We'll wait until everyone is off the plane," the taxi-bus driver said. "Stay here." There was another man there already, a gregarious type in his sixties, full of stories and opinions.

"Look," he said, eyeing my gear, "when I travel, I wear my ratty clothes. I carry my oldest bag." He pointed to a faded duffle slung across his chest. "Nobody will ever think I have anything to steal. Your bag"—he nodded at my ancient Mountain Equipment Co-op purse bulging with camera, drugstore purchases, and notebook—"it's fat. They'll think it's full of treasures. They'll think you're rich."

I clutched it tighter against my chest, wishing it wasn't quite so dark outside.

But my co-passenger had already moved on to other topics. Dési Bouterse—the current president—politics, and a proposed bridge to Guyana.

"It's going to be a disaster," he predicted. "There's no way Suriname should share the cost with Guyana. That river is ours. How are we going to protect it if Guyana owns half the bridge?"

The driver mumbled something indistinct in response.

"So," said the man, "can I assume from your comment that you're going to vote for Bouterse?" A challenge, but not a hostile one; there were elections coming up in just a few months. The driver was noncommittal, unwilling to show his hand.

"We've put him there," the man said. "It's our vote. He should do what *we* want. As soon as we give him the final authority, we've lost everything. He's responsible to us. Because we voted for him." He was getting agitated, warming to his passions, his arm gestures underscoring his point. The driver nodded but didn't respond.

"Where are you from?" The man seemed curious, interested and open.

"Canada," my quick reply. "But I have family here." I sensed a need to stake my claim.

"From Canada? How long are you here for?" The taxi-bus driver this time.

"Two weeks."

"You should stay longer. Make it a few months. Get a job working for the Canadian mining company. You could make lots of money. I see their buses all the time when I come to the airport, picking up new workers for the gold mines. You should stay."

~~~~~

Gold has been central to myths of empire. The fabled Eldorado lured European explorers to the jungles of South America from the sixteenth century on. Researchers pinpoint the first recorded explorations for gold to the eighteenth century, right around the time that the fictional Candide, the eternally optimistic hero of Voltaire's eponymous novel, was gallivanting around the continent with his loyal servant Cacambo. The pair stumbled into a city of unimaginable riches. After walking a road pebbled with jewels and gold, Candide stayed at the local inn, a space as grand as any European palace. The local townspeople worshipped a god, whom they thanked every day. There were no prisons and no courts. There was no religious persecution. There was no money. Instead, there was harmony, agreement, equality, and a commitment to learning. This, Candide learned, was Eldorado, a place of wonder, hope, and abundance.

That dream of Eldorado is still alive today. International mining conglomerates exploit the land, worming veins of gold into what is still largely a pristine rainforest, polluting rivers and streams, and extracting riches. Canadian mining interests are represented in the form of the Rosebel mine, owned by the Ontario-based IAMGOLD corporation. According to IAMGOLD's own data, Rosebel is a rich property that has, since 2004, produced over 85,000 kilograms of gold. They anticipate being able to mine gold until 2022.

Gold is also central to my own family histories. The story that's been passed down in the family goes something like this. One fine day in December 1913, my German great-grandfather, Theodor Wilhelm Heinemann, a spokesperson for the Compagnie des mines d'or de la guyane hollandaise, left on a trip. Perhaps he kissed his *buitenvrouw*—his "outside wife," or mistress—my Creole great-grandmother Adolphina, goodbye. Perhaps he patted my seven-year-old grandfather's head and chucked him under the chin, encouraging him to be a good boy. Perhaps his fingers traced his youngest daughter's cheek. Perhaps he waved. Perhaps he didn't.

What matters in the story is that my great-grandfather travelled from Paramaribo, the capital city of what was then the Dutch colony of Suriname, where he got onto the S.S. *Commewijne*, a Dutch ship bound for New York, taking with him a trunk filled with gold. After this, at least as my family experienced it, he was never seen or heard from again.

More recent genealogical explorations suggest that he then boarded a ship bound for London. But after this, the trail officially ran dry until 31 December 1918, when Theodor Wilhelm Heinemann died in Stuttgart, Germany, the city of his birth, at the age of thirty-eight, a victim, perhaps, of the Spanish flu.

When it comes down to it, those details of life and travel don't matter either. What matters, in this particular family story, is the gold. Nobody knows how big that trunk was. Perhaps it was nothing more than a small sack of nuggets, a memento for his German family. Maybe it was a small box. Maybe it was something more: a chest, a safe, a large box. In Heinemann family lore, that gold—however much it was—might have gone to prop up the fortunes of the William Heinemann publishing house in the UK. After all, if you look at a portrait of William Heinemann, the company's founder, there's a clear family resemblance.

"Look at that forehead," they'd say. "And that proud nose. And the hairline. See those eyebrows and the way they frame those dark eyes?"

"That," my relatives would say, nodding, "is a *true* Heinemann head."

And they'd be right. There *is* a clear resemblance. He could be an ancestor. The fact that William Heinemann also studied music and thought of pursuing a career as a classical musician just adds to the possibilities. Perhaps this love for music was genetic: my grandfather, me, and now, my son.... And so, maybe that's what happened.

Maybe that trunk of gold is bigger still. In my imagination, it's a treasure chest, sparkling not with precious gems in all colours, but glowing with the unearthly and ethereal tawny yellow of pure gold. The chest is filled with nuggets of different sizes. I scoop them up, feel their weight, and let their warmth run between my fingers like sand. Maybe the trunk is one of those seventeenth-century explorers' safe boxes made of wood and lined and girded with iron, with a large, heavy clasp on the outside. Maybe my great-grandfather alone had the key.

But perhaps the story has just grown and grown and grown, as all good stories do. Maybe there is no connection to a fabled publishing house. Maybe there was no large iron-girded trunk. Maybe there was no musical connection. Maybe it was just a single gold bar, a memento from work offered in recognition of my great-grandfather's services to the Compagnie des mines d'or de la guyane hollandaise.

Maybe there was no gold at all. Maybe it was just a story, something concocted over time to make sense of my great-grandfather's departure, a way to explain how a man could leave his lover and five young children alone on the edge of South America. Maybe it was something to make up for his absence, for the emptiness and the poverty, for the unrealized dreams. Maybe it was about his other family—another Creole wife and two more children and later grandchildren—in French Guiana, a family we didn't know anything about until late in the twentieth century. Or maybe, my academic voice whispered, it was a metaphor for colonialism itself, writ onto bodies and woven into the stories of those he left behind.

~~~~~

I have a single photograph of my great-grandfather. He was a tall, barrel-chested man with a mottled face, hair parted neatly on the right and slicked down against his head. In the photograph, he sports a trimmed moustache but no hint of a beard. There's an air of satisfaction or, perhaps, self-congratulation about him. He's wearing a dark three-piece suit, his right hand in a pocket, the chain of his pocket watch hanging across his chest. He's looking into the distance, facing slightly to the left, his jowly chin raised in an air of authority and confidence. His image projects success, I think, but then, I'm projecting too. In his stance, his bearing, and his body, I can see my uncles. I can see one of my cousins. The shape of the face. That nose—that *Heinemann* nose—the barrel chest, the forehead. That aura of self-confidence. I've seen all of them adopt this pose as well, their bodies and their bearings mirroring his.

Whatever happened to my great-grandfather and his gold?

~~~~~

We left the airport about half an hour later, after picking up an American woman working with remote Indigenous communities high in the Peruvian Andes. It had taken her twenty-four hours of travel on three different airlines to get to Paramaribo. Cuzco to Lima. Lima to Bogotá. Bogotá to Curaçao. And then finally, a hop and skip to Paramaribo. All this, and she had only a week off. She and I settled into an easy conversation about gender, health, and development, while the two men up front continued their discussion about politics, their voices rising and falling in Dutch and Sranan, the dominant Creole language. Mining rights. The problems with Brazil. Negotiations with Indigenous peoples and the Maroons. The newspapers.

~~~~~

My choir director grandfather was born in Albina, a small town at the edge of the Marrowijne River along the eastern border that Suriname shares with French Guiana. A once picturesque and thriving village, it was almost completely destroyed during the military rule and internal conflicts presided over by Dési Bouterse in the 1980s.

"Bouterse had boats in the river, and he just bombed it," my aunt Hanny told me, gazing into the distance.

"Destroyed the whole town. It was a beautiful place." There was a melancholy wistfulness in her voice. "We used to go there for holidays."

I looked at contemporary photos through my aunt's eyes. Derelict buildings collapsed into themselves, the wood at odd angles. In another photo, I saw burned-out cars, the remains of race-based riots that spun out of control during more recent gold-mining activities, piled haphazardly onto one another. But there were hints of a different past; colourful stalls lined the water's edge, an equally colourful row of boats were tethered to the shore.

In the early twentieth century, when my grandfather was a child, the town looked and felt very different. Fuelled by the gold rush, the town had grown, with people travelling there from all over to find their fortunes. Historical photographs depict a gracious, stately colonial town, whose buildings—tall, white, feathery, airy concoctions lining wide, sandy streets—resembled the grand UNESCO houses of Paramaribo's Waterkant that I'd seen in photos. It looked like a resort town, prosperous and wealthy, where the rich might come and play. Today, it is almost a caricature of its former self. But I may be romanticizing the past.

Early-twentieth-century gold mining in the South American jungle was no easy enterprise. Albina, the nearest centre to the mining operations, was accessible only by ship, or, in the case of military patrols, by internal boat travel, a route that required the navigation of weather, dense jungle, and several waterfalls. The journey along the river from the town of Albina to the mining operations themselves was a treacherous one, and mining companies relied heavily on Maroon boat operators in dugout canoes to manage the challenging journeys.

Natural forces were not the only challenges. Travellers and supplies had to pass through Indigenous and Maroon territories, and such journeys required careful negotiations with local leaders. The promise of riches also meant that gold-mining regions were subject to marauders intent on raiding mining communities, and individuals subject to violence. While they were comparatively well paid, gold miners themselves complained of poor working conditions that included lack of food, long working hours, threats, and unequal pay.

~~~~~

That midnight at Zanderij I wasn't thinking about earning money. I was just thinking about how hot and tired I was, and about how uncomfortable this kind of work might be. I was thinking that I'd hate a job like that. I was thinking that I wanted an air conditioner. And a bed. But the driver painted a rosy picture of planes and buses, and workers arriving and departing regularly. There was good work to be had, the driver insisted.

"Stay, and work," he urged. "Make some money before you go home."

~~~~~

The taxi-bus trundled on through the darkness, dropping passengers at their various destinations. Politics man waved us goodbye from his dark front door. We dropped the American aid worker at a well-known bed and breakfast in the heart of the city. Near my stop, the driver pointed out some takeouts. Javanese. East Indian.

"These are great," he offered.

"What I really want," I said, "is *pom*."

And in that instant, a sudden moment of recognition, a shared intimacy. *Pom* is a Creole specialty. A dish inherited from Jewish plantation owners and then transformed by slaves, it features Surinamese taro root, chicken, orange juice, and spices.

"*Pom* is my favourite," the driver said. "At birthday parties, when there's *pom* and *pastei*, I always take *pom*."

We fell into a companionable silence, each of us savouring flavourful memories.

"You know what?" he said. "I'll have my wife make you one. We live close by. She can bring it over to your apartment."

"It's okay," I said, my mother's warnings about crime and drugs echoing in my ears and my feminist self balking at the fact that he'd just offered his wife's labour to a random person he met in the middle of the night. "I'll organize something with my relatives."

~~~~~

By the time we arrived at the apartment building, it was past three in the morning. My aunt had stopped by earlier in the day and dropped off a whole basket of treats, and, keyed up, I spent the next hour rummaging through it. A mango, fresh from one of her trees. *Maizena koekjes*. Surinamese beer. Homemade guava jam stiff with natural pectin. A local phone card. An umbrella! And an envelope stuffed full of cash. The Surinamese dollar had tanked; I felt like a millionaire.

I was up early the next morning, my body and mind still exhausted but nevertheless eager to get going. The air conditioner murmured in the background, and I was simultaneously too hot and too cold. I missed the comfortable weight of my duvet. As I moved into the day, my nose adjusted itself to new smells, the sour sweetness of sulphur-rich water mixing with my sunscreen and insect repellent. The air was heavy, humid. My body was stiff and I felt dehydrated. But I wanted to go out. I had places to explore. Stories to learn. The world was waiting.

"Don't put anything valuable in your purse," my aunt told me when I called her to check in. "And keep it close to your body."

~~~~~

Be safe. Be aware. Keep an eye out. I followed my aunt's instructions to the letter. I emptied some cash into my pockets and hid my passport beneath my shirt. My phone was in my other pocket. Umbrella and water bottle in my bag. I was ready to face the day.

The heat washed over me as soon as I left the building. It wasn't even nine o'clock, and the thermometer already registered twenty-seven; thirty-three with the humidex, my mother would have said. The sun beat down on my neck. My eyes were wide open. There was so much to see.

My apartment building was located on a quiet street in the Rainville district, about ten minutes' walk from the downtown core of Paramaribo. I paused to admire the house across the street. The gate was freshly painted, standing firm and straight. The shaded verandah was idyllic, with dark wood furniture and a hammock, and bougainvillea—a fuchsia canopy. Next to it, another house was completely rundown, even as a jumble of toys and a tire hung down from one of the beams marked the presence of children. There was a sagging couch and, next to it, a wire cage with a monkey perched on top. Some straggly dogs lounged in the sun. The rusting tin roof clattered with the breeze, the edges lifting and falling gently. Rotting wooden shutters dangled from the windows. Farther on, a shuttered dwelling looked completely abandoned. Grey and weathered, it stood crooked and bent in an overgrown mess of weeds. The porch was decaying, the windows boarded up, faded rubber boots in a corner, neatly placed by the door. A few days later, I would see a woman in the garden, picking through the foliage.

Down the road there were mansions, sprawling compounds rising tall behind fences topped with barbed wire.

"There's a lot of money here," my aunt would tell me later when she came to pick me up for a drive around town. "People are rich." The underground economy, she said. Her euphemism for drugs and gold.

I turned towards a main street busy with cars, the traffic relentless.

"It's early in the month," the taxi-bus driver had said. "By the end of the month nobody will have money for gas. It will be quieter."

I picked my way across broken sidewalks and sandy greens towards the historic centre, my eyes darting. I was trying to take it all in, but there was too much to see. A school and the sound of children running and playing. A police station with a boat parked under the shade of a coconut tree. A tiny Moravian church with a rickety manse. In the distance, the minarets of a small mosque.

Security personnel outside every building. Look right before crossing, not left. Coconut palms. Election flags. Men gesturing towards me, honking their horns in appreciation. Keep your purse close. Is anyone following me? My senses couldn't keep up. There were so many impressions to sift through. I couldn't possibly make sense of it all. Who were these people? Where did I fit in? Who was I in this place?

And yet, other things seemed curiously familiar, drawing me deep into my tropical memories. A blast of calypso music from a passing car, and I was back in the summer of 1981, enjoying a Mighty Sparrow concert with my aunt and uncle in Barbados. A noisy school playground returned me to 1974, and my first day of school in Venezuela. Fruits and flavours stirred memories too. Suddenly I was climbing on the garage roof to pick tamarind pods and sucking the tangy flesh from their seeds. Watching a cousin grate taro root for *pom*. Sitting in the kitchen with my aunt Hilda in her Amsterdam apartment, watching her prepare *fyadoe*, a notoriously finicky Creole celebration cake that requires you to role individual raisins into dough to create a flower pattern on top. Walking with her through the market as she told off vendors she suspected of cheating her. Listening to the melodies and rhythms of a Dutch infused with tropical breezes, torrential rains, and four centuries of migrations that have spanned three continents. *Markoesa. Roti kip. Batjauw. Manjas.*

As in the Netherlands, I was both an insider and an outsider in Suriname. I would never completely be a visitor, a tourist; nor, however, would I ever completely be from there either. There were so many currents that I could not follow, so many understandings that flew right over my head. And all around me, a sea of bodies: brown, black, mahogany.

~~~~

I realized, suddenly, that I was white here. This was a revelation, though my cousin Elvira had warned me.

"They'll see you as *bakra*," she'd said just a few months earlier.

Bakra, the Sranan word for white. This was incomprehensible to me. After a lifetime in Canada, I had grown used to being an indefinable shade of brown; a chameleon who never quite fit in, I'd always been everything that a white person was not.

And now. A *bakra* in a brown land.

~~~~

My thoughts flitted back to the summer of 1981, to the last extended period I'd spent in the tropics. My aunt and uncle were living in Barbados then, and they'd invited me to join the family for the summer. Oma would be there, too, and we'd celebrate her seventieth birthday together, another treat. As memories tumbled over one another, I could barely keep up.

I was eleven when I'd left Alberta behind for a month, exchanging the heat of the prairie sun for the warm winds of the Caribbean. Every morning I'd run down the back yard, clamber down the stairs, and slip into the sea. In the late afternoons, we would head down to the beach, air mattresses in tow.

That summer, it seemed like it was just me and the ocean. My toes squelching into the white sands, my body bobbing in the waves, my eyes drawn into an underwater world of shells, corals, and sea urchins. I was an eel gliding along the ocean's floor, a mermaid bursting through the surface, a minnow darting among fluttering seaweed. In the sea, I was free. The ocean became home, an adventure. I learned its moods, rolled with its waves, gathered bits of shells in my hair, caked salt against my skin.

That summer, my cousins and I arranged ourselves in a row. Three cousins on the beach. Three sun-washed bodies basking in the sun. Three dark brown backs to the camera. Three smiling faces turned to the photographer. That summer, I made tissue-paper flowers—tulips, roses, chrysanthemums—and on my grandmother's birthday, I presented her with a jewel-toned bouquet. Later, we positioned ourselves on the verandah steps in our party clothes for an official birthday photo.

That summer, I learned to play canasta, ate Barbadian roti from a streetside stall, lost myself in the sounds of the market. That summer, I got up in the middle of the night to watch Prince Charles marry his fairy-tale princess, the bashful ingenue with the see-through skirt. I watched the fishermen dragging giant turtles onto shore. I shrieked when a tiny crab skittled across my toes, squirmed when salt water touched a blistered heel. I listened to the winds and rains of a hurricane, collected shells and sand dollars, each one slightly different from the others. I refused all afternoon siestas.

That summer I got sucked into an undertow. My cousins and I tossed, tumbled, and rolled like the stones on Middle Cove Beach, nothing around us but the roar of the surf, tiny grains of sand shifting and flying. Our bodies pulled in by an invisible riptide, churning in the ocean's power. Kicking, pushing, pulling, struggling with the water, searching for air, straining, aiming, angling for light in a rush of sound, pushing against the power, challenging it, moving finally forward, upward, anywhere but against the bottom, our legs scraping the rough ocean floor. Then the sea released us, and we popped up like dancing corks, gasping for air.

That summer I thought about mortality. I felt the power of the sea. I felt my own body, boneless ragdoll limbs, overcome by something that I was unable to grasp on my own. The ocean, as Dionne Brand observes, is life and death itself. It gives and it takes. It consumes and it retreats. The ocean is mysterious, unknowable, and the only way to measure yourself and your world. That summer, we dragged ourselves onto the beach, each of us silent, lost, sand caked against our legs, pooling in the bottoms of our suits. Our breathing slowed. Our bodies dried, the salty stickiness of the ocean baking itself onto our skin.

That summer, I swallowed sand, read my first Agatha Christie mystery, drank Shirley Temples with tiny paper umbrellas, and got stung by a Portuguese man-of-war. That summer, I celebrated water and wonder. I wasn't a teenager. I wasn't a child. I hadn't yet been told that my body wasn't good enough, that bikinis were for other bodies. I didn't know that tanning was work, necessary labour for girls and women. That summer, I grew a skin of deep brown, each experience layering itself onto my body. I drew sea and sun into my very pores.

<center>~~~~~</center>

Brown, I realized, as I thought back over that summer of 1981, is a story that emerges over time. It's about the communion of skin with sun, of encounters that are not planned or fixed, of time spent together, of chance meetings, of sensual pleasures in the water. Brown is not static or fixed. It moves and changes. Texture and depth, all of this shaped by history and environment. That island summer, each new experience added a layer of colour. Brown was not only in my genetics; it was the ocean calling me from inside a shell, a compilation of stories, each one imprinting itself onto my skin. I had layered my identity, painting myself deeper brown with every new adventure.

"We laugh at those *Surinamers* who have spent too much time in Holland," a tour guide would later tell me. "They are white. We call them *bakra*." Pale skin under a black exterior. But the guide's skin was dark and deep, a combination of history and sun.

Who was that brown girl with the carefree smile?

"*Bakra*," my cousin's voice reminded me, pulling me back to the present. "They'll see you as *bakra*."

I felt uncomfortable with this new visibility, with this glow. I needed to adjust myself. Reposition my identity, consider its effects on others. I found myself craving the sun, cursing my winter pallor, willing my body to brown itself. I wondered, briefly, if I should just avoid sunscreen. Maybe, I thought, I would brown faster. And suddenly, I longed for the suntan oil of the 1980s, those coconut-smelling products that would have fried me to a crisp in just a few short hours.

I snapped myself back. *You're being completely ridiculous*, I thought to myself. I never even used that stuff as a teenager. And besides, I was much too close to the equator. That old adage about brown people not burning? It's not true. I slapped sunscreen on my nose and across my cheeks. I spread some more across the back of my neck. Within a few days, my skin would warm into its brownness, and I wouldn't feel quite as exposed. The mirror, however, would continue to tell me that I was still *bakra* here. I just wasn't dark enough to be an insider. And yet. I could see myself in every body around me. I saw myself in the shape of a jawline, in the curve of a cheek. I saw my family in the breadth of a forehead, myself in the darkness of eyes. In my thoughts, I could hear my mother and her sisters laughing and sharing an inside joke. And in their voices, I could hear the sounds of my family.

Later that evening, my aunt picked me up for dinner, and we drove into the suburbs. My aunt Hanny and uncle Deryck, now in their eighties, live in a compact, low-slung house in the Kwatta district of Paramaribo, far from the downtown core. There, on the back verandah, in the shadow of their three mango trees—*mango trees!* my North Atlantic island heart rejoiced—we relaxed in the evening breeze and caught up on several years' worth of news and events.

The last time I'd seen them in person was sometime in the mid-1990s, well before my children were born.

Like his younger siblings, my uncle Deryck was born and raised in Suriname. In the early 1960s, after a period of study in the Netherlands and the UK, he brought his bride and his young daughter, Elvira, to Suriname. My aunt, a Dutch woman born and bred, can't imagine herself anywhere else. And it's clear to see she belongs. She knows this country's ways. She moves like someone born to this place. She shares their expressions.

My aunt and uncle haven't lived in Suriname the whole time, though. A military coup, in 1980, initiated within the first five years of Suriname's formal independence, scattered the family. One cousin came to live with us in Canada, where he still lives today. His sister moved to Zutphen, with our grandmother. And my aunt and uncle began almost a decade of nomadic travels that took them to New York; Washington, DC; London; Barbados; Antigua.... But Suriname beckoned, and when things had finally settled down, my aunt and uncle returned home. My aunt may well be Dutch, but her body and soul move to a Surinamese rhythm. My aunt and uncle are the only family members who have remained in Suriname, the only family members who still unequivocally claim Suriname as home. My other relatives appear to have a more complicated relationship with this place of their birth, alternately yearning for it and pushing it away.

My memories of Suriname, and, indeed, of my time in the tropics, are fundamentally influenced by my relationship with these two family members. It was their Paramaribo stairs I climbed with my newly earringed ears, their balcony where, as a four-year-old, I styled my grandfather's hair. It was the sand in front of their house into which I dug my toes. Later, in Barbados, when I was eleven, it was their daughter, my cousin Elvira, who taught me how to make *keksi*, a classic Surinamese light cake with endless eggs and rum-soaked raisins; their garage roof I climbed on to pick tamarind pods; their back steps that drew me into the warm waters of the Caribbean Sea; and their lime tree whose thorns pierced my skin. Their voices were an integral part of my experience, and so, perhaps it wasn't surprising that of all my relatives, they were the ones who seemed to understand my project best, the ones who embraced it, who seemed most invested. They were the ones who journeyed along with me, interested and intrigued by what I discovered along the way.

That evening, we talked and laughed over plates of curry and roti, my taste buds stirring other memories of the summer we shared in Barbados so many years ago.

~~~~~

On that first morning in Suriname, I had wandered through the faded glory of Paramaribo's historic centre, a UNESCO-approved collection of white colonial houses in various states of repair and disrepair. Along the Waterkant, a row of once-grand mansions faces the muddied café au lait of the Suriname River. They rise, one after another, tall, with white clapboard and wide verandahs on every floor. It was here, in front of these homes, that my ancestors first set foot on Surinamese ground. Where, as the archival materials in Middelburg reveal, slaves were walked before being sold, and where, as I'd later learn, processions of indentured labourers were led from ships to immigration depots and processing centres, and from there, to the plantations. Did they walk quietly? Did they talk? Did they falter, stumble, their bodies adjusting to solid ground after months aboard a ship? Did wealthy colonists stand out on their verandahs, looking out at the columns of brown and black bodies making their way down the dusty road?

Behind this row of houses is a maze of narrow streets filled with more colonial houses, these ones smaller, more contained. Some have been beautifully restored, their white exteriors gleaming in the sun. Most are faded. Sagging and their paint peeling, they bear the weight of long histories. In 1880, my great-great-grandmother, hailing from a tiny village in India now erased from maps, took up with a Chinese man and settled into life just around the corner on the Watermolenstraat. Her grandson, my great-uncle Harry, advertised in the local newspaper and taught violin lessons on the very same street for a number of years. "Theoretical and practical instruction on the violin," reads a 1933 ad. "A few spaces left." Somewhere, in this warren of streets, my Catholic East Indian grandmother, with her French first name and her Chinese last name and her Hindu grandmother, met my grandfather with his German name and his Creole blood, and from that point on, apparently stopped going to confession. Here, too, in the Thalia concert hall, my Creole grandfather and my Hindustani great-uncle made music together. French. Hindustani. Chinese. German. Creole. What brought them together? I could see hints of my family in the way people walked, in the sway of hips, in facial expressions, in gestures and words. I realized that we shared these histories, that they were stories that somehow united us, brown, black, and *bakra*.

Outside the central market, cars and mini-buses pushed themselves into every available space. Traffic was stalled. I followed the lead of other pedestrians and wove myself in and out between parked cars, inching along crowded and cracked sidewalks and paths. It was an obstacle course. Car horns blared. Along the river, a row of water taxis in a rainbow of colours waited for passengers. I held my purse tight against me, trying desperately not to look like a tourist. In the hot air, exhaust fumes mingled with the smell of fresh fish, roasted chicken, and spices.

At the market entrance, I was swarmed by men looking to sell me watches, necklaces, and, incongruously, rosaries.

"Want a watch, honey?"

"Beautiful necklaces!"

"All stolen," my aunt told me later, when I recounted my adventures.

Hands pressed towards my face, but I shook my head and moved on. The jumbly chaos was disconcerting, uncomfortable. I wasn't sure how to respond; I didn't fit in, didn't have the necessary social codes. There were too many people, too many voices, too many hands and arms gesturing towards me.

Inside the dark, cavernous market hall, I paused, my eyes adjusting to the low lighting. It was quiet here, cooler. I saw rows of vegetables: giant slices of pumpkin glowing a garish orange. Leafy greens. And *kouseband*—look! I could find these long beans in the Chinese section of our grocery store in St. John's, but here they were twice as long, bundles of green shoelaces dangling off the edges of tables. Peppers. Red. Green. Yellow. Short and squat. Long and thin. Ginger root, the dirt still clinging to it. Cabbages and cassava roots. So much okra.

And there, on the floor, a stack of young coconuts, freshly cut from the tree. Papayas. Sopadillas. Guavas. Passion fruit. So many mangoes. I felt like I was back in Barbados.

"This pile for ten SRD," a voice wheedled.

I couldn't resist, and was pressed to buy more.

"Mandarins? They're sweet. Papayas. Only seven SRD for this one."

I nodded, helpless, and a papaya disappeared into my bag.

"Nobody bought fruit when I was a kid," my uncle told me later that evening as we shared West Indian curry with roti, another long-missing flavour. "When we lived on the Tourtonnelaan, we had two mango trees as well as breadfruit, guava, sopadilla, and almond trees. Nobody shopped for fruit."

I'd spent the last six years looking for a single tasty mango in St. John's. My aunt and uncle had saved me the last mango from their tree, but it was already long gone, eaten immediately after my early-morning arrival at 3 a.m. I wanted to gobble all of this up, filling my body with the sticky sweetness of the tropics.

In the cooler area reserved for fish and meats, I walked past the fishmongers and the butchers, past piles of fish, their mouths gaping. Headless chickens, claws twisted together, their necks dripping juices onto a white tiled floor.

"Don't slip!" My aunt laughed, imagining the scene for herself.

Outside again, a sudden downpour, a brief respite from the sun's warmth. As soon as it came, it was gone again, and then it felt even hotter than before. A vendor cleaned fish, the scales flying and sparkling. Another grated taro root. I walked down the Jodenbreestraat into the city centre. In a quiet corner, under a canopy, a familiar figure: a woman holding copies of *De WachtToren*— The Watch Tower. Next to her, a man was selling *schaafijs*—snow cones—his cart decorated with a painting of a beatific Jesus beaming golden light over a trio of Nelson Mandela, Barack Obama, and Mahatma Gandhi.

I continued towards the central mosque and the synagogue. The mosque and synagogue stand next to each other, as they've done for decades, sharing a common parking space. I angled my camera and took a few photos.

"Everyone's amazed at this. Tourists are always taking photos," my aunt said later, almost as if she knew that I'd taken some pictures. "What they don't realize is that Suriname has always been about mixtures."

There was, in other words, nothing strange about this at all. The great Catholic Basilica of St. Peter and St. Paul, constructed around a Jewish theatre early in the nineteenth century and still bearing traces of this history, is just a few blocks away. The Moravian church is around the corner, just a short walk from the Lutheran church. In the suburbs, there's an open pyre for Hindu cremations. Wealthy Hindus have constructed temples in their own backyards.

There are small Moravian chapels in many neighbourhoods, and fifteen mosques scattered around the city.

Canada prides itself on multiculturalism, but it's got nothing on Suriname. As I took my first steps in Paramaribo, I realized that this place, with its long histories of migrations and mixtures, is my family writ large. This is the mixture that's moulded our bodies and experiences for hundreds of years; it's what we've inherited, what we all live.

In Canada, organizations like the Ku Klux Klan publicly rallied against mixed-race relationships in the 1920s and '30s. American miscegenation laws were struck down just fifty years ago, and even today, interracial relationships make up only a small minority—a mere 5 percent—of all relationships in Canada.

Living "mixture" hasn't been easy for my family either. Any number of relatives have stories to share. I certainly have my own.

"If God wanted the races to mix," a roommate's mother told her years before we ever met, "he wouldn't have created different races."

"I don't have anything against interracial relationships," an undergraduate dorm resident once mused during a dinner conversation. "But just think of what their kids would look like." It wasn't meant as a compliment.

My parents boycotted South African products during the apartheid years, and Australian goods during the White Australia policy years. Mixture is our reality; this is who we are. And Paramaribo was the first place where I saw this fully reflected in the people around me. I heard the sound of Surinamese Dutch, the lilt that has coloured the voices of my aunts and uncles. Several times I thought I saw my aunt Hilda sallying forth, her head held high, her steps determined. I imagined I spotted other aunts in the market by the shape of their jawline, and I heard my mother's voice in the spaces between words, the timing of phrases. My uncles were everywhere, their laughter ringing on the streets, their bodies, their bearing so familiar in the men I mistook for them. It was the first place where I felt like my family belonged. Is this what home looked like?

And yet, there was something odd about all of this. My relatives were, somehow, out of context. *I* was out of context. I knew how they fit into a Dutch landscape. I knew how *I* fit into a Dutch landscape. I knew how to find their voices, to follow their accents. I knew how their histories fit into Amsterdam, Zutphen, Nijmegen, Elst, Den Haag, Purmerend. Even Den Bosch. But in Suriname, it was different. They didn't quite fit. Or perhaps better put, I couldn't quite fit them in. They were like puzzle pieces that I couldn't place.

Or was *I* the puzzle piece that didn't fit? Why was I here? What was I looking for? Who was I in this place? I tumbled into impossibilities, and by the end of that first day, I was exhausted.

8.

DISRUPTIONS

L IKE ALL GOVERNMENT OFFICES AND SCHOOLS, the National Archives of Suriname opens early: seven o'clock, to be precise. Waking bleary-eyed at six thirty, I decided I wasn't yet ready to face the day. This new schedule had thrown all my conventional archival work patterns into disarray. Shower, breakfast, and tea—it was eight o'clock before I managed to call a cab. A compromise.

I'm usually rigid about my archival work. Unlike locals, who can pop in whenever they like, my research time—and that of others who come from away—is always limited. We don't have the luxury of coming and going whenever the muses strike us. Archives time is time away from our daily routines; it's almost like a suspension of time. But "real life" goes on while we're gone, and we'll have to jump right back in when we return. Archives time is both sacred and limited. And so we establish careful routines and rituals.

The taxi arrived, music blaring. The driver, a cheerful young Hindustani man, was full of stories about his haircut, his girlfriend, and his future.

"I still have to look good, you know," he said, smoothing his hands over a newly shaped haircut, a perfect part shorn into the left side. "She can't get too comfortable. She needs to be worried that someone else will take me."

He bobbed his head along with the music and pointed to a car dealership.

"See that car? That big white one?" he said, gesturing towards a large SUV. "That's what I'm saving my money for."

I listened with half an ear, anxious about my late arrival. I was already over an hour and a half behind. How was I ever going to catch up?

We quickly got snarled in the morning traffic around the market, and the driver cursed under his breath. Pedestrians were moving faster than we were. Twenty minutes later, we pulled out onto the Jagernath Lachmonstraat, a large artery that leads out of town in one direction and towards the archives in the other. By the time we arrived, it was almost nine, and I was finally wide awake.

The National Archives of Suriname opened in 2010 with the express purpose of housing colonial records previously held by the Netherlands. Slowly, since then, the materials have started going home, crossing the ocean from The Hague to Paramaribo. As I walked towards the building, my thoughts turned back to the early years of my doctoral research. I travelled to Paris in 2006, staying in a tiny hotel just off the rue St. Honoré, a location I had chosen not for its proximity to posh stores and the Louvre, but because it was within easy walking distance of two things I enjoyed the most: archives and music. Just a short walk from the Bibliothèque nationale de France in one direction, the hotel was also, tantalizingly, right around the corner from Alphonse Leduc, a fabled music publisher.

My supervisor had warned me about the intricate processes involved with accessing materials at the Bibliothèque nationale de France, talking me through the various steps I'd need to follow. First I'd need to produce a letter from her explaining the reason I was there. That hurdle cleared, they'd give me a library card. Then, at the door to the manuscripts reading room, they'd give me two more cards, one red, one green, and I'd have to pass the green card to someone and the red card to someone else, and then I'd get a seat and the materials would arrive. If I wanted to leave the room for any reason—even something as simple as going to the bathroom—I'd have to reverse the whole process. She also warned that I'd have to dress appropriately. No sandals. Nothing casual. Professional. Above all, I shouldn't look North American.

"Sit straight," she said. "No slouching or lounging about."

The instructions were long and convoluted, and I don't even remember all the ins and outs anymore. But my general impression was one of gatekeeping. These documents were meant to be protected, and only certain eyes could have access to them.

That trip to Paris taught me much about the relationship between archives and national identity. The Bibliothèque nationale de France is not just a repository for esoteric, sometimes mouldering documents to be read by people like me. It is France's *patrimoine*—its legacy, its heritage, its inheritance—and the archivists took this responsibility seriously.

In the years since, I have found myself in both formal and informal archival spaces. In Berlin, on the hunt for flute manuscripts from the court of Frederick the Great, an avid flute player and composer, I had to surrender my passport and wait three hours for materials to appear. In Lausanne, chasing the complaints of an eighteenth-century doctor's myriad patients, I shared a much more casual work environment with flip-flop-wearing university students working on class assignments. I've grown accustomed to the requirements of different archival spaces; I've moulded myself to what they expected. I could play the consummate professional. I could play the academic. I could play the student. I could look the part. I had the right credentials. I had the requisite introduction letters from the right people. And with my computer, camera, pencils, and magnifying glass—all in a clear plastic bag—it was apparent to all involved that I had the right tools.

But I'd never visited the tiny reading room of the National Archives of Suriname. With its work tables clustered close together, it was by far the most compact space in which I'd worked. It was difficult to spread out, especially when there were more than a few people working at the same time. And yet, despite its size, the reading room was an active and busy place, with people regularly coming and going throughout the day. It was also one of the noisiest reading rooms I had ever encountered. In Middelburg, I was one of only four individuals leafing through documents, and I was the only one to stay all day. While The Hague was busy, with researchers lined up even before the doors opened, we were an army of professionals ready to settle in for the long haul, spending hours and even days in silent pursuit of our stories. We'd stretch legs and bodies every hour or so. Sometimes folks would head out for a smoke or some fresh air, but they almost always returned, making the most of the seven-hour window available to them.

In Paramaribo, things were different. I didn't need a passport. I didn't need a letter from my university. I didn't need green and red cards. I didn't need to carry everything in a clear plastic bag. In fact, I didn't need any kind of formal identification. Everyone had access to this national heritage, regardless of their background, regardless of their education, regardless of their history. All they had to do was sign in: name, address, phone number, and research interest.

During my time at the National Archives of Suriname, patrons came and went throughout the day. I saw the usual students and professional researchers; dogs of a similar breed, we learned to recognize one another, nodding in acknowledgement as we arrived in the morning. But I also saw others—an elderly woman with her daughter, working together to solve a family history mystery; a pair of young women with heads bent close to a screen; another woman with a notebook reading carefully through slave registers on micro-fiche, jotting down notes as she went; a mother with a baby in her lap looking at plantation stories, and a wide-eyed toddler wandering the room, a bottle dangling from her mouth. What journeys had brought them to the archives? What stories did they hope to find? What mysteries did they want to solve? These were not career researchers; they were ordinary folks looking into their own pasts, seeking evidence to support stories they'd been told, or documents that could fill in blanks and silences.

Some of them would never have been allowed to set foot in a European or Canadian archive. A mother and a baby? A toddler and a bottle? Others, lacking passports or other forms of official identification, wouldn't have been able to navigate the various checks and balances that archival spaces normally put in place. To whom should archives belong? I wondered. And who should be allowed to access them?

~~~~~

That morning, I decided to start with microfiches, old technology that allowed me to read scans of original materials not accessible to the public. My techno kids, full of conversations about gaming computers and driverless cars, would have been appalled. But I saw this as an appetizer before my main course. Just a few hours, I promised myself, and then I'd ask for the real thing.

I dug in. Ten o'clock came and went. Eleven. I pretended I didn't need to use the restroom. I ignored hunger pangs. And I continued. By half past eleven, I couldn't wait any longer.

"I'd like the slave registers, volume thirty-three," I said, my fingers already itching.

But the archivists shook their heads.

"Sorry," one said, her large red earrings fluttering. "The archives elevator is broken down. We can't get any materials." Archives elevators bring documents from their climate-controlled storage areas, often in basements, up to the reading room. They're essential to the routine functioning of the archives. No elevator meant no archival materials.

I hadn't expected this. "When do you think it will be fixed?"

A shrug from the red-earringed woman. "Possibly next week?" she hazarded a guess. "The repair person is out of the country right now."

A week? But I had only two weeks in Suriname! The archives staff shrugged; there was nothing they could do.

"Sorry," the red-earringed woman said, "but you can give us a call to see if it's fixed sooner than that."

There was a change of plans, I told my aunt and uncle over a dinner of Javanese treats. My uncle didn't seem surprised. He knew his country. He also knew the repair person.

"He's in Guyana right now," he said. "Supposed to be back next week."

"What will you do?" my aunt asked. I did the only thing I could do and turned to the city itself. If paper documents couldn't tell me a story, then perhaps the streets and buildings could. And I knew exactly where I was going to start.

9

ROOSJE

~~~~~~

I N PARAMARIBO'S OLD CITY, about ten minutes' walk past the Catholic basilica, lies the Nieuwe Oranjetuin cemetery. In use between 1756 and 1921, this cemetery, so named because it's located in a spot where previously there was an orange grove, holds the remains of some of Paramaribo's most illustrious residents, many of whom, in centuries past, paid with sugar for the privilege of being buried there. I'd had the cemetery on my itinerary since before my arrival. I love cemeteries. The quiet. The solitude. The stories. I look at the names etched into stones. I look at the messages left by friends and family, at tattered bouquets, and small stuffed animals. I look at the way that people are remembered on the tombstones. And I look at shapes and sizes. There are so many lives, all gathered in a small plot of land.

In early 2009, within the first year of our arrival in St. John's and just after our sons had started learning how to play chess, we drove past a cemetery down the road from the university. My younger son, Tóbin, then four, pointed eagerly out the window. "Chess pieces!" he said with enthusiasm. In the years since, the boys have humoured me on summer holidays. Acknowledging what they see as their mom's odd personal eccentricities, they've allowed me to explore all the old cemeteries we find along our way. *It's okay*, their patient and knowing smiles seem to say. *You can go and check it out. We love you anyway.*

Newfoundland has many historic cemeteries, some forgotten in long-abandoned communities. In them, eighteenth- and nineteenth-century gravestones buckle against the wind, leaning in different directions. The salt air has almost worn away the names, but a careful rubbing can bring these histories back to life. Cemeteries are spaces for thinking and for reflecting. They are as much about life as they are about death; indeed, the way we care for our dead can tell us a lot about how we care for the living. And so I've crouched over leaning slabs in Petty Harbour, squinted at inscriptions in the hills above Greenspond, and whispered to spirits in Lumsden. I've walked through tall grasses to the abandoned cemetery near Shallow Bay, lost my shoe in the deep mud of another somewhere in the vicinity of Cape Freels. I've listened to the ocean lapping against the shore, singing lullabies to the souls who rest there. I've thought about the pasts that brought people to the island I now call home.

~~~~~

The archives were inaccessible, but the city—and the cemetery—beckoned. It seemed like a perfect opportunity. I set off at a jaunty pace, eager to reach the cemetery as quickly as possible. It was early, earlier than the previous morning in any case, but still not early enough, according to my aunt and uncle.

"Too hot by nine," my aunt said, even though she's often shivering before seven. My aunt's body doesn't like the extreme heat. Even as a younger woman, her ankles would swell and she'd be uncomfortable.

Sure enough, within a few minutes of leaving my apartment, I could feel my T-shirt sticking to my back. I walked past an elementary school, marvelling at school children in jeans running around on the playground, laughing and calling. My body was panting; it couldn't keep up with the heat. In my pocket, my Surinamese dollars were getting damp with sweat, and later, I would be ashamed to pass them on to store clerks. I adjusted my stride, slowing down to accommodate the temperature. Even then, by the time I arrived at the cemetery twenty minutes later, I was a soggy mess, and I was in for further disappointment. The gates were locked, a rusty padlock hanging forlornly from an equally rusty chain, and the cemetery's brick wall was just a hair too high for a good look. I walked the whole length of it hoping for a way in, all the while peeking in through breaches and cracks, and squinting between the gate's iron bars. But I could see almost nothing at all. Overgrown and untended, the cemetery was buried, most of the graves lost under long grasses and shrubs. Others had been damaged or destroyed. Poking my point-and-shoot camera through the rusting fence, I zoomed as close as I could, and clicked the shutter button. Looking at the photos later, all I could see was a single grey stone lump in an overgrown field.

~~~~~~

People of all sorts have rubbed shoulders in Paramaribo, from the monied slave-owning elite, to visiting mariners and sea captains, poor Europeans seeking their fortunes, free blacks, former slaves, Chinese merchants, and former indentured labourers. Boundaries aren't neat and tidy in Suriname; I couldn't expect the cemetery to be either. And that's what drew me there in the first place. Could this place tell me a bit more about those messy pasts, about how it was that these people lived, loved, and died together?

Among bones of the muckety-mucks interred at the Nieuwe Oranjetuin cemetery are those of Frederika Rosette Dessé, whose tombstone lists Anthony Dessé, the man who owned my ancestors, as her "devoted and attached friend." As I'd already learned, Dessé was one of the most powerful plantation owners in the country. In 1863, when slavery was abolished, he owned many plantations—among them Leasowes and Clyde, Good Intent, Inverness, Sarah,

Catharina Sophia, and Paradise—and more than 1,000 slaves. It stood to reason, then, that Frederika Rosette—mother to his eight children—would be buried at the Nieuwe Oranjetuin.

But this story, just as so many others in slave-owning societies, is much more complicated. Anthony Dessé seems to have arrived in Suriname at some point in his late teens. It's thought that he came from Guadeloupe, or perhaps from Santo Domingo. In any case, he wasn't a white European man, but rather of mixed racial background. After his arrival he somehow worked his way up the social and economic hierarchy, moving from plantation administration to owning prime plantations and hundreds of slaves.

At one point, he also owned Frederika Rosette. Named Roosje on the small Plaisance plantation, she was manumitted in 1838 along with her eldest child, a son named Edmund. Just over a decade later, Dessé petitioned for Roosje and Edmund, as well as seven other children—Edwin, Elvira, Ethelrid, Eleonora, William Henrij, Henriette Dorothij, and James—to take the last name Dessé. Roosje, meanwhile, changed her whole identity, moving away from her slave name—a diminutive, childlike first name, and a last name tagged on upon manumission—to the much more regal Frederika Rosette Dessé, a transformation that was supposed to demonstrate that she had arrived in elite Surinamese society.

I had no idea how well the new Frederika Rosette Dessé might have been received in elite Paramaribo society. I suspected it wasn't well, but I did wonder. While there was a large population of free blacks, and while some freed slaves did inherit the wealth of their owners, their skin colour and mere presence must have challenged the basic premises of a slave-owning society.

I thought about the case of Elisabeth Samson, the real-life heroine of a novel by well-known Surinamese historian and writer (and, because Suriname has the same negative degrees of separation as Newfoundland, my uncle's schoolmate and my cousins' high school history teacher) Cynthia McLeod. Born free to a freed mother a century before Frederika Rosette, Elisabeth Samson had it all. She owned several plantations. She owned slaves. She wore the finest clothes and socialized with the wealthiest colonists. In addition to her own plantations, she inherited plantations from her lover after his death and managed them brilliantly. And in 1767, a full two hundred years before *Loving v. Virginia* struck down anti-miscegenation laws in the US, Elisabeth Samson became the first black woman in Suriname to legally marry a white man. At her death, three years later, her estate was worth over one million guilders. By all accounts, Elisabeth Samson had broken the colour barrier, inserting herself—through her wealth—into the highest echelons of Surinamese colonial society. And yet, even as she played her part, she never really fit her role.

I wondered how Roosje and Elisabeth navigated their social responsibilities. What was it like to live in a world organized by and for white people? I wondered if Roosje and Elisabeth partied with them, and I wondered how they felt about it. In a particularly revelatory passage in her novel, McLeod describes Elisabeth Samson at a public event, and reflects on the golden locks piled upon Samson's head. Until that point, I hadn't even considered how fashion would have interacted with race. What did it mean for a black woman to wear wigs—*de rigueur* in eighteenth-century polite society—designed for the whitest of white powdered faces? I thought, too, of lace fluttering against black wrists, of diamonds and sapphires and gold sparkling against a black neck, and of the swell of black breasts rising coyly over the light-coloured cottons, silks, and taffetas so popular among young women of the fashionable elite. I thought of all the contradictions at play and of how these women might have managed the deep brown-black of their skin, so out of place in white society.

My aunt and uncle didn't think that Roosje would have fit in.

"No." My aunt shook her head. "Not a chance."

And yet, I know that the complexities of colonial life meant that Roosje and Elisabeth wouldn't have been the only ones to have crossed the colour barrier; there were others mixing it up with the elite. And Dessé himself wasn't white either. How were these gradations of colour understood in polite society? What did people choose to see and what did they choose to ignore?

The previous day at the archives, I'd stumbled through an electronic copy of parts of the 1811 census. This document grouped people into two main categories: free and slave. Within those, there were subcategories: free white, free black, and free *gekleurd*—or coloured; that is, mixed race—and black and mixed slaves. While women like Elisabeth and Roosje would probably have found themselves in the "free black" or "free coloured" categories, I was at a loss to understand the boundaries of these categories. The range of categorizations boggled my mind. Who policed them? Who determined if someone was black, coloured, or white? And what did this mean for how they lived their lives?

What was clear was that Roosje would have had to navigate polite society somehow. Given Dessé's social position, she would have had to manage the masquerade. I imagined her as a serious woman, an observer who watched everything carefully, learning and cataloguing. And perhaps I imagined her this way because that's how I would have been in her shoes. Living in white society was serious, watchful business. Given Roosje's situation, as the freed companion of a powerful man who claimed hundreds just like her as his property, she likely had little say in the matter. It's possible that Dessé told her that things would be fine, that she wouldn't have to worry. But if I'd been Roosje-turned-Frederika, I wouldn't have believed it. A careful observer of slave society, she would already have known how hard it was to navigate the intricacies of polite society, how easy it was to fall out of favour. The wrong dress.

The wrong dance step. A misinterpreted smile. Her black skin. She would have known the challenges of fitting in.

I projected my own social awkwardness onto this woman. I don't thrive in large formal settings. Instead, I shrink, seeking out the darker, quieter spaces. My sensibilities chafe against social and gender norms. I know nothing about makeup, dress, shoes, or dissimulation. I don't have a tinkling laugh. A rather stuffy cellist once told me he could never date me because my laugh was too loud. I avoid the camera. I don't know how to pose. I'm interested in political commentary, not small talk.

It wasn't fair, though, to impose all of this on Roosje. She was her own woman, with her own interests and her own personality, and it's possible that she knew everything she needed to know. She'd been observing the fashionable elite for years. She'd grown up next to them, worked in their houses. She'd listened to young girls' laughter, observed their tears, and followed their progress as they learned to play the guitar. She'd learned the intricacies and intimacies of colonial life from the sidelines, and in some ways she would have known the colonists better than they knew themselves. From her vantage point, she'd watched their lives unfold, and now she was part of that same world, a wealthy woman just like them, wearing a tightly strung corset under a full beribboned dress of palest pink silk, her curls teased into ringlets, a langorous satin ribbon woven through them.

If she loved fashion and the life of high society, Roosje would have had plenty of options available to her in Paramaribo. Merchants advertised all sorts of fancy goods in local newspapers: gloves, dresses, stockings, pomades, and a variety of fine fabrics, from the most common muslin to silks, satins, cotton, wool, and more, with one offering "extra fine muslin embroidered with floral bouquets in the latest tastes." Consumers could enjoy a global marketplace of products: Westphalia ham, Havana cigars, Marseilles soap, Madeira wine, French fruits in brandy, Italian straw hats, East Indian muslin, Irish butter, Scottish herring, English candles.... There were musical instruments too. In 1821, a merchant offered discerning colonists the possibility of owning one of two recently arrived fortepianos, "being the commissioned work of first rate masters." Presenting a fashionable, stylish, tasteful, and well-bred self clearly mattered, and merchants were only too happy to oblige. I imagined Roosje's daughter Eleonora in a muslin dress, her brown face bent over the piano keys as she practised her scales.

The social calendar was busy. Suriname's first theatre company, Thalia—an organization that still exists today—was founded in 1838, the very same year that Roosje was manumitted. Just two years earlier, in 1836, a pair of brothers had established the Harmonica Society and presented a series of thirty-six subscription-based concerts, each one advertised in local newspapers. The concert programs offered a potpourri of musical works, from Mozart overtures to Rossini arias and works by Spohr and others. There was even flute music, including solos and duets by Anton Bernhard Fürstenau and Jean-Louis Tulou. Tulou and Fürstenau were stars, the pair of them, two of the top flutists of the period. They were also prolific composers. I'd played Fürstenau duets. I'd played studies by Tulou. And there they were, listed on concert programs in a small colonial city in South America.

Later, after I returned to St. John's, I would search out the compositions listed in the newspaper. *Rondeau Brillant. Fantaisie.* I

5. (Facing page) The Waag Gebouw, or Weighing House, along the Waterkant in Paramaribo, Suriname. Concerts hosted by the Harmonica Society took place here. Anonymous, "Nieuwe Waag aan de Waterkant te Paramaribo (Het Nieuwe Waag Gebouw en Bank der Colonie Suriname)," 1829–1830. Object number RP-P-2017-1664, Rijksmuseum.

found virtuoso extravaganzas designed to showcase all of the flute's technical attributes. The music danced and dipped, rippling and swooping through the flute's upper registers, a sparkling cascade of sound. This was audience-pleasing music if ever there was any, and I imagined delighted murmuring and generous applause from the assembled gathering. As the music sparkled and skipped, I realized that Paramaribo, a small outpost at the edge of a deep, dark rainforest, was also intimately linked into global markets, and its citizens clearly bought into the possibilities of a cosmopolitan identity. Wealthy planters like John Bent, Elisabeth Samson, and Anthony Dessé may have lived far from the centres of power, but they led lives of luxury and comfort that rivalled those of family, friends, and colleagues in Europe.

Roosje and I wouldn't have been allowed to play the flute in the nineteenth century. Wind instruments weren't considered seemly for young women. Had we been born into a family of means, we'd have been schooled in guitar or piano, but only just enough to make us marriageable. And that's clear from the flute methods Tulou and Fürstenau wrote, which feature drawings of well-dressed, upper-class young men with gentle cowlicks and pursed flute-playing lips. It's just as well times have changed.

Harmonica concerts took place on the second floor of the storied Waag building on the waterfront. Now home to a trendy bodega, the Waag was a weighing house, where everything that

passed through the Surinamese economy—from foodstuffs to textiles to slaves—was weighed and measured. It would have been well known to both audiences and performers alike. It's likely that Frederika Rosette knew it, too, but for entirely different reasons. If I were Roosje, I'd have been profoundly uncomfortable there.

In the 1930s, a hundred years after these concerts, my grandmother's brother Harry, a violinist, advertised music lessons from a series of apartments in the white colonial houses along the Watermolenstraat, around the corner from the Waag. My grandfather, meanwhile, showcased his choir in a range of venues, including the Thalia theatre. Sometimes, in fact, my grandfather and great-uncle performed together. Thalia. The Waag. The Watermolenstraat. My musical DNA was deeply woven into the landscape of this city.

~~~~~

On the way back to my apartment, I passed Fort Zeelandia, the colonial fort located in a shaded—but also haunted—area seemingly removed from the bustle of the city.

"We don't go there often," my aunt had told me during our first drive through the city together, regret and sadness in her voice.

Fort Zeelandia has endured over the centuries. Named Fort Willoughby in 1650 by English settlers travelling from Barbados and seeking to establish a permanent colony, it was taken over and expanded by the Dutch in 1667. In recent years, Fort Zeelandia, a small but distinctive five-pointed citadel located just past the mouth of the Suriname River, was the site of the infamous *Decembermoorden*—the December murders—where fifteen political dissidents were shot in December 1982, their brutalized bodies left at the fort's front gate during the military coup orchestrated by Dési Bouterse. Bouterse himself, president of Suriname since 2010, has disavowed any responsibility for the event, and because of a range of complicated political manoeuvres, criminal proceedings have been started, thwarted, and restarted numerous times. Inside the fort, pockmarked brickwork along turret walls offers a poignant visual remembrance of the gunfire that marked this bloody period in Suriname's recent political history.

Suriname's longer history is knotty and complex; violence flows through the rivers that wend their way through the rainforest. As a colony, Suriname survived on the labour of enslaved and indentured people and on pushing Indigenous people and, later, Maroons deep into the jungle. It was at Fort Zeelandia that the enslaved were punished for their resistance to the inhumanities of the slave system: Fort Zeelandia, where a man named Tata Colin faced a tribunal for inciting mutiny on Leasowes plantation, just next door to Sarah plantation; Fort Zeelandia, where three others were held in captivity for several months before facing death after having been found guilty of setting several fires in and around Paramaribo in the autumn of 1832; and Fort Zeelandia, where the formerly enslaved Roosje-turned-Frederika Rosette might have found herself if she'd run afoul of Dessé.

As I stood looking out over the river, my fingers tracing the pockmarked brickwork, I contemplated these pasts. I imagined the waters filled with tall-masted ships discharging goods, products, and enslaved and indentured people, and later, filling their holds with all of Suriname's riches destined for northern ports: coffee, sugar, and, eventually, cotton.

The museum guide led us to a dark room at the base of the main turret.

"This is where Cojo, Mentor, and Present spent their final days," he said, referencing the famous trio charged and convicted of setting fire to Paramaribo.

I walked into a damp, cave-like space with thick walls that muffled sounds. It would have been pitch black when the door was closed; the incarcerated men would have seen nothing, not even each other. Their only remaining senses—smell, sound, and touch—would have grown stronger over time. Did they listen to each other breathing, find comfort in each other's smells? In this deep darkness, did they reach out for each other's bodies for comfort, to soothe their fears? Did they work together in this prison, or in their isolation, did they turn away from one another?

Cojo, Mentor, and Present, and their counterpart Tata Colin, probably never learned to read, but like Roosje, they had seen all the finery that the wealthy colonial elite enjoyed: the mahogany furniture, fine cigars, parasols, rich fabrics, gold, and silverware. They'd heard the fortepianos and the flutes. They'd tended the French gardens carved into the rainforest. They'd also understood that unless things changed dramatically, none of it would ever be meant for them. Resistance was the only option, and they paid for it with their lives.

In the shade outside Fort Zeelandia, I paused in front of a gaudy plaster monument. "I heart SU," it read, the letters painted in the red, white, and green striped pattern of the Surinamese flag, the heart a blot of red between them. The paint was chipping, the red slightly faded. *What is Suriname?* I wondered. *What did it mean?* A group of Surinamese and Dutch scholars has argued that Suriname "is seen as a country whose population has been artificially constructed." Suriname, in other words, is an idea concocted and put into play by the Europeans who managed it. The product only of fraught colonial histories, it is an impossibility that can never really exist on its own terms.

My uncle called it something else.

"Suriname is a *broko pranasi*," he had said during our first dinner together, grasping for Sranan words to make his meaning clear. Translated literally, the phrase meant "broken-down plantation." I nodded, because that's what I was expected to do. At the time, I didn't really understand what he meant. I wasn't quite sure how to make sense of the words and the meanings they carried. But his comments stayed with me, becoming a lens through which I would come to see all my interactions in this place.

~~~~~

Roosje didn't get much opportunity to celebrate her newfound social status. In 1853, just a few years after her Cinderella-like rebirth, she passed away. Though she is listed in the official records as "unmarried" at her death, her tombstone in the Nieuwe Oranjetuin nevertheless acknowledges her long relationship with Dessé. Dessé himself died in 1868, five years after the abolition of slavery, and just a week after his daughter Eleonora's marriage to her first husband, Edmund Oldfield, a British-born doctor, in Berbice, British Guiana. After Oldfield's death at the age of forty-nine, Eleonora managed Leasowes plantation and later married again, this time to a Dutch-born plantation agent and administrator named Severinus van Lierop. She passed away in 1905 and is buried in The Hague. Her older brother Edmund, meanwhile, was also a plantation owner. In 1882, he married Mathilde Petronelle Landt, with whom he had a daughter. He died in 1888 after a long illness, and like his mother before him, was buried in the Nieuwe Oranjetuin. Another brother, Ethelrid, undertook medical training in the UK and later, in the Netherlands. He died in 1889 in Barbados at the age of just forty-six.

It was fairly easy to trace the life journeys of Dessé's heirs. The elite leave many traces of themselves: portraits, news articles, judicial records, birth and marriage records, and obituaries. But I wasn't as interested in Eleonora, Edmund, or Ethelrid. The person I wanted to know most about was Roosje. Knowing about this woman, who began her life in slavery and ended it in the most posh resting place of all, should have revealed much about my own family history. But just as the cemetery itself was hidden under layers of overgrowth, so too was Roosje's story, a mystery that lives on only in her tombstone.

~~~~~~

Cemeteries are a sore point in Suriname. The large cemeteries in Paramaribo have long since run out of space, with no possibility for expansion. In 2009, the government approved a bill that allowed cemeteries to clear graves, removing headstones and making room. In early November 2009, the Roman Catholic cemetery, whose oldest tombstones dated to 1917, was granted permission to clear 600 graves. It started with 175, all of which were carefully listed for descendants. Rural plantation cemeteries haven't fared well either. Forgotten as plantations were abandoned, any tombstones that remain are now buried in rainforest growth. Mudbank erosion, meanwhile, led in the 1980s to the somewhat grisly discovery of human bones, the remains of anonymous enslaved Africans and their descendants buried in a long-forgotten cemetery that had slowly disintegrated into the water. What happens when we disturb the remains of the dead? How can memories live on when evidence of lives disappears?

In contrast to forgotten burial grounds, nobody has called for the clearing of the Nieuwe Oranjetuin cemetery or for the removal of any of its graves. Instead, in 2016, just a few short weeks after my second visit to Paramaribo, the local government announced an initiative to clean the cemetery with the intent of turning it into a park, and hatched a plan to make this a retraining project that would allow formerly incarcerated men to transition back into society.

My aunt wasn't on board with the plan.

"It's a colonial cemetery filled with colonial people," she said. "Maybe the Dutch should be responsible." In other words, why should the local government pay for its maintenance? Still, I found myself wishing I had been there, wishing I'd been able to take part in this cleaning operation; this was the kind of archival work I loved to do. I wanted to dig, get my hands dirty; I wanted to discover. I wanted to be there as this cemetery re-emerged from under years of tropical growth. It didn't matter that someone had taken an inventory of the cemetery early in the twentieth century. I wanted to be there to find it for myself. In person. On the ground.

Instead, I resigned myself to watching the whole process unfold online after my return to Canada. As the months passed, I witnessed the rebirth of this cemetery, looking on as workers pulled brush and cut grass, rebuilt the brick wall, and cleaned out garbage. By early April 2017, most of the work was complete, and the cemetery had been transformed. Where my camera had picked out a single early-twentieth-century tombstone rising out above tall grasses, photos on the Surinamese Built Heritage Society page showed hundreds of graves—tall and flat, large and small, brick and stone, new and old. Some graves had collapsed, the brickwork disintegrating over time. Others were heavily damaged. Slowly but surely this cemetery has emerged again, and with it, too, those whose bodily remains rest there.

Frederika Rosette Dessé was probably a wealthy woman at her death. And, as any good mother of the time would have done, she managed to secure the fortunes of her children. But underneath the trappings of wealth and status, she had nevertheless been born into slavery and lived most of her life as an enslaved woman. As a free woman of colour, she had to navigate a social and cultural world that wasn't ready for her. While Dessé's wealth and status enabled her burial in the Nieuwe Oranjetuin cemetery, Roosje remained, even at her death, an outsider.

Perhaps her tombstone still stands, and maybe, now that the cemetery has been cleared, I can go back and visit it. Or perhaps it's long since disappeared. Her legacy, however, continues: in her freedom, her name, and her children.

SLAVENREGISTERS

I N THE END, my archival exile wasn't nearly as long as I'd
anticipated. A few days later, with Roosje's nearly impossible-
to-categorize life still at the forefront of my thoughts, I
headed back to the achives.

"I'm looking for slave registers," I said, handing the archivist
my handwritten request. About ten minutes later, the first boxes
appeared.

Unlike the declarations in the Dutch Chamber of Accounts—
loose sheets of crumbling, pulpy paper gathered together into thick
files—the plantation slave registers are thick, bound volumes of
heavy paper. In them, the plantations are arranged alphabetically
by district. These documents also served a different purpose from
the records in The Hague. The Dutch records were designed only
as a sort of accounting exercise to compensate enslavers. These volumes, however, are more like censuses; in them I learned of births,
deaths, sales, escapes, and manumissions. In many ways, these are
the hard facts of slave societies, the evidence not only of human
purchase and sale, but of a society that had absolutely no qualms
whatsoever about the practice.

I soon learned that it was the everydayness of these records
that I found most disturbing. Because, you see, it's possible, after
spending several months with this material, to start to believe that all

of this was normal. It's possible to start to count the way plantation administrators counted, to begin to think the way they thought. I was reminded once again that there was logic to this system of dehumanization, and it was that logic that troubled me. It's easy to discard systems that seem chaotic, irrational, confused, but what do you do with a system that presents itself as entirely rational, and that seems, at least on the surface, to be objective? After all, a colonial voice whispered in my ear, what's the difference between these ledgers and the census? And why *not* account for the power of one's labour force?

I'd worked through denial, the first stage of grief, in Middelburg and The Hague. But as I sat in this reading room in Paramaribo, I moved into the second stage: I found myself resisting. I didn't want to enter into a colonial mind. I didn't want to imagine myself as an enslaver. I didn't want to count the enslaved, to list them, to mark myself as an owner of other humans.

I thought back to some guest teaching I'd done a few years earlier, with a group of graduate students. I'd assigned *The History of Mary Prince*, the first known published slave narrative written by a woman. Born in Bermuda, Mary Prince was enslaved in Bermuda, the Turks and Caicos Islands, and Antigua. Later in her life, after travelling with her final owners to Britain, she claimed her freedom and, with the support of the Anti-Slavery Society, published an account of her experience of slavery. This short book, published three times in 1831 alone, became an important element in British abolitionist struggles. Two years later, Britain abolished slavery in all of its colonies.

I'd assigned the work before, to undergraduates, and we'd talked through various elements of the publication. We'd considered Mary's position as an enslaved woman, looking at how both her gender and her status affected her experiences and, inevitably, how they also played a role in her storytelling decisions. We'd thought about the details Mary had included and those that she'd left out, the most lascivious of which came to light only later, during a court trial for libel.

But this group of students was different. They didn't want to read Mary Prince's *History*. Some of them *couldn't* read it. They shook their heads as I glanced around the room.

"No," they said, one after another. "I couldn't."

The violence was too much, and they had turned away. All fully committed to their learning, they'd started reading but hadn't been able to bring themselves to finish. It was too distasteful. Too painful. Too much.

Here in the reading room, as I thought back on that class, I could understand their revulsion, for it mirrored my own experiences in Middelburg. But my resistance in Paramaribo wasn't about denial. It was about anger.

The slave registers, or maybe more accurately, what they represented, were repellent, offensive. It was impossible for me to imagine chattel slavery. It made no sense. It was so fundamentally antithetical to my understanding of the world as to be completely illogical. I couldn't fathom it. But the existence of these ledgers—these seemingly objective and rational accounts—meant that I *had* to confront it. In the ledgers, it was all too real.

I had to heed the words I'd shared with my students a few years earlier: *I couldn't just look away.* This wasn't just theoretical. Transatlantic slavery thrived for more than four centuries. During that time, it was considered normal to buy and sell humans, to traffic them across oceans, to enslave them and all their offspring for the economic benefit of plantation owners and the Europeans for whom their products were destined. There was nothing outrageous about it. This particular system of human trafficking ended less than 150 years ago. Variations of it continue even today.

That was the reality we had to confront in the classroom. We couldn't look away, no matter how distasteful the situation, no matter how uncomfortable we were. We had to face this. We had to look Mary Prince in the eye, and we had to listen to what she had to say.

In some ways I could understand my students' reactions. How could we, as readers, respond to Mary Prince? How could we even begin to acknowledge the enormity of her enslavement? How could we ever atone for it?

But was that what we were meant to do? Was atonement even possible? Or were we, as readers, meant instead to be witnesses, and in this way, to acknowledge that even today, we are all still part of this history, that we are all participants in the afterlives of slavery. This is the argument that Caribbean nations have put forward as they seek reparations for these painful histories. Slavery is a crime against humanity, and its effects transcend generations. Slavery didn't end upon abolition; rather, these histories continue to influence contemporary lived experience throughout this region and beyond.

What might reparations look like? In Middelburg, I'd read through some visitor comments to a small exhibition about the slave trade housed in the archives. A noisy group of teenagers had been through just before me, so I waded through a few pages of relative silliness. But then, I paused at a long commentary offered by a different visitor: "I was born in Suriname" began the entry.

> I'm the descendant of both the slave and the slave owner. When I moved to Middelburg as a teenager, I was surprised to discover that slavery was not at all part of the Dutch history curriculum. There could be changes made here. Let us learn from the mistakes of our ancestors. Respect and Freedom. 250 years of slavery is impossible to understand. On the first of July we celebrate freedom!

Education. Financial compensation. Formal and honest apologies. These are big issues. It's hard to account for something as monstrous as the transatlantic slave trade. How do we live in the present in bodies still affected by the everyday violence of slavery? How do we live and move through landscapes that still reflect this history? How do we navigate cultural and educational systems that still fundamentally deny the horrors of slavery and indenture? And how do we acknowledge the complicated pasts in which we are all embedded? In the words of Guy Emerson Mount, these questions amount to this: "How do we forgive the unforgivable? How do you repair the irreparable?"

Perhaps the answer lies in the visitor comment itself. After all, according to Saidiya Hartman, stories may be the only reparations the Caribbean will ever receive. In them, we can sift through that mess of emotions that make us who we are: loss, longing, fear, grief, love, awe, joy, anger, frustration, resentment. Only by making room for this discomfort can we begin to think of moving forward.

In the end, it was Mary Prince's depiction of her enslavers that allowed my students a way in. Contrary to what the British may have thought, slave owners were not genteel, gracious, civilized Britons whose hard work furthered the ideals of the British nation. Mary Prince presented them as violent, sweaty, and depraved individuals who sought—and got—pleasure out of the violence they inflicted on others.

And there I was, a continent away from my university classroom, sitting in front of a grey archive box housing a thick, bound volume of slave registers. Like my students, I didn't want to enter into the colonial mind. I didn't want to imagine myself as an enslaver. I didn't want to think about a system that did this to people.

"No," I wanted to say. "No."

Before I knew it, my brain had scampered off on an adventure of its own making, anger and resistance giving way to rage.

How to Buy a Slave: A Practical Volume Designed to Facilitate Favourable Negotiations. By Sonja Boon

First, recognize that some slaves will cost more than others and plan accordingly. Find ways to appeal to your trading partner's vanity. Make him look good and you will own the world.

My pencil scratched across the page, the weight of my rage almost gouging the paper.

Pack your trunk carefully. You don't want to give the game away too soon. Pull out the items one by one, laying them out like priceless gems. Allow the wonder to enter into the trader's eyes before you pull out more. All of this could be yours, your gesturing arms seem to say as they sweep over the goods arrayed between you. All of this for that lovely slave you've got there.

My imagination skittered ahead, careening through the archival scraps that littered its path.

In the flickering candlelight you stroke the guns, draw your hands over the cotton, dust your fingers in a bag of flour. You offer your trading partner a mirror, maybe two, maybe more. "You look fantastic! Some tobacco, sir? And here's a snuff box, too."

How much for the slave? you think. She's young. Her body is strong. You squeeze the flesh on her thighs, pull behind her ears, look deep into her mouth. You resist the urge to examine the darkness between her legs. Not now, you think. Later.

You nod. This is the one. But you'll have to be careful. The other men will want her too.

"A virgin?" You need to ask. Slight nod. Untested, but that will have to do. Baby-making hips, and a round, fleshy bottom. She'll sell for a good price on the other side. Some owner will be a lucky man. Lighten up the proceedings. Things are getting serious here. You don a feathered hat, wrap the finest white cotton around your chest, pull a pinstripe along your leg. Produce a stoneware plate and the finest glass mug.

"Coffee, sir?" An eyebrow raised in question. "Or perhaps a spot of tea?" The man gestures to the gin.

"Ah," you reply, "the good stuff." And then the negotiations really begin.

Off kilter now, I fell into a ghoulish, macabre rhythm.

I could offer you a mirror
I could offer you some hats
I could offer you some fabrics
What might a man about town think of that?

I could offer you some spices,
Some butter and flour, too.
Sugar, you say?
Yes, of course. That I can certainly do.

But let's keep this all between us,
We won't share it with the crew ...
Shhh, be very quiet now.
There's so much work to do!

Perhaps you're a man of fashion
And fabrics are your passion—

Cotton? Linen? I've got pinstripe, too—
It's perfect for a man like you.

Not a single person has them
You'll be the only one in town!
Come look into the mirror, now—
You look great! Take away that frown.

It was getting petty, but I couldn't seem to stop myself. My hand-writing had become a scrawl, loopy and loose. My mind was spark-ing and spinning. I'd seen the sales lists in Middelburg. I'd seen what it took to make a deal, clinch the sale, buy the slave. The traders ran their own department stores, with the finest goods on offer. Cheese. Flour. Sugar. Salt fish. Butter. Spices. White cotton. Pinstripes. Gingham. Frisian lace. Tobacco. Mirrors. Hats. Snuff boxes. Guns. Knives. Stoneware. Glassware. Copperware. You name it, they had it. The transactions only continued in Paramaribo. Newspapers advertised auctions promising strong men, furniture, silverware, and cows.

How much was this slave actually worth? What could you sell her for? The questions flicker through your thoughts, but you push them away. You're making a deal, lost in the game. Not now, you think. I've got work to do. And the negotiations continue. Push and pull, back and forth. You nod, smile, curse, cajole.

But then suddenly you're there: one final copper kettle and the deed is done. Pull out your quill, dip it in ink.

"No. 54 woman." Short and sweet. Give her a name, anything that sounds good. Sophonosbia. Ajuba. Quassiba. Sounds fine. Min-erva? Fidella? Celestina? Fanciful, yes, but you want something sim-ple, classic, elegant even. Pure. She is a virgin, you think. Beautiful. And now it comes to you: Belle, you say. That's it, that's right.

Perfect.

The candle flickers from dusk until dawn and then through another cycle again. You haggle and bribe. You wheedle, whisper, seduce...

The art of the deal. Was that what this was all about? The seduction of bargaining? The power of sales? I thought of shopping mall salespeople eager to make a sale. I thought of their faces, their glow. The commission they imagined. The commission they needed. The game that I played in response. My irritation. My annoyance. My frustration. My grudging acknowledgement that they were just doing their job as they'd been told to do it. And I thought, too, of the economic system that demands this push and pull, and how we're all so firmly embedded in it.

I don't want to equate my experiences at the local mall with the transatlantic slave trade. But I do want to suggest that we're all implicated in the economic systems that structure our lives. Sellers cannot exist without buyers, and the two are intimately linked through the products they exchange. We might disagree, fundamentally, with the principles of the economic systems that structure our lives, but we can't escape them. This was true, too, of the slave trade. Buyers and sellers were locked in an uneasy and uncomfortable tango, dancing together right down to the bottom.

For plantation owners, just as for traders, the bottom line was money. The trade was about little else. For traders, this meant keeping a close eye on their human cargo in order to ensure its safe arrival. In all instances, they had to maximize their profits—this is why they inspected the enslaved so closely, why they negotiated so carefully. Plantation owners, enslavers themselves, undertook calculations on how best to manage slaves most efficiently. I thought back to a passage I'd read in John Newton's *Thoughts upon the African Slave Trade:*

One thing I cannot omit, which was told me by the gentleman to whom my ship was consigned, at Antigua, in the year 1751, and who was himself a planter. He said, that calculations had been made, with all possible exactness, to determine which was the preferable, that is the more saving method of managing slaves: *"Whether, to appoint them moderate work, plenty of provision, and such treatment as might enable them to protract their lives to old age?"* Or, *"By rigorously straining their strength to the utmost, with little relaxation, hard fare, and hard usage, to wear them out before they became useless, and unable to do service; and then, to buy new ones, to fill up their places?"* He farther said, that these skilful calculators had determined in favour of the latter mode, as much the cheaper; and that he could mention several estates, in the island of Antigua, on which it was seldom known that a slave had lived above nine years.

This capitalist tango was a complicated one. We cannot assume that all those who owned slaves supported this system. Many did not. But the ultimate irony of a slave-based system was that you could free the enslaved only by first purchasing them. In other words, you had to play the game. Resistance, it seemed, was possible only from within. And that's exactly what some did.

In Suriname, a man named Jan Houthakker, himself formerly enslaved, purchased more than 100 slaves over a twenty-year period. He didn't buy them to work his plantations or ease his domestic life; he bought them to free them. Houthakker purchased and manumitted young and old, single people and whole families. Some families came intact, purchased as a group from a single owner. Other families had already been separated by the realities of slavery, and a series of purchases was necessary before they could be reunited and freed under a single name. I could follow all these transactions in the slave registers. Consider, for example, the case of Willie,

Johanna, and Patientie Koen. Willie and Johanna, born in 1845 and 1843 respectively, were the property of one F.W. Faerber, from whom Houthakker purchased them in January 1860. Patientie, their mother, born in 1808, was the property of L.M. Kohn, from whom Houthakker purchased her one month later, in February 1860. The three of them were manumitted together, as a family, on Christmas Eve 1862, six months before abolition, taking the names Jacoba Patientie, Christiaan Willie, and Cecilia Johanna Koen.

While Houthakker offers a remarkable example of resistance, his story is embedded in a much larger narrative. Born Flink, Houthakker had been owned by a group of three men. Of those, two had previously been enslaved; their owner, too, one Mary van McNeil, had been enslaved. It seems that Houthakker's vocation was a responsibility, an inheritance gifted to him by those who came before him, and it was clearly something he took seriously. As the slave registers show, this same responsibility was something that some of those who were freed through his work also took up. Thus Ferdinand Touh, who was freed in September 1854 (and whose last name—spelled backwards—is an obvious homage to Houthakker), freed Ernstina Frederika Omzigtig and her three-year-old son, Julius Ferdinand Omzigtig, in November 1859. So, too, did Salomon Adam Schelts, freed in December 1857, later free a child—Rudolf—on 24 December 1860.

~~~~~

It had felt good to release my rage, but my fictional venting hadn't been particularly helpful. My rage had fizzled itself out by this point, giving way, instead, to resignation. If I wanted to understand this history, my family's place in it, and how these pasts continued to affect contemporary realities, then I needed to enter that history, no matter how uncomfortable or how angry it made me. I needed to find a way to resist from within. Feeling its weight in my hands,

I gently placed the first ledger on the table, balancing its spine carefully to protect it from harm. The volume showed its age; the cover was—strangely—attached only with a few strips of white Scotch tape apparently added by a recent caretaker. Opening it released a slight mustiness, another reminder of the book's age. Inside, the plantations were listed in alphabetical order, just like the papers in The Hague: *Belladrum. Bellevue. Burnside. Clyde. Diamond. Good Intent. Hamilton.* Some were small operations, with only a handful of slaves. Others, like Burnside, were large, their records going on for pages, their slaves running into the hundreds. I flipped ahead. *Mary's Hope. Nursery. Paradise.* Sarah was two hundred pages farther along, after *Perseverance, Plaisance, Potosie,* and *Rhynie.*

Each plantation organized its information slightly differently, but the main parameters remained the same: the official records required name, sex, age, and mother. In the final columns, administrators included other relevant information: infirmities, deaths, sales, and escapes, details rarely included in the General Accounting Chamber declarations. In 1854, twenty-one enslaved men, ranging in age from sixteen to forty-four, escaped from Burnside plantation. Another eight men in their twenties escaped in early 1863, on the eve of abolition. I wondered what happened to them. And I wondered, too, what happened to the women and children who remained. Hampton Court's records show a spate of slave purchases from other plantations—eighteen in 1855, followed two years later by another five. The administrator at Inverness recorded a transfer of sixty-one slaves from Leasowes and the escape of fourteen men and boys—including two young children named Ferdinand and Abraham, aged eight and seven respectively—in 1854.

By contrast, things appeared remarkably stable at Sarah plantation. For the most part the enslaved at Sarah were born, fell ill, and died on the plantation. Of the more than three hundred slaves listed in the records, only two were listed as "runaway"; another six were written off for no specific reason at all. Twenty, the majority of whom were women and girls, were manumitted—given their freedom—between 1854 and 1862. I wondered why things were so different at Sarah. What made them stay, while so many others fled from Burnside? Were the conditions better, or, perhaps more ominously, were the punishments worse?

~~~~~

I didn't see any of these details the first time I opened the volume. Instead, my eyes scanned the names, hungry for those I needed to find. Frederik, born in 1798, mother unknown. Edward, born in 1818, mother deceased. Eva—listed as Eve—born in 1827, mother deceased. Frederika, her apparent twin. The names tumbled out of the ledger, one after another, confirming the records I'd seen just a few months earlier in The Hague.

But then, some differences. By the 1850s, the administrator had started including exact birthdates. Jack 2, born on 12 November 1851. Joseph, born 9 December 1855. Wilson 2, born 26 August 1857. I'm not sure why this mattered to me, but it did. Maybe it's because these extra details meant that administrators were paying more attention. Maybe, it said, things were changing. But this level of detail wasn't necessarily the case at other plantations. And so maybe it was just about a single administrator who was pickier about his job, more concerned with tiny details. I'm not sure, and I doubt I will ever know.

Madleentje, my great-great-grandmother, was born on 28 April 1855. Madleentje shimmered in my imagination, her face coming in and out of focus. She smiled, an imp with a row of white teeth, a dimple in her right cheek, her cheeky eyes promising trouble. It didn't make sense, of course. I couldn't possibly know what she looked like. How is it, I wondered, that people become real when we give them specific birthdays? What's the difference between

1855 and 28 April 1855? Madleentje was a spring baby, I now knew, born at the beginning of Suriname's major rainy season. For nine months, her mother had carried her, feeling her grow and change. And then, she'd laboured during the heavy weight of season change. Was Madleentje born during one of those flooding tropical downpours, the ones where everything stands still in what the locals call *witte regen*, white rain?

I already knew that Madleentje was Frederika's fourth child. I knew that Frederika was about twenty-eight years old when Madleentje was born. I knew that Madleentje had two younger siblings, Wilson and Leander. But what the Dutch records—designed to account for restitutions for colonial enslavers in the aftermath of slavery—hadn't been able to tell me was that Madleentje had another sibling—a sister, Annette, born in 1843.

Frederika was sixteen when she gave birth to Annette. When I was sixteen, I wrote maudlin poetry and dated a flute player who already knew he wanted to become a mortician. I spent part of my summer at a flute camp in Ramsgate in the UK, where we paraded around the grounds dressed in togas made out of our sheets, argued about nuclear weapons, and accidentally shot the fuses by having too many hairdryers on at once. I watched bratpack movies and wished I had Molly Ringwald's hair. *Pretty in Pink. The Breakfast Club.* I had absolutely no reference point at all for Frederika's experiences.

~~~~~~

Annette was the one who got away. In October 1862, aged around nineteen, and just eight months before the abolition of slavery, Annette was manumitted under the name Annette Juliane Jurgon. Here, suddenly, was a new family member, one none of us had ever known about.

As I looked more closely through the registers, I found another. Lodewijk was born in 1844 to Frederika's sister, Eva. Like Annette, Lodewijk got away. But how? The records told me that in 1859, when he would have been fifteen, he was struck from the register. No reason was given. Had he escaped? Had he died? Did he just disappear?

Two teenagers with two babies.

Two babies who grew into teenagers.

Two teenagers who got away.

I sat in my chair, quiet in my thoughts. Next to me, another researcher was buried in letters of some sort. Across the room, a man in flip-flops was trying to convince the archivists to help him out. He had stories, so many stories, but not quite enough detail to access the records.

"We're sorry," they kept telling him. "We need a bit more information."

He grew more and more agitated, his voice rising, but they couldn't help.

Outside, the sun had risen farther in the sky. The security guard was snoozing, his chair tipped back against a pillar, his chin sinking into his chest.

Who were Annette and Lodewijk? I wondered. How did they manage to get away, when their younger siblings hadn't? I didn't have a lot to go on. It's clear that the children of plantation owners, administrators, or overseers had a greater chance of being manumitted. Lighter skin was a plus. So was where they worked: house slaves employed in domestic positions for administrators or owners were much more likely to be freed than field slaves. And mothers who bore many children were also rewarded. I imagined different scenarios, turning them around in my mind as I looked out the window.

We're sorry, the archival materials taunted me. *We need a bit more information.*

The problem was this: like the flip-flopped man, I didn't have enough to go on. When I returned to my apartment later that afternoon and went online to search through historical newspaper and census records, I found only a few more hints. In 1879, the Court of Justice found that Annette Jurgon, previously residing in Nickerie and then living in Paramaribo, was to be placed under care. But I didn't know what that really meant. One year later, on 15 April 1880, she died. She was thirty-seven years old. Lodewijk, meanwhile, didn't appear anywhere at all.

In my gut, I knew that I was still missing something, and it niggled. I examined the records again. Until 1855 at least, Frederika and Eva seemed to have led remarkably parallel reproductive lives, giving birth sometimes within months of each other.

Annette and Lodewijk, born in 1843 and 1844.

Cornelis and Sultan, born in 1847.

Janny and Amsterdam, born in 1849.

Madleentje and Joseph, born in 1855.

Twin cousins almost, born of twin mothers. What was I missing? It took another year of reading and rereading the transcriptions I had made of the register before I figured out that there was an outlier. Jack Abraham, born to Frederika on 12 November 1851, appeared to have had no "twin," no cousin who almost shared his birthday. And Eva, a woman in the prime of her childbearing years, had somehow managed to avoid pregnancy for six years before going on to have three more children. It wasn't impossible, of course, but seemed highly unlikely.

And so it was that I found another probable ancestor. Marlon 2—so named to distinguish him from the first Marlon, an elder born in 1780—was born on 20 August 1851. Jack Abraham and Marlon 2, born in 1851. Now it made sense.

Two years later, in late May 1853, Marlon 2 was manumitted under the name Jacob Schove by one of the plantation administrators, H.J. Blancke. And then, like his brother, Lodewijk, he disappeared.

I'm not sure why I hadn't noticed Marlon 2 earlier. Perhaps it was because his mother was listed as Eva—not Eve, as she was listed in relation to all her other children. Perhaps it seemed too unlikely. But there are no other Eves in the slave register for Sarah plantation. A second and third Eva, listed in the declaration for Sarah plantation in The Hague, led me to a woman who suffered from leprosy, and a child of thirteen. Neither could realistically have been Marlon 2's mother.

Annette. Lodewijk. And now Marlon 2/Jacob. Why did any of this matter? What was the point of it anyway? Why rummage through these registers at all? I thought back to my fictional trader, inscribing names into his ledgers. *Belle*, he had said. *Belle for the beautiful one.* Annette, Lodewijk, Jacob. Regardless of who had given birth to them, it is likely that all of them had been named by the plantation's owners, directors, or administrators. Their stories, created for them, were not their own. They had no control over their names, no control over their bodies, no choice in their enslavement, or even in their freedom. But then I thought of John Newton, who denounced the slave trade after several journeys as a trader, and of Jan Houthakker, who did what he could to undermine the system from within. It was time to bargain with the past. Was there a way of creating a different narrative, building something new out of the ugliness that had brought my ancestors into the world? Could I tell a different story?

In the Netherlands, at the Leiden University Library, I'd read a book about enslaved children. The historian, Geert Oostindie, had observed that while plantations were places of violence and oppression, with low life expectancies and high death rates, they were also places filled with intimate memories and experiences. The plantation, he wrote, was where your own umbilical cord was buried, that of relatives and maybe your loved one. The place where you had learned to walk, not only to the coffee fields where you had to work, but to the forest where you lived more freely and where the planter was the lesser one. The place where you had seen and perhaps experienced abuse, where you had to bury your younger brother, your mother, but also the place where you knew the best fishing spots, had fallen in love for the first time, where you had learned to dance and had heard stories about the clever spider Anansi who always outwitted the Whites.

At a rational level, I knew all of this to be true. The slave registers and General Accounting Chamber declarations, with their maternal family trees, their owner-assigned last names, and their intricate webs of purchases and sales, had already revealed some of this. But I didn't want to think of plantations as intimate spaces. I scribbled and scribbled my resistance in my notebook. I spilled my emotions in words, filling pages and more pages. How could something so dehumanizing, in a system that was designed to turn people into objects of trade, also hold within it love, intimacy, warmth, tears, music, joy? How could a plantation be home, with all the emotions we attach to that concept? How could any human being possibly bear these contradictions?

~~~~~~

A few years earlier, in 2013, I had participated in a collaborative art project developed by a St. John's–based visual artist, Pam Hall. Pam has long been interested in the domestic, and this project, "Building a Village," was no different. The premise of "Building a Village" was simple: Pam asked her participants to explore the question, *What does home mean to you?* Pam would send a house model—photocopied onto white cardstock—to any interested party to decorate as we saw fit. Then we'd return the finished houses to her, and she'd exhibit them as a collection, a village of tiny homes. Pam requested a dollar to cover the cost of postage, but other than that, we were on our own.

An enthusiastic if somewhat incompetent crafter, I signed up right away and waited for my house model to arrive, eager to get started. But once it arrived, the cardboard model languished on my desk as I tried to sort out how best to approach it. I overthought every step of the process. There were variables to consider. I had to think through authenticity, truth, representation, equity, justice, honesty. I had to ponder my pasts, my futures. I had to consider my artistic desires (and also, it must be said, my inevitable artistic limitations).

~~~~~

What does home mean to you? In Paramaribo, Pam's question fluttered through my mind. Back in St. John's, I'd sat with her collaborative house project for months, struggling to articulate what I was searching for.

The question haunted me. Taunted me.

In the meantime, as the months passed, contributions to Pam's project grew. She kept us all up-to-date on social media, sharing photos of the new houses as they arrived in her mailbox. Some were intricate, some colourful. Some were the work of professional artists, others the submissions of interested and keen crafters. Some just wanted to explore stories. No two were even remotely similar.

My own cardstock house model gathered dust on the corner of my desk. The more I thought, the further my webs unspooled themselves, the more tangled they became.

And then, suddenly, a moment of clarity. Home, I realized, was not something fixed at all. Movement had marked my pasts; it also marked my presents. And so, certain of something at last, even if that something was unmoored, I collaged scraps of historical maps to the outside of my house, foregrounding the cities and regions that mattered in relation to my family history, while still leaving room for some sea serpents and other fantastical creatures of the wild ocean.

On the inside, I attached my vision statement: "Home," it said, "in a mode of migration." And that, I thought, was that.

But my archival reflections were telling me a different story. Three generations of my enslaved ancestors had lived not only in the same country but on the very same 500-acre tract of plantation land. For over sixty years, they hadn't migrated at all.

In the archives, I wrote and wrote. I wrote because in my heart, I knew that Oostindie was right. My enslaved ancestors had been at Sarah plantation for several generations. For better or for worse, Sarah was home. It was where they were whipped and where they were raped. It was where they died and where they were buried. But it was also where they sang and danced, where they played games, where they fell in love, and where they mourned their dead, grieved for the missing. Sarah plantation was everything they knew; it was who they were.

But how could I possibly imagine the plantation as home? It felt wrong but it also felt right. It felt like a betrayal. It felt like a relief. It hurt. It made me angry. It made me long, although I have no idea what I was longing for. I didn't know what to do with my emotions. I didn't know how to honour my ancestors, their experiences, their memory. What could I do with 500 acres of plantation slavery? How could I navigate the space between love and violence, life and death?

This is my family. These are my people. This is my inheritance. I wanted to shout it out loud, to make that claim loud and clear. Because somehow, I thought, if I claimed these lost ancestors, I could give them life beyond these damning ledgers. I thought I could make sense of these contradictions. What I was really asking, I suppose, was this: If I yelled loud enough, could I make all these emotions go away?

II

BROKO PRANASI

EW ACTIVE PLANTATIONS remain in Suriname. Katwijk, originally developed as a coffee plantation sometime around 1748, continues to produce coffee today. Alliance, meanwhile, produces a range of citrus fruits. But this doesn't mean that the plantation regions have gone silent. Where once the enslaved and indentured laboured, their descendants continue to live in tiny villages whose names recall plantation pasts. And while the rainforest has taken over much of the landscape, physical memories remain. Balls and chains. Giant vats for stirring cane sugar into molasses. Straight lines of canals and dikes marking both plantation properties and the inevitable Dutch propensity for water management. If the enslaved carried their stories in their bodies, the country of Suriname remembers too, bearing witness through its own scarred landscape. It was time to venture beyond the city limits.

The boat's nose nudged itself into the opening of the Warappakreek, the operator guiding it into a narrow passageway. The creek was dark and still; the jungle, as we continued, ever more overwhelming. Mangroves stretched their roots into the water. Overhead, branches swayed, creating a canopy of leaves. All around us, flies and mosquitoes. As we motored farther in, the creek grew narrower, at some points appearing almost to close in on itself. Apart from the constant buzz of insect wings, it was eerily silent.

The Warappakreek is a small tributary that comes off the much wider Commewijne River, which itself forks away from the Suriname River. Centuries ago, hundreds of plantations lined the banks of both river and creek. Today, only shadows remain; the plantations have collapsed into themselves, leaving only tiny traces on the landscape. The Warappakreek lies at the heart of Surinamese plantation history. One of the first areas to be settled by planters, it also endured, the homes along its banks broadcasting the fortunes of their owners.

As we travelled the creek, it narrowed further. Originally, it had stopped completely, a dead end in the darkness of the rainforest. But plantation owners, eager for a more efficient way of bringing goods to and from their properties, decided to extend the creek right out to the ocean. And thus was created the Warappa Canal, a channel that stretched from Bent's Hope plantation right out to the sea.

These things are apparently easy on paper when you have a seemingly endless supply of enslaved labour at your disposal. But as the current owners of nearby Reynsdorp plantation discovered, it's a completely different story today. Armed with a digger, they set to work in 2007.

"We thought it would take us a couple of weeks," Marsha Mormon told us, incredulity still evident in her voice almost a decade later. "We thought we'd just start digging and keep going."

Mormon is a Creole woman in her thirties who originally arrived in Suriname in search of her family history. A descendant of slaves from this region, she came armed only with the knowledge that her grandfather was the owner of a plot of former plantation land. That land, somewhere in the depths of an overgrown and abandoned plantation, proved uninhabitable, and so she settled at a neighbouring plantation, Reynsdorp, instead. Marsha was positive about her projects and hopeful for the future. She and partner Bas Spek are creative entrepreneurs, drawing on the histories of this place to design a future for themselves and the local community. Since their arrival, they've developed a small museum that houses the various artifacts they've dredged up from the canal, a garden that features plants and herbs important to the different ethnic communities who have come to call Suriname home, and a pair of rental accommodations. They've worked with the government to improve the dock and, with it, general access to this region. They've welcomed tourists and also researchers, and through them, they've learned more about the history and ecology of this place they call home. One researcher, rummaging around in the far reaches of the former plantation, found an as-yet-undocumented species of banana tree. Another focused on birds.

In the end, it took seven months for Marsha and Bas to excavate the canal. Seven months with modern industrial equipment. Chopping. Digging. Dredging. Stabilizing. Over and over and over again as the banks continued to erode. All in the humid heaviness of the tropical rainforest. For the enslaved delvers, it must have been soul-breaking work.

~~~~~

Gliding through the canal, I was amazed at their original prediction of two weeks. Not only would a project like this require digging, but it would also require constant and continual vigilance. The canal's banks are soft and muddy, and the mangroves voracious, their roots stretching farther and farther. New roots appeared almost daily as if by magic.

"There's no way to turn around here," our tour guide said, catching my interest in the boat operator's chainsaw. "You wouldn't want to get stuck."

We also had to worry about the mud. The creek's sides are constantly collapsing into the water; the soil is soft and glutinous. The coastline, too, is prone to erosion. Already, whole plantations have slipped away, in the process revealing uncomfortable histories. In the 1980s, skeletons of the enslaved emerged from the mud. Scientific analysis revealed stories of physical hardship, illness, and disease. All of this rattled around inside our heads, as our boat continued its journey.

~~~~~

There were eight of us on the tour, including a couple from Rotterdam, their skins leathery from a sun-baked holiday in Curaçao, and a family of four from Leiden, travelling together with a local friend. Of the group, only three of us had been in Suriname before.

"I was born here," said the mother from Leiden, and I visualized her wrapping belonging around herself like a warm blanket.

Just earlier, in a feat that would have made any Newfoundlander proud, she had launched into a conversation with our boat operator, an otherwise quiet and somewhat taciturn, moustached man who kept his peace as the rest of us chattered among ourselves. After fifteen minutes of rapid-fire Sarnami, the Hindustani Creole language, she looked triumphantly over at her son, an overgrown teenager on the cusp of adulthood.

"He's related to you," she announced.

The teenager sighed; he'd heard this before.

"I'm related to everyone," he said.

I had no response. If this was a competition, she'd already won. I wasn't born in Suriname. I'd never even lived there. Suriname was a complicated family tree and a collection of stamps in passports. What precisely was my claim to belonging?

My first days in the archives had been challenging. I'd struggled to listen for my ancestors, but I couldn't hear them, their voices muted by the weight of colonial ledgers. Maybe they just kept their heads down. Did the work. Didn't fuss. Sometimes survival depends on making oneself small. But even then, they must have had a vast store of stories. Surely they could have explained the everyday madness that was slavery? In the quiet stillness of the Warappakreek, I wondered.

There is no way through this region other than by boat. There are no roads. Any walking paths are long gone. The small canals that once marked the dividing lines between plantations have silted in, and only a few forlorn brick pillars mark the spots where sluices once stood. In the dense darkness of the jungle, plantations are nothing more than memories. From above, however, clear contours remain: here a boundary, there a former canal.

Two hundred years ago this creek would have been busy, alive with work and activity. There would have been paths on either side, and bridges linking the two sides together. And a constant bustle of boats, gliding up and down with goods for the plantations. It would have been a noisy place, the chaos and overgrowth contained and corralled into neat plantations, into some of which were carved formal French gardens. I listened for the music that might have influenced Johannes Helstone and Dario Saavedra—the string quartets that accompanied evening plantation soirees; the drums and singing that must have spilled from the dwellings of the enslaved and later, indentured—but everything was quiet. The rainforest had reasserted itself, and as we moved farther into the canal, the silence grew. None of us spoke; we were in awe of our environment, lost in thought.

We approached a small wooden dock and pulled in. This was the entrance to Bent's Hope plantation. The air was thick and humid, alive with the beating of thousands of insect wings. Voracious mosquitoes danced around our limbs, burrowing into our flesh when we weren't paying attention.

"They've even bitten me in the backside!" the mother proclaimed. "I itch everywhere!"

"They bite through jeans," the guide said, and she was right. I could already feel welts rising on my hips.

We stamped our feet and swatted with our arms, our DEET-soaked bodies no match for feasting beasts.

"Vitamin B is supposed to work," the guide offered. "But you have to start taking it a few months in advance." She had wrapped a cloth around her head and seemed impervious to the onslaught, while the rest of us continued our swatting dance.

The guide led us down a small path. At the end, in a small clearing, lay the rusting carcass of an old steam-powered sugar mill, its skeleton bones askew on the jungle floor, slowly being consumed by the foliage. A large wheel, still standing, was disappearing into a bamboo forest. A few metres away was a steam tank, forgotten and forlorn, its hulk embraced by vines. In the early nineteenth century, this was the heart of Bent's Hope's operations.

Bent's Hope was to be the pride of John Bent, the same John Bent who once also owned Sarah plantation. Purchased in 1828, Bent's Hope was his dream plantation in a dream location. Bent's Hope lies right at the point where salt water meets fresh water. According to an early-twentieth-century eyewitness nostalgic for the plantation days of yore, this region lay at the heart of Surinamese plantation culture. The Warappakreek boasted gracious houses filled with grand decor and possessions. In other words, this was prime plantation real estate. All that mahogany, all those silk parasols, all those cigars? Those two fortepianos? This region was a likely destination for them.

Here, Bent decided to set up a modern sugar cane plantation, ordering the latest in sugar-producing technology: a James Watt steam-powered sugar mill. But to make this work, he needed money, and lots of it. While he managed to acquire the necessary funds through creative arrangements with financial institutions, it's clear from early newspapers and other records that this gamble did not necessarily pay off. Some of Bent's properties, among them Sarah plantation, were placed under sequestration and threatened with public auction. Others he sold off. He also appears to have used some of his slaves as leverage. The slave registers include a list of over 260 slaves registered to the names of J. Mackillop, R. Dent, and J. Young, all purchased from John Bent in December 1833 "on condition of re-purchase over a period of three years." Mackillop and company seem to have functioned like a pawnshop, guaranteeing the possibility of re-purchase even as they gave out money that Bent clearly desperately needed.

But Bent's Hope was in a race against time. By the 1830s, the plantation economy was in decline. The slave trade had ended. The glory days were over, and when John Bent died in 1848, this plantation, too, was put under sequestration. Bent's Hope had become Bent's Folly. Just over a decade later, in 1859, Bent's Hope and its remaining 165 slaves were sold to another British subject, Hugh Wright, for 30,000 guilders at public auction, in violation of British law. And by Emancipation, the plantation was empty, the enslaved likely transferred to another plantation. Many other plantations along the creek had also been abandoned. These rusting iron bones we examined are all that remains of Bent's Hope.

I wanted to spend more time at Bent's Hope, to walk quietly and feel the energy of this space. I wanted to hold on to it, capture it somehow. And just as in Middelburg, I wanted to revel in the silence. This was a plantation. A living archive. Sacred space. I needed time to think, reflect, process. But tours are difficult. People have questions. They make comments. They shuffle around, take up space, get itchy, get bored. They want to move on. There's a script to follow and a schedule to keep.

As a child, I'd been taught the rules of proper etiquette for girls, and those teachings ran deep. *Don't keep the others waiting. Sit straight. Be polite. Don't ask too many questions. Don't take up too much* space. *Keep your knees together.* There were other people with other needs. My own would have to wait.

I took as many photos as I could and then slowly made my way back to the boat.

~~~~~

Later, back at my apartment, I read that fifty years after the abolition of slavery, there was nothing left of the Warappakreek's former glory. In the words of an anonymous correspondent, writing in a local newspaper in 1909,

> Nothing ... is to be seen except dense growth of *parawa*, *branti makka* and mangrove trees, the latter easily distinguishable by their very long roots hanging down the brinks of the Creek to the very bottom, until behind this dense mass of vegetation is to be heard the barking of a worthless cur, or the crowing of a cock, then one realizes that the place is inhabited, or moored to the root of the mangrove tree may be seen a corial or two indicating that is the landing-place or entrance to some particular farm-ground or other. To get ashore one must be an expert in the art of scrambling on all-fours or by holding on to the overhanging branches of "branti-makka" at the risk of getting the prickles into your hands.

The anonymous author continued:

> ... following your course along the creek you next arrive at the confluence of the water from the sea and the creek.... Here is the abandoned estate Ponthieu, next is Bentshope an old abandoned sugar estate, opposite to which on the other side of the creek is the abandoned estate Clifford-Kocshoven (now in the possession of a Chinaman who is busy cutting open the frontage to establish

a fishing industry). At this point the creek runs almost dry and is therefore not navigable by low tide, so that to go along the creek the journey must be regulated according to ebb and flow.

Abandoned but for worthless curs and Chinamen, any hint of civilization lost. This is imagery of loss, desolation, and decay, a story of a once grand region now derelict, left to fend for itself. Even the creek itself had collapsed, its silted heart a barrier in low tide.

But it wasn't just the Warappakreek. The colony of Suriname itself was collapsing, another eyewitness claimed. Where once it had been place of wonder, hope, prosperity, and progress, Suriname had fallen on hard times: "Where are the coffee ships, the sugar ships, the cotton ships that once so frequently sought out our harbour to collect the rich products from our plantations? Everything has changed," he lamented. "It's now a miserable, shabby, sorry rubble."

Everything had changed. These words weren't just nostalgic, they were a eulogy, a longing for a past that was fundamentally beyond reach. Today, there's a new harbour in Paramaribo filled with containers stacked several high, but where are all the ships that once sailed the grand Suriname River? Where is the wealth? Where are the riches? What happened?

These are selective witnessings, of course, stories told by those who benefitted from the fruits of enslaved and indentured labour and lived lives of comfort in this hidden city in the jungle.

And yet.

Suriname is a broko pranasi. My uncle's words came back to me. In Surinamese proverbs, known as *odos*, the idea of the *broko pranasi* is always linked with the Maroons coming in the dead of the night to lay waste to the plantation. A *broko pranasi* is about willful devastation and destruction, about ravaging and ruin. It is about the rusting, decaying carcass of a former society slowly being consumed by the jungle, of a once grand colony crumbling into a shadow of itself. But it is also, simultaneously, about the resistance and resilience of the enslaved, a coming-to-terms and transformation. It is about hope in decay.

"Suriname is a *broko pranasi*," my uncle had said during our first dinner together, repeating the words. "But it is *my broko pranasi*."

~~~~~

I've always imagined ruin as a site of romance. I have feasted on ruin, seeking stories in the collapse of the past and in the fragments that remain. Ruin is both a material reminder of what once was and a promise of what could be. Nostalgia brings the two together, mythologizing the past. We can project all our longings and desires onto ruin.

As someone who specialized in early music, I know this perhaps better than anyone. At its heart, early music is all about nostalgia; it's a search through the ruins for an authentic, true, and "real" musical past that can somehow be brought to life—through performance—in the present. In my performances, I have drawn inspiration not just from the musical score, but from the larger context in which the music was written: I play on copies of historical instruments, use historical techniques, and spend hours foraging through the archives for long-forgotten eighteenth-century masterpieces.

I thought back to a chamber music concert I'd performed at an American art museum many years ago. Four of us were rehearsing a program of eighteenth-century French music. Couperin, Leclair, Rameau, and Blavet—it's some of the most luscious music ever written. The music was at times tender, gracious, charming, and sublime, at others raging, furious, impassioned. We'd drawn sighs from the pale seventeenth-century painted faces looking down on us from the gallery walls, and applause from the audience that surrounded us. For all of us gathered there that night, early music offered the seductive promise of bringing the past to life, of bridging the centuries through sound.

The eighteenth-century European elite were also fascinated by ruin, so much so that at their country homes and castles, they constructed artificial ruins at perfect vantage points: here a broken arch, there a fallen column, some crumbling bricks. Some members of the aristocracy even built ruin gardens, complete with hired hermits for authenticity. These artificial ruins were a conduit for the emotions: wealthy landowners could gaze upon or dwell among their ruins, drawing on them to provoke a sentimental response in the form of tears or swoons.

Today, in contemporary Newfoundland, the leaning saltbox, clapboard siding weathered in ocean winds, evokes the apparent rustic authenticity of a simple outport life, the worn boards and peeling paint symbolic of the struggle and perseverance of the resilient Newfoundlander who for centuries has scraped a living from a harsh landscape and thrived in forbidding weather.

Popular publications, meanwhile, teach eager readers how to distress and age furniture, so that it has that comfy shabby-chic look. The semblance of history, it seems, is all the rage. But just as eighteenth-century aristocrats faked ruin, so too are we rummaging around in mythical pasts of our own making, histories that never happened, could never exist. Our furniture is carefully worn, consciously weathered; our denim deliberately crafted with holes for effect. Just as it was for the eighteenth-century elite, ruin has become a design accessory, a prerequisite for contemporary living.

In Suriname, I'd tried to capture the complexities of ruin through photography. Online, I'd posted countless photos of Paramaribo's distinctive white colonial houses. Some of these buildings have been beautifully restored; others, however, sagged. With the damp and the heat, it's almost impossible to maintain such properties well. It's even harder in Suriname's volatile political climate and fragile resource-based economy. One photo in particular provoked a passionate commentary from a friend. I'd posted a picture of a worn colonial structure propped up with support beams, vines winding through the faded balcony trestles and rusting corrugated metal sheets arranged along the front serving as a protective fence. My friend was deeply distressed by the photo.

"If people really cared," she said, "they'd never have let it go to ruin. They'd fix it up and care for it. They'd allow its beauty to shine." On a surface level, her comments made sense. Paramaribo's historic centre, a UNESCO World Heritage site, is lined with rows of white colonial houses, all of them beautiful, gracious buildings. To maintain its heritage status, the city has a responsibility to maintain the buildings. But many are poorly kept, with peeling paint and rotting windowsills. The one she'd commented on, along the fabled Waterkant, was clearly rotting, actively disappearing even as I tried to capture it in time.

But to me, there was something more to it, something else going on. Ruin, I wrote in response, was part of its beauty; in fact, it was essential to it. It wasn't evidence that people didn't care. Quite the opposite. The support beams and the fence showed that people *did* care. They cared a lot. They just didn't have the means to fix it up yet. Ruin, I wanted to say to my friend, is fecund and rich. Decay is a site of growth. It is ripe, generative. Ruin is about potential, about the promise of the past embedded in an unknown future. It is the only way to see beneath the surface, to look under the skin. The decaying colonial structures evoke nostalgia and longing, but they also suggest resilience. Like the leaning saltboxes that litter outport communities in Newfoundland, these structures carry their histories in their bones. They stand today as a testament to people who made their home in a place that was never meant to be home, people who crafted identities, made families, survived. They offer poignant evidence that survival itself can be evidence of success.

Ruin makes memory visible. It writes memory onto structures, embeds it in landscapes. But these ruins are not the fanciful aristocratic imaginings of the eighteenth-century elite; these are, instead, the markers of lives lived and lives lost. Collapsing and crumbling buildings are memories of difficult histories inscribed in the landscape, leaving physical scars that are still sometimes visible from the air. These histories can't be scrubbed away; they can't be painted or renewed. Decay is living essence of the past. It's alive. It's uncomfortable. It's ugly. It hurts. But it's also deeply moving and very beautiful. Ruin is about strength in the face of destruction.

Ruin, I wanted to say, is about understanding the relationships between past and present. It is also about imagining possible futures. As Brian Dillon has written, ruins "are freighted with possibility, even with utopian promise." Ruin, in this sense, is about hope—hope for a future that is different, a future built up from a powerfully violent past. Paramaribo's historic wooden structures seemed to balance carefully, one gust of wind ready to blow them over. From large colonial mansions in the downtown core to the tiny houses along the Frederik Derbystraat that were once owned by the free black population, many of these buildings are already well over a century old; many more are older still. They've weathered storms. They've been battered by winds. They've survived a military coup and a civil war with the Maroons. They've outlasted slavery and indenture. Some of them lean, precarious, the corners no longer straight, the shutters not quite even. And yet, still they endure, their wooden siding worn silvery grey with time. The structures are fragile and strong, vulnerable and resilient. Their bones are raw and exposed, their histories on full display.

I thought back to my research visits to Middelburg and The Hague. Middelburg is a picture postcard, its seventeenth- and eighteenth-century homes lovingly restored, its bombed-out core carefully reconstructed. In The Hague, stately nineteenth-century rowhouses line narrow residential streets, even as glossy modern buildings rise in the city's centre. In both cities, ruins have been almost completely erased from the streetscapes. It's easy to forget, then, that history has never been orderly, that some lives mattered much more than others, that the wealth in one part of the world was dependent entirely on the oppression of peoples in other parts of the world.

~~~~~~

The stillness of the abandoned plantations gave me a chance to reflect on my time in Suriname. Paramaribo had been a shock to me, to all my senses. Past and present collided with each other. I couldn't make sense of this city of extremes: wealth and poverty living side by side; rotting, boarded-up shacks cozied up next to beautifully restored homes, barbed wire fences to keep undesirables out. I didn't know how to handle the jumbliness, the noise, the chaos. It was all too much, even for someone like me who generally loves excess. Too many colours. Too many patterns. Too much *music*, even. I couldn't find the rhythm. I didn't know how this place fit together; there was no system, or at least, no order that I recognized.

In the rural plantation regions, these extremes were even more pronounced. Earlier in the day, we had stopped at Alliance plantation. Formerly a number of separate plantations that were joined together into one—hence Alliance—it is now the largest citrus-producing plantation in the country. We docked and walked into the community—the *kampong* in Javanese—a cluster of small earthen homes with corrugated metal roofs lined up in a grid next to a canal. In the distance, past the sluice, we could see the school. Beyond that, our guide said, lay the plantation itself.

We were there for a short refreshment break: drinks and hot Surinamese Indonesian *saoto*: a hearty meat, egg, and vegetable soup. Our guide warned us about the spicy condiments, but the teenager who was related to everyone paid her no heed.

"I love spicy things," he said, aiming a solid squirt of hot sauce at his bowl. As he sipped, the sweat started rolling off his brow almost immediately, and the soup was quickly discarded.

We were sitting at a table under a covered verandah of one of the houses. It was a small dwelling with a rudimentary toilet around the corner.

"Don't flush," a handwritten sign read. Instead, there was a bucket of water with a cup. Scoop and pour.

I wouldn't have expected a hot, spicy Indonesian soup to cool me down, but it did. We sat in the shade of the verandah looking out at a small grove of orange trees between the houses, while our hostess, a woman of Javanese heritage who didn't speak Dutch, smiled and nodded.

"These are the slave dwellings," said the man from Leiden.

"Really?" asked one of the Rotterdammers, with lazy interest.

"Yes, of course," replied the man from Leiden.

"Huh," said Rotterdammer, looking more closely. "Then they lived a better life than I imagined."

I wondered what he meant by this; I wondered what he saw when he looked at the houses. The dwellings were spotless, but simple at best, with whole families gathered into two or three small rooms. Kitchens, such as they were, were outside. There were no windows, just square holes carved into the walls, with faded curtains fluttering in the gentle breeze. It wasn't clear if there was electricity.

This wasn't the time or the place to get into a discussion about possible slave dwellings and what constituted a good living. Later, I would learn that these houses were built for indentured contract workers brought in from China, British India, and Indonesia. Thinking about the East Indian heritage that I hadn't yet had the opportunity to examine, I wondered how many people might have called these tiny houses home a century ago. Were they for families, or just for groups of men and women? And where would children have lived?

In 1863, at Emancipation, Hugh Wright—the same man who had purchased Bent's Hope just four years previously—was awarded 150,000 guilders in compensation for the 507 people enslaved at Alliance. But the plantation only grew in activity in the period following the abolition of slavery. Over the next several years, some 4,000 indentured contract workers were employed at this plantation, about half from Indonesia and half from British India. Now, little remained of Alliance's glory days. There were a few sluices, a school, and a handful of simple houses. The once grand plantation house was in a state of profound disrepair.

I wondered about the promise of Suriname's ruined landscapes. What new stories could they tell? There was so much that was still unfinished, so many histories left undone. What futures were possible in this complex place? In a world increasingly reducing to the lowest forms of populist politics, what might this land of ruined, resistant, and resilient landscapes have to offer? What alternative stories might it have to tell? What can a scarred landscape littered with ruins offer to a future?

Our tour guide nodded when I shared with her my family history.

"I'm half Creole—from Saramacca—and half Javanese," she replied. "In the future, I think it will all be like this. All of us mixed. That will be Suriname. That will be who we are."

Bent's Hope is gone, its history visible only in rusting machinery and hints of canals. But our families, our histories, remain. Was this—this intermingling of pasts and presents—the radical promise of ruin?

On 1 July 1863, the Netherlands abolished slavery in Suriname and the Antilles. That day became known as Keti Koti—the breaking of the chains—an event still celebrated in both Suriname and the Netherlands today. It was exactly four years before Canada became a country and exactly fifty-three before the Battle of the Somme, that day of reckoning that became Memorial Day in New-foundland.

For as long as I can remember, July 1 has been a celebration. When I was young, we'd head out to the Royal Canadian Legion early on Canada Day to get a good spot in line for the annual pancake breakfast made by town luminaries. The mayor in an apron. Two big pancakes. Two sausages. Two squares of butter. And a big container of syrup. We'd plop ourselves at one of the picnic tables and dive in, wishing we could go back for seconds. In the afternoon, we'd head out to watch the parade, screaming and yelling so the clowns would notice us and throw candy our way, and shrieking as firefighters shot cold water out the hose of the 1929 fire truck. If we were lucky, the RCMP Musical Ride would be in town, their sixteen horses moving in formation. Then we'd make our way down to the park in the river valley, where we'd sing "Happy Birthday to You" and eat birthday cake. That same sense of celebration continued into adulthood, even as I traded small-town Alberta for life in the big city. Sun. Song. Temporary tattoos. Cake. Parades. Victoria. Toronto. Vancouver. Variations on a theme.

Canada has a complicated, troubling colonial history, but parades and cake and fireworks make it really easy to pretend that this ugliness never happened. Slavery. Indian residential schools. The *Komagata Maru*. Chinese head tax. Japanese and Ukrainian internment. The MS *St. Louis* with almost 1,000 Jewish refugees on board. I didn't focus on any of that when I celebrated Canada Day. I didn't think of violence or genocide or internment. I knew the stories; I just wasn't listening. I was the embodiment of Canadian multiculturalism, remember, and these stories didn't fit that narrative.

Perhaps it's not particularly surprising, then, that I hadn't picked up on alternative meanings of the first of July as they played themselves out in my own life either. In my two years of living in The Hague, I'd never noticed Keti Koti celebrations, focused as I was on Canada Day. Before moving to Newfoundland, I'd never even heard of Memorial Day, which honours the hundreds of Newfoundland men who were killed in the folly that was the Battle of the Somme. I didn't notice because I was singing birthday songs and waving a flag, a maple leaf tattoo on my cheek.

～～～

These days, I start Canada Day early, at the Sunrise Ceremony at Signal Hill—a misnomer if ever there was one, since it's usually shrouded in fog. The ceremony starts at six o'clock in the morning. The flags fly at half mast and we stand for a minute of silence, the Atlantic wind accompanying the Last Post. As the flags rise, we sing both "Ode to Newfoundland" and "O Canada," competing nationalisms on this windswept rock in the North Atlantic. An ocean away, in Rotterdam and Amsterdam to the east and in Paramaribo to the south, others are gathering, too, to celebrate the breaking of chains. I recalled the entry in the visitors' book in the Zeeuws Archief: "On the first of July, we celebrate freedom." July 1 is layered with meanings. Celebration. Mourning. Violence. There is no easy remembering.

～～～

By this point in my research journey, I'd learned much about my Creole histories. I should have been filled with elation, but instead, I found myself growing uneasy, unsettled. I wasn't sure anymore what this journey meant or what I was trying to prove. In the days that followed my plantation tour, I found myself overcome with a strange lethargy, as though my body was too heavy for itself. Each morning I got up later and later, and my last few days in Suriname passed by in a haze of TV watching. For the first time ever, my research schedule went completely out the window. I knew I was wasting time, time that I'd never recover, but I couldn't seem to stop myself. I didn't even care what I was watching. I needed to escape. To get away for a while.

There was so much still to work through. So much still to try and understand. But I was full. Over-full. My brain hurt. I couldn't seem to focus. I was stalled. Overwhelmed. Nothing made any sense anymore.

Casting about for some way to occupy myself on the day before I left, I decided to head off in search of the Musicus Helstone monument mentioned in newspaper articles about my grandfather's choir. I don't know exactly what I was looking for or exactly why it mattered. I think I wanted something I could grab hold of. Something solid and certain in all of this jumbled mess of memories, histories, and legacies I had been trying to avoid. Music. My grandfather. I hoped they would ground me.

The monument on Paramaribo's Kerkplein was bigger than I'd expected, an imposing angular structure of concrete and tile featuring the letters M and H and a giant eighth note. In a corner, a small relief bust of Helstone himself. In 1963, on the hundredth anniversary of the abolition of slavery, my grandfather had brought his choir to this monument to lay a wreath in honour of a man who had been born into slavery and later made his name in the concert halls of Europe. Now, just over half a century later, it was my turn to pay my respects. Musicians like Helstone had paved the way for my grandfather. And my grandfather, in turn, had paved the way for me.

According to my mother and my aunts, Opa left a strong impression on many of his students. He was imperious and demanding, a perfectionist who terrified those who encountered him. Opa was quick to point out mistakes and set impossibly high musical standards that his own children were never able to achieve. I was the standard-bearer, my musical autobiography and his woven together through our shared studies in The Hague. It was time for me to pass the story on.

I found myself thinking back to a wintry Christmas choral concert in St. John's in 2013. In the silence before the music started, I could hear my heart beating, its rhythms swelling in my chest. Next to me, my husband's heart joined mine, our bodies counting time together. We held our breaths. Suspension. Anticipation.

Outside it was snowing, the first few flakes of December. Inside, around us, some quiet shuffling, a stifled cough. Gower Street United was full that evening, the audience 800 strong. Around the altar, in the choir loft, and arranged in rows and organized by uniform, 250 young singers, ranging in age from seven to eighteen. And there, right in the front, a microphone clutched in his eight-year-old hand, was my son. It was his first public concert. We'd ironed his shirt, bought special leather shoes, and found matching black socks. We'd even combed his hair.

Tóbin's voice broke the stillness, his clear, pure soprano rising confidently into the air. It shimmered, soared. My heart slowed, filled, and broke.

Two years earlier, when he was six, his smiling grade one teacher had told us that he'd admonished her for singing out of tune.

"*Madame*," he had said, "*tu chantes faux*."

Recounting this tale to her sister, my mom had asked her a simple question: "Does he remind you of anyone?"

"Yes," replied my aunt. "Papa."

My younger son's body is filled with music. His sinews, bones, blood, and soul vibrate with song. It's his musical inheritance, a genetic legacy passed down from a choir director great-grandfather born exactly one hundred years less two days before him, a birth-right that had travelled across oceans from the edges of the South American jungle to a rocky island outpost, an instinct come to rest in a small, tenacious body that lives for harmony.

"*Madame, tu chantes faux.*"

Behind my son's clarion call, I could hear my grandfather's long-silent voice, and I knew that he was smiling.

~~~~

Next to the Musicus Helstone monument, on the spot of the original Oranjetuin cemetery, stands the octagonal Dutch Reformed Church. On past walks in this part of town, its doors had been closed. But now they were open, and I stepped inside. I needed a moment to regroup. The church was simple, quiet, its pews arranged around a high pulpit, the pipe organ rising behind them. A woman bustled over, her arms gesturing in different directions as she shared the history of the church. Lost in thought, I didn't hear a word she was saying. I nodded, smiled, and put some money into the donation box, but I hadn't processed anything.

The next morning, it was time to leave. Before the plane even reached Miami, I was homesick for Suriname, an odd yearning that I couldn't place, couldn't quite make sense of. During my doctoral research, I'd learned that eighteenth-century physicians understood homesickness as a disease of the spirit. According to the eighteenth-century Parisian salon hostess Suzanne Necker, homesickness was related to air and breathing. A devout Swiss Calvinist transplanted into the highest echelons of Parisian society, Necker was overcome by life in the French capital, discombobulated by a social world that felt completely foreign to her.

"I need the air of my homeland," she wrote to a close childhood friend. For the first time, a full decade after reading these words, I understood what she meant. My body was longing, yearning. I missed the hot sun, a heat so intense that I could feel my skin tightening with every step I took. I wanted the sweat trickling its way down my back. I wanted to hear the lilt of Surinamese voices, the cluttered, chaotic energy of the market, the blare of Hindustani music from passing cars. I wanted the evening breeze. The rush of heavy rain flushing everything out.

St. John's, once I arrived, felt strange. There had been three winter storms during my two weeks away, and the landscape was white, snow piled high along the edges of the driveway. But it was as if I were removed from all of this; as if I were outside my body, as if it were all happening at a distance. The kids' voices, the cold, my husband's questions—everything was muffled.

The air felt wrong. The wind pushed too hard. The landscape wasn't right. And I kept looking for mangoes. At the grocery store I bought papayas, but it wasn't enough. Later I caved, buying a crate of ten mangoes that pushed us well beyond our usual food budget. The kids were thrilled—it was a rare splurge.

"You should go to Suriname more often," my older son, Stefan, said, his mouth full, juice leaking from his lips.

But the mangoes had been picked too soon. They weren't ripe enough; their flavour and texture were all wrong. Their deep, juicy heart was missing.

~~~~~

I had returned to St. John's with a collection of notebooks bulging with observations and ideas, a computer full of data and photographs, a suitcase filled with fabric, and a hare-brained idea that somehow I could pull all of this together into a quilt that could represent Suriname. My basic plan was simple. If a country is made up of peoples—and those peoples have collectively determined (by chance or by choice) to make up an imagined community—then it must be possible to represent that community, and my part in it, in textile form. There must be a way to bring that diversity of voices and histories together. In my mind, I was already making the world's most beautiful quilt, a document in textile that would lie resplendent across our bed, telling my history in colour and pattern. It didn't matter that I'd never made a quilt. This quilt would make sense of all that was clattering around in my brain. It would tell my stories for me.

But the odd lethargy wouldn't leave me. I fingered the fabrics, running my hands over the colourful patterns—Javanese, African, Maroon, Surinamese; it didn't help. What story was I meant to be telling? Whose story was this? I owed something to myself, but I also owed it to my family. I had responsibilities to them. They were invested in this too. My cousin Elvira, who first invited me to join the collaborative family tree. My aunt Rita and uncle Gott, in Purmerend, who welcomed me into their home during my return to the Netherlands in 2014 and shared conversations and memories. My aunt Hilda, who gave us a classic Surinamese cookbook as a wedding present way back in 1995. My aunt Liska and uncle Ber, whose home and menagerie have long been a happy refuge. My aunt Sheila, who first pressed me to think about my histories. And Elvira's parents, my aunt Hanny and uncle Deryck in Suriname, who had made that history their own and who continued to live it every day. My aunt Hanny had even prepared a whole series of electronic documents for me, from nineteenth-century almanacs and books about Suriname, to a collection of family photos and examples of Surinamese choral traditions. But beyond the addition of two new names—Annette and Lodewijk—to the family tree, had I added anything at all to what they already knew before I started? Was I telling a story they wanted to hear, a story they'd approve of?

I'd bought all my fabric in Paramaribo, at a place called Ready-Tex, a curious collection of buildings that houses a contemporary art gallery, a tourist shop, and a store that sells all sorts of random household things, including fabric. Indonesian batik. Javanese batik. African fabrics. Maroon cottons. Red. Blue. Yellow. Black. Green. I gathered a number of bolts, already designing quilt patterns in my head.

In front of me, a woman was buying children's prints. Bunnies on a light blue background in a soft cotton. When it was my turn, I dropped my collection on the counter.

"I'd like a metre of each," I said in Dutch.

The Javanese clerks were intrigued.

"What will you do with these pieces?" they asked. "Will you sew with them?"

"Yes," I replied. "I'll bring them together into a patchwork." I tried to explain with my hands.

They nodded, and as they measured and cut, we started a conversation about cotton, sewing, travels, and Canada.

"You can't buy this kind of fabric in Canada?" they asked. They seemed surprised.

"Not so easily. Well, not where I live, anyway."

"The *bakras* in Holland also buy small pieces," they said.

I was curious about where I fit into their equation, but it wasn't a question I could ask. Did they see me as *bakra*, too, but just not a Dutch one? Or did they see me as something else entirely? The fact that they used the term suggests that they saw me as something of an insider, but I wasn't sure. I applauded myself for my ability to blend in. But less than ten minutes later, a toothless man flashed me a grin and tried to sell me some cheap tourist junk on the Waterkant. Clearly my disguise had slipped.

In Suriname I'd evaluated everyone's responses to me, measuring my value—and my right to belonging—in relation to how they acted and what they said. I recognized that I was doing the same thing in St. John's: I was measuring my interests, and my needs, against those of my relatives. There was a lot riding on my work. Any story that I told was part of their story too. And who was I to tell it—someone who had inherited a history she'd never lived? I closed down. I didn't know how to proceed. My histories were in Suriname, but I couldn't find myself.

What story was I meant to be telling? I realized that I was struggling with, through, and against my family's expectations, or perhaps, what I assumed to be their expectations. But it was also *my* story to tell, I tried to reassure myself. The archives had shown me the way in; they would also show me the way forward. I pushed the lethargy away and pressed on.

~~~~~

The Netherlands was one of the last European countries to abolish slavery, lagging well behind England (1833), Sweden (1847), Denmark (1848), and France (1848). Even then, freedom did not come immediately. The Dutch instituted what they called an "apprenticeship period," ten years of transition during which the enslaved were now contract workers paid for their labour. No longer forced to stay on the plantations where they had been enslaved, some chose to move to the city; others moved to different plantations. *And then, of course,* my snarky inner voice sniped, slipping back into the conversation, *they all lived happily ever after.*

One by one, my ancestors entered into the records no longer enslaved, but as free citizens. In March 1866, Philip Elias Redout married Bella Emelina Bobson, a woman also previously enslaved at Sarah plantation. Three years later, the newspapers announced another marriage: on 28 February 1868, Sultan Timotheus Redout, then eighteen years old, married Rozetta Johanna Hasselbaink, probably a seventeen-year-old recorded as Renata Johana Hasselbaink in the 1862 accounting declarations and Rosette in the slave registers. She was also from Sarah plantation.

The newspapers were quiet for a while after this, but twenty-six years later, in 1894, Sultan's oldest brother, Jack, announced his marriage to Frederika Margarethe Gessel with an advertisement in a Paramaribo newspaper, thanking all those who had celebrated with them. In June 1895, he and his wife placed an even larger advertisement for an open house to celebrate their first anniversary. Guests were welcome from 10:30 at their home on the Rust en Vredestraat, it read. The 1921 census, meanwhile, listed other ancestors still living in the plantation regions in the west of Suriname. Joseph Elias Redout was living at Burnside plantation, right next door to Sarah, in the Coronie district. And my great-grandmother Adolphina, who was born in the west in Nieuw Nickerie and had lived in Albina in the east with a German man and also in Paramaribo, was back in the Coronie district, now listed as living at the former Perseverance plantation.

You would think that the story ended there. After all, by 1921, Opa, my grandfather—the child of Adolphina Redout and Theodor Wilhelm Heinemann—was already a young man of sixteen. In fact, a year later, in 1922, he was listed as a schoolteacher at the Wanica School, one of several schools managed by the Moravian church. He married my grandmother in 1935, with my uncle Deryck, their first born, following a few months later.

But as much as I had learned to this point, tracing this long story of slavery was only the beginning of my family history, and so it couldn't possibly tell me everything I wanted to know. Half of my family—Oma's half—hadn't even arrived on Surinamese shores by the time slavery was abolished in 1863. My Hindustani great-great-grandmother didn't leave India until a decade later, in 1873. And it would be seven more years—in 1880—before she went to live with a Chinese man. Migration? Mixed race? We were only just getting started.

12

JOORAYEE

I T WAS SUPPOSED TO BE EASY to map out the East Indian side of my heritage. There's a lot of material to work with. Far more than just accounting declarations and slave registers. There are immigration records. Ship logs. Business records. Oral histories and autobiographies. There are even photographs. *It was supposed to be easy.* Famous last words.

Like the enslaved who came before her, my great-great-grandmother Joorayee Radha had no past. She appeared in the archival records fully formed, a woman of twenty-five, her history missing and her future stretching out before her. But there was one significant difference. Unlike the enslaved, Joorayee Radha had a five-year fixed, limited-term contract. Five years is so very different from a lifetime.

Joorayee Radha arrived in Suriname in January 1874, just over a decade after abolition. Suriname was changing. The ten-year "apprenticeship" period that followed the end of slavery had come to an end. While some of the formerly enslaved continued as agricultural workers, many were less than keen to continue working on plantations. The plantation owners, meanwhile, were still complaining. Their livelihoods—and their wealth—depended on a stable, cheap source of labour.

The Dutch had already begun to experiment with Chinese labourers. In The Hague, I had looked through some of the business materials of the Nederlandsche Handel-Maatschappij, the Dutch Trade Company, which purchased and ran a few plantations in the late nineteenth century (including de Resolutie, where Joorayee Radha was later sent). Among the papers in the file were the reports and notices for a relatively short-lived employment immigration venture, a shareholder-based company that sought to import Chinese labourers to Suriname to work the cane fields. The proposal for the Surinamese Immigration Society outlined the rationale for the scheme as follows:

> Everyone knows that slavery in the colony of Suriname was abolished two years ago, and that the Negroes now work under contract for paid wages, as they are bound by law; but one does not know what the outcome of that system is; sometimes one reads in the newspapers that emancipation has borne the finest fruits and the colony is in full bloom; then again, that production has decreased at a shocking rate and the colony is rapidly deteriorating. The truth is that to the extent that emancipation has not failed, that the desertion of the blacks, and yes, even murder, which some foresaw as the outcome of this process, have not taken place and that the Negroes have, for the most part, even remained at work, which surpasses what one might have expected from such uncivilized people after the acquisition of liberty; but it is equally true that their work is irregular, inadequate, and insufficient to sustain normal production; that they are gradually abandoning heavy work and the sugar industry (and this is—and should be—the main culture of the colony) in order to hire themselves out to work with the by-products.

Like the researcher I was trained to be, I had transcribed these words dutifully. But then I added a row of exclamation marks, my version of yelling in the archives. Perhaps unfairly, I pictured a group of portly moustachioed men, stomachs contained inside natty silk waistcoats, top hats by their sides, cigar smoke swirling around them as they contemplated their fortunes and their futures.

What is wrong with you people? That's what I wanted to say. But there's no point in arguing with the dead.

Clearly, at least according to the directors of this organization, something needed to be done. After all, the whole purpose of the colony was to produce sugar, and the labour on sugar cane plantations was hard labour, much harder than that on coffee or cotton plantations. Not that these investors were planning to do the work themselves; no, their wealthy, European bodies were not made for manual labour. Another solution needed to be found. Chinese labour seemed a workable solution.

But, according to a handwritten annual report delivered at the society's meeting on 27 December 1867, the organization was having problems meeting the requirements of the gender-based quota system. The government said that women had to make up one-quarter of each shipload of labourers. But Chinese women, the society discovered, were not particularly predisposed to leaving their country, with the result that this regulation had, in the words of the shareholders, "seriously constrained the society's operations from the beginning, and resulted in significant disadvantages." In other words, they were losing money. The cigar smoke swirled ever more thickly.

The directors hastened to add that they weren't against such a ruling; they were aware that successful colonization would require some women. This was not a problem, they assured their shareholders, offering a practical solution:

On these grounds, and in particular, because the female population in Suriname is now much larger than the male, and that the conducting of marriages between Chinese [men] and Negresses does not appear to have met with any objections we have proposed to the government the repeal of this provision, and have also obtained it.

I had to stop reading once I got to the end of that paragraph. The paternalistic tone, the *fait accompli*. Exclamation marks were no longer enough. *You, too, could have the Creole wife of your dreams. They're right there, like juicy mangoes, ripe for the picking.* I bit my tongue. I had nothing. I could picture the directors in their Amsterdam chambers, arranging labourers like puzzle pieces as they sought the best solution for their own profits. It was like playing the boardgame Risk, moving armies around, playing God. The needs and concerns of the labourers were incidental. As long as they worked and as long as they reproduced, everything was fine. There was nothing in these records about the labourers themselves, about their desires, their longings, their fears. It was as if none of this mattered at all.

~~~~~

Ultimately, the Chinese experiment was a failure. And so, following the lead of other Caribbean countries, the Dutch negotiated with Britain, arranging to bring labourers—"agriculturalists" or, simply, the derogatory "coolies" in British terms—from what was then British India to work on Surinamese plantations on five-year contracts. The first, sailing aboard the *Lalla Rookh*, arrived in early June 1873. My great-great-grandmother, Joorayee Radha, who stepped aboard the Liverpool-based ship, the *Kate Kellock*, together with her toddler son, Sahatoo, in October of that same year—contract numbers C/37 and C/38 of a total of 466 indentured labourers travelling on that ship—was thus among the earliest British Indian arrivals on Surinamese shores.

I'd first encountered Joorayee and Sahatoo online, in immigration records included in the digital archives of the Dutch National Archives in The Hague. Joorayee's immigration record states that she was 1.513 metres tall and *donker bruin*—dark brown—in complexion. She was Hindu, and according to the transcribed record, she hailed from the village of Aburpore in the district of Faizabad, in the north of India. She and her son were sent to one of the largest sugar plantations in the colony, the Nederlandsche Handel-Maatschappij–owned de Resolutie, where she lived and worked for five years.

6. A map of de Resolutie plantation, ca. 1871. Labourer dwellings and provision grounds are depicted in the very bottom of the drawing. National Archives of the Netherlands, Nederlandsche Handel-Maatschappij (NHM), 1824–1964, catalogue reference C85.3.1, inventory number 13222, Public Domain. *Photo credit: Sonja Boon.*

In January 1880, by then mother to three children (one of whom died in infancy) and partnered with a Chinese goldsmith and merchant named U-A-Sai, Joorayee Radha was granted leave to stay in the colony. That record, desperately short on details, is almost all that remains of her story. Like the majority of her compatriots, she left nothing in her own words. Sahatoo, meanwhile, is equally silent. According to family lore, he was illiterate and never wanted his photo taken. It's almost as if he deliberately silenced himself, hiding away from any possibility of later revelation.

But I had so many questions. I wondered, as I read this record, why Joorayee travelled alone, a single mother with a child. I wondered what made her choose to travel so far, what she might have been hoping for, or conversely, what she might have been running from. How she may have ended up on the boat. And I wondered, too, why she stayed. Many of her shipmates returned to India after their contracts ended. Why didn't she? I wondered about the two children born in Suriname, and about how it was that she ended up in a relationship with a Chinese man, a relationship so uncommon that it's not even mentioned as a possibility in any studies of British Indian migration to Suriname, most of which suggest that the Hindustani community stuck together, or, alternatively, that some women ended up in relationships with Creole men.

All that archival material—all those records, books, and photographs—was supposed to build a firm foundation, a context into which I could place the almost-absent Joorayee and her son. But I soon learned that piecing her life together was going to be a process of moving sideways, crab-like, through the archives. I scrabbled for fragments and hints left by others, filling in the gaps—there were so many gaps—with speculation and my own desires. As I worked through the material that remained, I found myself inventing her histories, creating stories, and testing them out. I climbed into her skin, rooted around in her body, and dug among her possible memories in search of a range of possible pasts.

~~~~~

I pulled a memoir towards me, that of a relatively privileged man who left a detailed record not only of his life in Suriname, but of his life in India and the circumstances that led to his indenture. I was hoping that his memories could help me fill in some of the blanks, particularly around Joorayee's life before she left India. But almost as quickly as I opened it, I found myself pushing the book away. According to the author, a man named Munshi Rahman Khan, all women were evil, grasping charlatans who wished nothing more than to destroy men like him. Not a single one was trustworthy. I wondered about Joorayee, a single mother with a small child, and about how she'd fare in his eyes. I imagine she'd have been the worst of the worst for him, a fallen woman eagerly looking for a weak man to dupe into taking care of her. I hoped that she had steered clear of men like these; that she recognized their attitudes for what they were, and that she was able to avoid life with those who wished her harm. I hoped that her Chinese partner, the faceless U-A-Sai, treated her well.

But I don't know. What I do know is that she was on her own. It was just Joorayee and Sahatoo. Two dark brown bodies, mother and child. And it was this aloneness, this isolation, that stuck with me. She had no family stories to draw on, no partner, no mother, no sisters, no cousins. She had no memories to cocoon her as she journeyed across the oceans, as the ship steamed on and on, day after day, into an endless horizon. Joorayee and Sahatoo were alone. Alone before they left port in Calcutta and alone after they arrived. How can this be? How can a woman appear out of nowhere? I could not be that woman without a history, that mother without her family, that lover without her love.

It's not like I hadn't encountered archival silence before. As devastating as my journey through the accounting declarations and slave registers had been, I had, in some ways, anticipated silence there. This is, after all, what slavery does. It tears families apart. It erases kinship. It dehumanizes the enslaved, turning them in property, numbers. But I expected something different from stories of indenture. And somehow, I expected *more* from events that took place less than 150 years ago. I thought that things might have improved, that colonial authorities might have learned something. I thought wrong.

~~~~~

Joorayee Radha's emigration process likely began in Faizabad, a historic city and one of the key centres of the 1857 Indian Rebellion against the British East India Company. There, she and her son probably stayed in the emigration depot until enough recruits were signed up, coerced, or captured. Then, according to Khan, a train would take emigrants from Faizabad to Lucknow, while another zigzagged them back to a town called Mughalsarai. Eventually, they'd end up at Howrah train station at the edge of the Ganges River, which another emigrant described as a rush of people and noise, with endless platforms, trains, and railway lines.

This was the heyday of the steam engine. The East Indian Railway had run its first train—from Howrah to Hooghly—just twenty years earlier, in 1854. Mughalsarai was linked to the system in 1862. Faizabad junction railway station, meanwhile, was completed in 1874. Trains were both modern and extremely popular, so popular, in fact, that the train company introduced a new class—fourth class, for standing passengers—to help cope with the volume. And so it was that Joorayee and her fellow emigrants, many of them the poorest of the poor, got to ride the most modern form of transportation and enjoy one of the great inventions of the Industrial Revolution. What must this have been like for a young woman who had likely known nothing beyond her small village and the crops she tended?

I studied a map of India and traced Joorayee's likely route. I'm usually comfortable with maps, but I was disoriented by India; this map, cluttered with the names of tiny villages and towns, confused me. So close to Nepal and China; I hadn't known this. There was no hint of my great-great-grandmother's village, and I wondered how tiny it must have been. Looking online, I learned that it would take one and a half hours to fly from Mughalsarai to Kolkata. Twelve hours on public transit. But Joorayee and the others would have been standing in a train that jostled and jumped along a track, a train that, in the 1860s, took ninety minutes to travel thirty miles. I wondered if there were windows. I wondered what they were thinking. I wondered if they were fed. I wondered if they talked, or if they stayed silent, their gazes focused only on the slivers of landscapes that passed them by.

I thought of Joorayee, probably only a hair taller than my grandmother, petite and dark, her body sinewy from agricultural work, skin stretched taut against a face turned towards any hint of fresh air coming into the train carriage. I thought of her son, small, hiding between her legs, looking around him, so much to see, cowering sometimes in the noise, but also, like any toddler, eager to escape at the first opportunity. In my image of him, I could see my own train-loving eldest son, Stefan, when he was small, his body swathed in steam at the train museum, mesmerized by the sound, size, and power of the steam engine. I saw him reaching forward towards the wheels, crouching by their mechanisms to see how things worked, and later, at the library, hunting down every single book about trains.

"The past is remembered and told by desire," writes Lauret Edith Savoy. And so it was that in the absence of a rich archival record, I began to create stories for Joorayee Radha, exploring different scenarios, plotting a range of different adventures. In one version of her story, Joorayee and her husband travelled together, a hopeful young couple looking to better their situation in the world. But tragedy struck, and he died somehow—at the emigration depot, perhaps, or on the train—leaving a grieving widow and son. In another version of the story, she was already a widow, a woman in mourning who left her older children with her husband's family, and took the youngest, too young to leave behind, to start a new life. In yet another version, she fled her village, desperate to escape a violent household. Or perhaps she was an orphan, abandoned on the street, a girl who found some measure of economic security in sex work before signing on for a Caribbean adventure, lured by the promise of health care, housing, and regular pay in an apparently Edenic location where she could rebuild herself. In my worst dreams, she was a victim of capitalist enterprise, grabbed as she was walking down a dirt path, then dragged to a depot by a greedy agent looking for women to meet his gender quota. In this version of the story, she was held against her will, her child in her arms, their futures hazy and uncertain.

But what if all the stories I had created for her were wrong? What if there was nothing sympathetic about Joorayee Radha at all? What if Khan was right? What if Joorayee was a grasping schemer? What if she was dangerous? What if she lied? What if she was mean, cruel even? What if she was abusive? What if I just didn't like her?

I imagined Joorayee at the train station, head veiled, eyes downcast, hand holding tightly to her small son's arm as she shuffled forward, her body jostling against those of others around her.

I imagined the ripe smell of bodies too long in close quarters, of steam and coal. And the heat. Monsoon season was just ending, but it would still have been well over thirty degrees. Was Joorayee regretting her decision? Was she afraid?

I've taken solo journeys with a toddler. I know exactly how ropy such experiences can be. But I always had a husband at one end of the journey and doting grandparents on the other. I had a passport and I spoke the languages of security personnel and airport staff. But most of all, I was on holiday; every time I've travelled I've made completely free choices, and I've always had a secure home to return to. I couldn't bear the thought of Joorayee's isolation. No matter how I imagined her, as a single woman with a child, she was an outcast and she would have been shunned by other emigrants. She was likely illiterate and wouldn't have been able to read the terms of the contract for herself. The emigration agents might have promised her the world; after all, it was in their best interest to recruit as many women as possible. While she might have understood a smattering of English, she wouldn't have understood Dutch at all. And she'd had no adult family with her, nobody with whom to share her feelings about the enormity of this journey. She'd been alone.

I thought back to my archival research in Paramaribo. I hadn't been able to request the immigration records for the *Kate Kellock*; the documents were badly damaged. Instead, I looked at the immigration log of the *Medea*, which had arrived a few months earlier, in late 1873. Paging through the log, I quickly got caught up in caste names, confused by their sheer number and variety. *Chuttree, Loodh, Munibar, Pathau, Thakoor, Brahmin....* Later, when I asked a colleague about the caste system, she barely even looked at the list I'd painstakingly transcribed.

"It's complicated," she said, and as I perused a book about Hindu women and pondered my great-great-grandmother's life, I understood how true her statement was. It *was* complicated, with gradations that made no sense to outsiders. In India, this system mattered, but the whole process of indenture undid it completely. From Khan, the memoirist, I learned that at Howrah, the indentures were told to strip and bathe, all of them together, and in that moment, the first caste boundaries were broken. Then they each received the same package of clothing, and thus the second boundaries were broken. No longer individuals, they became an amorphous mass of brown, labouring bodies swathed in white. This is exactly what I saw in the photographs. Groups of men in white gathered together at the depot in Paramaribo. Groups of women in white squatting in a field. Serious faces aboard a ship. Whatever social differences might have separated them in India, by the time the emigrants arrived in Suriname, all hints of those differences had fallen by the wayside. In their new uniforms, they became anonymous. Ghost workers traversing an ocean, leaving their histories and past lives behind. Maybe this is how Joorayee and Sahatoo began to disappear.

~~~~

In my best dreams, Joorayee had a mother who taught her daughter about life and love.

The kitchen is a space of mystery, Joorayee, I imagined her saying. *You take different elements, one spice at a time, and you bring them to your nose. Draw them into your body. Pull them down to your toes. Feel them warm you from the inside. Only then can they tell you what they need.* I could hear her voice clearly—assured, calm, and confident.

You must find love in the heart of ginger, she continued, drawing on lessons she had learned from her own mother before her. *Like the man you will marry, the garlic must be young and fresh, with a sharpness that reaches deep into his soul. You will lie together with cumin, peppers, and turmeric, making love on a bed of cilantro.*

And in my dreams, Joorayee loved this husband that her mother had chosen for her with such care.

He was everything that you said he'd be, Mama, I heard her say. *He was cilantro and garlic, sweetness and bite.* Her voice caught, tripping over the comma, and I know that in my dreams, this faithful lover, faceless still, died, leaving his wife, her mother, and her young son to grieve his passing.

I know this isn't Joorayee's story. It's the one that I created for her. I found her a past; I tethered her to something larger than herself. She was no longer C/37. She was a woman with a history, with desires, longings, passions, and motivations. More than this, she was a woman surrounded by love.

This story is, of course, much less about Joorayee than it is about me. It's not at all about her desires, longings, passions, and motivations. It's not about how she understood love. It's the story *I* can live with. I needed this for her because I couldn't bear to think of her alone. And perhaps I couldn't bear it because I couldn't imagine it for myself. Her life—her complete isolation—was unfathomable to me. In my version of the story, she was part of something bigger. She had a history, a family, a culture, a palate. She was loved, and she loved. And in my version of the story, it was this love that sustained her, this love that meant that no matter where she was and no matter what happened to her, deep inside herself, she was never alone.

There was absolutely nothing in the records that could tell me if any part of this story is true. I didn't know if Joorayee was loved, or even if she loved in return. It was just a story. Maybe she didn't need this story at all. But I had yet to make sense of this Madonna and child, to understand the motivations behind her decision to travel to a New World about which she knew nothing. And so, in the absence of anything else, it was the story I needed to tell myself.

I could only assume that Joorayee made a conscious decision to travel to Suriname. After two centuries of slavery, anything less than choice was unbearable. And yet, I knew that the idea of choice, too, was likely limited. Joorayee and her son came from a deeply impoverished region of India. Drought. Bad harvests. Debts. Hunger. The observations in an 1883 *Report on the Colonial Emigration from the Bengal Presidency* painted a stark picture of suffering: "Although the scarcity in the Western Provinces and Oudh had not yet reached the more acute stage of famine," the author wrote, "it was sufficiently severe to urge crowds of half starved adults and emaciated children to the different recruiting centres with the result that the Calcutta depots eventually became asylums for a large number of people in a more or less anaemic and unhealthy condition."

I didn't want to see Joorayee as a victim of circumstance, her decisions buffeted entirely by forces outside her control. I wanted her to be a free agent, capable of making choices for herself. More than this, I wanted her to have a happy ending.

~~~~~

What was life like for the women who travelled to Suriname as indentured labourers, and particularly for those who came on their own? I buried myself in research, and before I knew it, I had a tall stack of books and articles on my desk. I was, of course, neither the first nor the only one to ask this question. There's been considerable debate about whether or not women's lives improved as a result of indenture, or whether the system just further perpetuated—and even exacerbated—the social inequalities they already faced at home. There's support for both sides of this equation, and ultimately, I suspect that in the end, much came down to chance: some women, by virtue of their age, their physical attributes, their general health, the plantation they ended up in, their backgrounds, the people in their local communities, their support systems, their domestic relationships, their personalities, and more, had good experiences. Others, by contrast, did not. Was Joorayee one of the lucky ones?

According to the initial agreement signed between Britain and the Netherlands, there were supposed to be forty women emigrants for every hundred men. This was never an easy proposition. Indian recruiters found it difficult to recruit women, and colonial authorities assumed that any women they did manage to recruit were sexually suspect.

But there is evidence that some women were able to turn this gender imbalance to their personal advantage. Some women had relationships with many different men at the same time, and played them off against each other, a situation that would have been unheard of back home in India. Others moved between partners, casting one aside as a better option arose. Still others entered into relationships with planters, although it's not at all clear if these relationships were consensual. On the surface, then, it seemed that at least some women enjoyed a degree of sexual freedom that would likely have been unknown in their home communities, and that they were able to leverage this to their advantage.

I paused, thinking back to an intriguing annotation that I had come across during my first trip to Suriname in February 2015. A woman named Matai Chatarpali arrived in Suriname in April 1898 with her husband aboard the English ship *Avon*. The record stated that by 1904, her situation had changed dramatically: "Chatarpali 313/Aa wants to know nothing more about her husband Prtipal 312/Aa," the scribe noted. "[She] has taken another man and is pregnant by him." At the time, I'd laughed, but a year later, surrounded by my stack of books and articles, I wondered.

Women could also benefit from the breakdown of the caste system, making it possible for someone like my great-great-grandmother to enter into relationships that crossed race and faith boundaries. And emigration to a faraway land must have been an appealing option for women who existed outside conventional family groupings: the widows, prostitutes, abandoned women, fallen women, the women who were trying to escape their marriages. Moving outside the rigid conventions of their Indian lives gave them an opportunity to remake themselves on their own terms. This might especially have been true given that on the plantations, these women earned their own money. It was still significantly less than what men made, but it was their own, to use as they saw fit. And it's impossible to ignore another factor: while many married women returned to British India with their families at the end of their contracts, a sizeable number of women stayed, despite the fact that free right to return was specified in their contracts.

But all was not necessarily rosy. Women emigrants were subject to high levels of physical and sexual violence—from recruiters, ship's crew, fellow emigrants, plantation administrators, fellow workers, and others. Men fought over women. They abused women. They raped them. They prostituted their wives for financial gain. They mutilated women. They even murdered women out of nothing more than jealousy and suspicion. Rates of sexual violence were so high on plantations that, according to one researcher, special legislation was needed to protect women from violence.

I learned that even the promise of social mobility was fraught. While some women (and some men) benefitted from entering into relationships with partners of a higher caste, such relationships could be illusory. Formal Hindu marriage was forbidden in Suriname until 1940, and these relationships could easily fracture upon return to India. While caste may not have mattered as much in Suriname, it was integral to social life back home. Is this why some emigrants never went back?

The economic picture wasn't as positive as it initially seemed either. By the time British Indian labourers set foot on Surinamese shores, the sugar market was starting to suffer. De Resolutie, the plantation where my great-great-grandmother was indentured, was developed as a model, modern plantation in 1865, the biggest and best sugar plantation in Suriname. But just twenty-one years later, in 1886, it was sold, its housing, labourers, and state-of-the-art equipment sent on to Marienburg plantation.

So, in the end, was indenture a good option for indentured women like my great-great-grandmother? One researcher, Pieter Emmer, thinks it was. For him, emigration was a "colonial escape hatch" that gave women a way out of narrowly defined lives in India. Emmer's conclusions, based on broad data sets and quantitative analysis, sounded promising, and I wanted to accept them. I would have loved to see my great-great-grandmother's decision to sign on to a five-year contract as a form of empowerment through which she positively determined the course of her own future. I would have loved to see her decision to emigrate as a conscious strategy for change.

The problem with this vision is that things are always much more complicated than they seem. Emmer's data sets are invaluable in revealing large patterns, but they can't get below the surface; they can't reveal the nitty-gritty of lived experience. And they certainly can't get at what interested me most: what happened in the century that followed, and what remains for those of us who have inherited these histories. Because what struck me about the oral histories of indenture that I read was the sense of surprise. It was almost as if many of the emigrants never reconciled themselves to what happened. Even decades later, they weren't sure how or why they had ended up in Suriname. And they never really recovered from any of it. That sense of loss and yearning permeates contemporary writing, too, as novelists and memoirists interested in the indenture period struggle to make sense of this history and of their place in it.

I couldn't find my place in this story either. I still couldn't see Joorayee and Sahatoo. They remained abstractions, names on a page. I couldn't make sense of who they were in this sea of emigrant labourers.

Perhaps this was because, for the most part, our encounter had been digital. Because the 1873 records of the *Kate Kellock* were too fragile to handle, I couldn't "touch" Joorayee and Sahatoo in the way that I could my enslaved ancestors. The touch of paper—whether thick and rich or pulpy and crumbling—is part of how I've come to understand the stories that I was piecing together. There's a tactility to working in archives, and until I was forced to work only with digitized transcriptions, I hadn't realized just how much I would miss it. As I looked at the transcribed, computer-generated sans serif letters of Joorayee Radha's immigration record on my twenty-nine-inch monitor, I realized that I had come to rely not only on the "hard evidence" of historic records, but also on the actual documents themselves. It's not just the text that matters, not just the *words*. The *handwriting* tells stories. The *paper*—its texture, its size, its shape, its colour—tells stories. And so, too, do the ink, the wax seals, the ribbons, the labels. Even the folds in the paper can offer insights. This is how the lives of those who came before me were made real to me.

I struggled with the immigration records, but in different ways than I had struggled with the slave registers and General Accounting Chamber declarations. I struggled to find meaning in the words on the screen. More importantly, I struggled to find connections, to make this story my own. It didn't seem possible to me that individual life stories could be reduced to a series of pixels on a computer monitor. How could I find a life—how could I find *my* life—in any of this?

Even after all my reading and thinking, my great-great-grand-mother remained almost completely hidden. All I had left of her was some biostatistical data—her name, sex, age, height, birth-place, and skin colour—and annotations about her reproductive and conjugal history. To put it bluntly, this wasn't much from which to build a story. This record couldn't tell me about questions of agency and empowerment. It couldn't teach me about who I was, where I came from, and where I was going. Somehow I needed to accept this. And perhaps I also needed somehow to accept that I wanted something for her that would have been impossible to real-ize. Maybe the questions I was asking were the wrong questions. Maybe love was the wrong conversation. Maybe agency wasn't about choice. Maybe voice, as I wanted to understand it, wasn't an option. Maybe empowerment wasn't even a prospect.

The more I read, the less I seemed to know. The fragments wouldn't arrange themselves. Some of the materials relating to the immigration depot had crumbled to dust as soon as I touched them. I had too much information and nothing at all. I couldn't see Joorayee and Sahatoo.

Where are you? I asked. I'd read so much. I'd read studies. I'd read oral histories and song lyrics. I'd read fictionalized accounts and memoirs. I'd combed the archival records in The Hague and in Paramaribo. I could tell you almost anything you wanted to know about indenture. I could rattle off the names of all the ships that came to Suriname. I could tell you exactly how many labourers returned to India after their contracts ended, and how many stayed. I could tell you who lived and I could tell you who died. I could point you to interesting oddities in the archives, and pull up a range of intriguing photos. I could follow some of the new immigrants through generations, tracing their family trees from the 1870s right through to the 1960s in the immigration records. I could tell you about the history of de Resolutie plantation and its unfortunate fate. But the serious faces on the "Coolie Depot" photos remained mute. They wouldn't tell me a damn thing.

13

OCEANS

ITHIN A FEW WEEKS of my return to St. John's, I went looking for the *Kate Kellock*, the ship that brought Joorayee and Sahatoo to Suriname. It was a lark, a shot in the dark, something—*anything*—that could offer me a new way in to Joorayee Radha's story. At the time, *Kate Kellock* was nothing more than a name attached to a shadowy shape that I called a ship. Imagine a brown bottom, somewhat trapezoidal in shape, with three circles to represent portholes, a tall mast running straight up the middle, and two white sails, one slightly wider than the other for aesthetic value. At the very top of the mast, I would draw a red flag, for colour. This, in any case, is how I've always drawn ships: simple line-drawn boats rocking gently on perfectly sculpted blue waves. In the sky, birds flying towards an equally perfect yellow circle of a sun. Don't laugh. Remember, I spent most of my childhood on the prairies, land-locked and far from any oceans.

My ship, I knew, would have a crew. Picture a series of stick figures clambering around the ship and its sails. And I knew that on its 1873 voyage—the one that interested me most—it carried a human cargo: more than 450 indentured labourers travelling from rural areas in northern India to plantations in Suriname. Among them were Joorayee Radha and Sahatoo. I would have drawn them into my ship as serious faces looking out from the portholes. A bigger face with long hair to represent my great-great-grandmother, and a smaller one with large eyes and an O for a mouth to represent my great-grandfather.

Around the ship, I would draw that series of jaunty waves—blue, of course, but possibly, if I was in a colourful mood, a hint of aquamarine—but I would add whitecaps for good measure. After all, as I was to learn later, just a few short years after ferrying my ancestors to Suriname, this ship ultimately sank in stormy weather. But even during the voyages that preceded the wreck, these journeys between continents and across the open ocean must have been one hell of a ride.

I've been able to find only a single image of the *Kate Kellock*. Sails billowing, she stands tall and proud on the water, statuesque with four masts and endless sails. When Joorayee saw the *Kate Kellock* for the first time, her sails would have been rolled away, but still, the sight of the giant iron-hulled ship must have been awe-inspiring. As it left port, sails unfurling, the *Kate Kellock* was transformed from skeleton to queen, ugly duckling into swan—majestic, graceful, and powerful. She would also have been noisy, the rumble of her engines and the roar of wind in the sails, snapping and clapping in the wind. Did the ship's power inspire hope or fear? Or was Joorayee too overwhelmed to name her feelings?

~~~~~

By the time I decided to go hunting for the *Kate Kellock*, I was flailing, casting a wide net to see what might emerge. I didn't expect to find much. I certainly didn't expect to find what I was looking for in St. John's, right on my own university campus. Not only were there archival materials on my campus, but they were right across the way, less than five minutes' walk from my office. Sometimes research sends you in the strangest directions.

So it was that I found myself on a rainy Friday morning in March 2016, walking down from my office and past the music school and then winding my way through the rabbit warren of hallways and offices that is the Henrietta Harvey Building, in search of the Maritime History Archive. I was feeling oddly bodied. Not *disembodied*, exactly, but as if my body didn't fit in this part of my research journey. Ships. Seamen. Oceans. I'm not a maritime historian; I don't even know the proper names for the parts of a ship. I had to look them all up, and I'm still not sure I have them right. More than this, though, I have learned to map myself through land, rather than through water. How could I begin to make sense of an ever-moving ocean?

This was entirely new terrain. I was used to diaries, letters, and music manuscripts. I'd managed to figure out slave registers, and immigration records. I'd learned how to work with photos. But I had no idea what I was going to do with ships. It's not as if the Maritime History Archive itself was strange; the main reading room felt like a comfortable, if slightly shabby, living room. On the walls, paintings, portraits, and drawings, each one slightly askew. In the corner, a wobbly coat rack. Looking around, I almost expected to see doilies on furniture and a bow-tied and bespectacled man in a slightly ratty cardigan ready to serve me tea. There was no tea, of course, nor a bespectacled man. Instead, behind a glass-fronted door to the right of the information counter, I spotted shelves of archival boxes and knew I was in a familiar place.

For all its unassuming presence, the Maritime History Archive houses remarkable collections. In addition to rich information about Newfoundland's maritime history—including diaries, journals, photographs, and commercial records—the archive acquired 75 percent of all the crew agreements and log books of all British-registered ships sailing between 1857 and 1942. That glass-fronted door, I realized, offered only the tiniest hint of a window into a collection that includes some 55,000 boxes of materials. Researchers from around the world travel to St. John's to immerse themselves in the materials housed at the Maritime History Archive. I requested records for the *Kate Kellock*, which sailed the seas between 1865 and 1878, and burrowed in to see what I could find.

C.W. Kellock & Co., a ship-brokering company that still exists today, was founded in 1820 by Daniel Tonge, a master mariner and ship owner. Several permutations later, a man named Charles Walford Kellock assumed the helm, and in late 1864, C.W. Kellock & Co. was officially born. Given this timing, it seems as though the *Kate Kellock*, registered in 1865 and one of only a few ships that were part of C.W. Kellock & Co.'s own fleet, was also one of the first ships built to fly under the new company flag. It also seems likely that Kellock named this ship, built in one of the most famous ship-building regions of Britain, after his wife, Catherine Wignall, a clergyman's daughter whom he had married in 1859. *Kate Kellock*. Formal, with just a hint of familial intimacy, *Kate Kellock* rolls easily off the tongue. It was a perfect name for a flagship vessel.

A search online for Charles and Catherine Kellock turned up a large half-timbered house with a curving, paved laneway in the small village of Buerton, Cheshire, home to Mr. Kellock, esquire, and his lady bride. The house looked grand, pride of place for an ambitious and rising star in the ship-brokering trade. "Highfields," I read in a 1902 publication, "is a black and white timbered mansion in the Elizabethan style, erected in 1613, and is situated on a rising ground in a park of 200 acres; it contains some very fine old oak, including a carved mantel-piece dated 1616." I conjured up the small, rickety, precarious wooden structures I had seen in Paramaribo, leaning as they released their histories to the soil. One of these things was not remotely like the others.

An iron ship, the *Kate Kellock* weighed 1,175 tons and plied the waters of the Atlantic and Pacific, transporting goods and people between the United Kingdom, North America, India, and Australia.... Listen to those facts just tripping off my tongue. Size. Weight. History. The truth is that I had no clue what they meant. I didn't know enough about ships, or shipping history. I didn't know how ships were built and operated, or, indeed, how they were run. I didn't really understand the ins and outs of ship brokering. But I had to start somewhere, and so I plowed on.

I ordered all the log books and crew agreements I could find, every record available for every journey taken by the *Kate Kellock*: 1865–66, 1867–69, 1872–73, 1875–76, 1877. In the beginning there were too many details, especially in the crew agreements. I wanted to consume it all, absorb everything into my system. Did I need to know what seamen ate? What clothes they wore? Was it important to understand their social hierarchies? What about their origin stories—were their hometowns, ages, and previous shipboard experiences relevant? My brain quickly filled with data, facts and figures tumbling through one another.

~~~~~

The *Kate Kellock* appears to have undertaken three "coolie journeys," transporting British Indians from the depot in Calcutta to a range of ports in the West Indies in 1872–73, 1873–74, and then, after a short break while contracts were suspended, in 1875–76. But before this, in 1869, it had transported an entirely different clientele.

I opened the records and followed the *Kate Kellock* to Australia. The *Nieuw Rotterdamsche Courant* listed the departure of the *Kate Kellock* from London to Melbourne, a twenty-seven-day trip, in its 27 September 1869 issue. Melbourne was booming. Declared a city by Queen Victoria in 1847, it was named capital of the new Colony of Victoria shortly thereafter, in 1851. The Australian gold rush brought more wealth and more people. In 1852 alone, 370,000 immigrants arrived on Australian shores, hailing from many different parts of the world, among them the US, France, Italy, Germany, Poland, Hungary, and China. Soon, Melbourne was the largest city in Australia. Newspaper ads show a range of ships advertising for passengers, each offering sumptuous cabins and the most modern comforts.

~~~~~

Boats and ships and things that travel on water haven't been part of my landscape. Unlike Newfoundlanders and Britons, I don't carry islandness in my bones. I am a child of the prairies, but living on an island means reckoning with the sea on a daily basis, and this is something that I have had to learn.

I've never spent more than twenty-two hours on a ferry. In 1994, I took my first trip to the Faroe Islands. Búi and I took the train from Manchester to Aberdeen and then climbed aboard the vessel that traversed the sometimes rocky waves of the North Atlantic. For us, the oceans were calm and the sun shone; indeed, on the return journey, people were sunbathing on the top deck. It took a while to adjust to the ship's rhythms, but after almost a full day of sailing, my body had fully assimilated itself. The constant rumbling of the engine rattled my bones, the heavy sweetness of diesel painted itself into my nostrils. More surprising than either of these, however, were my sea legs. My body had adjusted to the rocking of the boat, bending and stretching with the gentle waves. By the time we disembarked in Tórshavn, the capital city of the Faroe Islands, it wasn't the boat that was rocking, it was solid land itself. My legs searched for the waves, and I almost stumbled when they couldn't find them. The land seemed to swell and lurch; my body didn't know what to do.

A few days later, we took a small passenger ferry to Mykines, the westernmost of the eighteen islands that make up the Faroe Islands. The ferry arrived late, and there was much agitated chattering as arriving passengers disembarked. Then it was our turn to climb aboard.

The trip is only forty-five minutes, and on a good day, there's much to occupy the imagination and feed the spirit. Puffins bob in the ocean and along the shore; dramatic cliffs and stark mountains open out to lush valleys. But it soon became clear that this wasn't going to be a good day. The boat tossed and rocked, waves slapping against its sides. All around me, people were reaching for seasickness bags, their faces grey. There was little conversation; this was an endurance test.

I have a strong stomach by nature, a genetic inheritance from my father's side of the family. But even I was having a hard time. And so I tried to turn my focus inward, drawing on my musical imagination to steady my balking stomach. I had performed a whole flute recital in my mind before I noticed the two men leaning against the side of the boat. Grizzled and weathered, they were deep in conversation, their faces animated, alive with energy. Unlike those who cowered behind me, these men appeared completely unconcerned by the churning waters.

What was their trick? What did they know that I didn't? Their bodies rocked and swayed, keeping time with the ocean's heavings, first a knee bend here and then another there. Moving together with the sea in a sinewy dance, their bodies traced patterns they'd perfected over decades. As I watched, I learned. I leaned into the water, releasing my desire for control. I allowed the waves to guide me, letting the ocean show me the way. Slowly, bit by bit, my stomach settled, my panic subsided.

Later, after we'd clambered onto shore, Búi told me what all the heated conversation before our departure had been about.

"They were saying it was the worst crossing they'd ever taken," he said. "And the boat almost couldn't dock."

~~~~~

What did it mean to imagine oneself through sea, rather than through land? I wondered. There is a timelessness and an endlessness to water. "Water," Dionne Brand writes of her Tobagonian childhood, "is the first thing in my imagination." But there are no landmarks to guide you through the oceans; there is nothing to call you home. Coordinates mark invisible points in the vastness of an otherwise unmappable space.

~~~~~

The *Kate Kellock* was in port in Melbourne for just over two months. An advertisement published in the Christmas Day edition of *The Argus* made it known that the ship would sail in a few days and invited prospective passengers to tour its "superior" saloon accommodations. Another advertisement made it clear that the captain, one George H.A. Bevan, would take no responsibility for his crew's actions while in port. Alcohol. Ladies. Fights. Desertion. I'd already learned that anything that could go wrong probably would. Bevan was smart.

Every port town has its stories. The British Contagious Diseases Acts, passed in the 1860s, which sought to protect British army and navy men from the pernicious effects of venereal disease in port cities like Liverpool, allowed police to detain any women suspected of prostitution. But sailors weren't innocents either. In port towns around the globe, families kept their daughters close when the ships came in. The whisper network churned into high gear. *Some* seamen behaved well. Others? Not so much. Soon after our arrival in Newfoundland, we learned that among Newfoundlanders, at least, Faroese fishermen weren't held in particularly high regard.

After returning to Liverpool, the *Kate Kellock* left port again in 1872; this time, however, the ship had been outfitted for indentured labourers. I unfolded the crew agreement for the 1872 journey, mindful of the cracks worn into the paper. The paper was crusty, still salted by sea air. Having been folded for over a century, it didn't want to open. I teased the pages gently, but the documents wouldn't lie flat. Instead, they lay there, awkward, like a ballerina tangled in her own legs.

The *Kate Kellock*'s 1872 crew was a diverse bunch. Shaped by a series of complicated events including death, criminality, and desertion, this crew drew its members from as far afield as Mauritius, Barbados, Quebec, Antigua, and the US. Curiously, one sailor even hailed from landlocked Ohio. I wondered how these men worked together, what languages they shared. More than this, I wanted to know more about life aboard one of these ships. The ship as ecosystem, that's what I wanted to know; the ship as a space of encounters. I wondered how the sailors communicated, not only with each other, but with the emigrants, and how they made sense of their new status. I wanted to know what life was like on board the ship, the rhythm of a day, the conversations.

But like the slave registers, the crew agreements would get me only so far. I needed more. And for that I needed to climb aboard; I needed to move away from *terra firma*. If this was a world that was foreign to me, I reasoned, then, like a sailor, I needed to allow my knees to bend and stretch with the waves around the Cape of Good Hope; I needed to orient myself away from the shore to the point where water meets sky, a seemingly endless seascape interrupted only by ships, storms, and flying fish. I needed to feel the ocean in my limbs, my body. And so, I reached for a log book. *Come*, I said to Charles Littler, the fifteen-year-old apprentice who had signed his first contract with the *Kate Kellock* in 1872. *We're going sailing.*

I began to relax when I read through the log books. Now I was on much more familiar footing. Here were the account of the captain's struggles with recalcitrant seamen, his hiring of new crew. More interesting still were the tiny hints of emigrant lives and experiences that seemed to emerge almost between the lines: the husband who complained—in English!—about his wife's mistreatment by a sailor, another male emigrant who brought his arguments and frustrations to the ship's doctor. What was it to live together in such close quarters—crew members and emigrants—for such long periods of time?

It was more than a little disappointing to discover that the records I was particularly interested in—those that recounted the details of the *Kate Kellock*'s 1873–74 voyage—are among the few not housed in the Maritime History Archive. The archivist pointed me to the National Archives of the United Kingdom, and I sent in an order. The quote came back two weeks later: seventy-nine pounds stirling for eighty-five pages of records. Six weeks, the email said. I had no choice but to wait. It was still cheaper than a flight to London, but when it came right down to it, I'd really rather have had the trip.

It felt like Christmas when an email arrived to tell me that my materials were ready and all I had to do was follow a link. There it was, the complete file: the crew agreement and log books for the 1873–74 journey of the *Kate Kellock* from Calcutta to Paramaribo. I wanted to dive in right away, but I waited; I had to do this right. There's only one chance to open an archival file for the first time. I'd already messed up in the Netherlands. I'd learned my lesson.

~~~~~

It was George Bevan who captained the *Kate Kellock*'s 1873 journey. The ship left Liverpool on 15 May with a full crew, most of whom hailed from the British Isles. But there were a few North Americans on board as well, hailing from Maryland, Boston, New

York, and Nova Scotia. While the ship had a clear plan—Liverpool, Calcutta, Suriname, New York, Liverpool—the terms on the crew agreement were much broader: "Liverpool to Calcutta and any parts and places in the Indian Pacific and Atlantic Oceans, China and Eastern Seas and Continent of Europe calling for orders if required and back to a final port of discharge in the United Kingdom term not to exceed 3 years." In other words, I translated, they could find themselves sailing anywhere on the globe, as long as it happened within three years.

Four months later, in early September 1873, the *Kate Kellock* docked in Calcutta. Nine sailors were sent before the magistrate due to refusal to work. Found guilty, they were docked two days' pay and sentenced to fourteen days in jail. Another crew member, requesting leave to go to church, returned several hours later, completely intoxicated. The captain noted all of this in his log book, each entry witnessed by his first officer. In the meantime, over the next weeks, the ship readied itself for the emigrants. The captain brought on five new crew members, whose primary duties would be to see to the emigrants. Dr. Bepin Behary Dutt, a British Indian emigration agent and Edinburgh-trained doctor, joined the ship in an official capacity as Surgeon Superintendent to the Emigrants. As an emigration agent, Dutt stood to gain a tidy commission fee upon the successful delivery of the emigrants to Suriname. What nobody knew at the time was the prominent role that he would come to play on this particular journey.

On 6 October 1873, the *Kate Kellock* steamed away from Suriname Ghat—Suriname dock—in Calcutta, travelling down the Hooghly River towards the Indian Ocean. By 17 October, they were on the open ocean, far from any hint of land. I imagined Joorayee on board the *Kate Kellock*. After a few weeks on board, she'd have developed a rhythm, a ritual that gave meaning to these endless days on the water. I saw her step out onto the deck, raise her face to the sky, and breathe deeply. The women's quarters were dark, and after so many days at sea, the air was dank, heavy, and sour with sweat and straining bodies. And so, Joorayee drew fresh air into her body, filling her lungs, releasing the dark. Taking her son by the hand, she moved toward the sides of the ship. Leaning her body against the railings, she scanned the horizon, searching for land, just as she had every morning since they'd left the Hooghly River behind. But there was no land to be seen. Just a vast ocean of nothingness. She filed this away in her memory, another check mark for another day. Sometimes she and Sahatoo would see other ships in the distance, and she'd pick up her son and point. But the ships would never come closer. Instead, they would slowly disappear, leaving Joorayee to wonder if she'd ever seen them in the first place.

~~~~~

Things started going awry just two weeks after the *Kate Kellock* left port.

According to the coordinates noted by the captain, the ship was still near India at this point, journeying south from Calcutta towards the British cinnamon, rubber, and tea colony of Ceylon in the Bay of Bengal. Two emigrants—a husband and wife—made a formal complaint that a crew member had purposely touched the woman on her lower thigh. She was "most provoked by being touched by any other man than her husband," Bevan wrote in his log book. The crew member in question, John Evans, the second officer, denied the accusation. Bevan, a seasoned captain who had already experienced his fair share of complicated shipboard situations, was nevertheless uncertain about how to proceed. "I feel quite powerless and unable to come to any decision myself," he wrote, "and confine myself to seriously cautioning Mr. Evans against touching or in any way meddling with the Emigrants in any unnecessary way most especially the Females ..." This wouldn't be the first or the last time that a ship captain had to intervene in crew–emigrant tensions. Less than three weeks later, the same emigrant returned to Bevan to complain of assault by two other crew members, threatening mutiny if things didn't improve.

Emigrant ships were not necessarily safe places for women. My thoughts turned to Joorayee. I realized, now, how much my understanding of her was influenced by the fact that she was a single mother travelling with a child. Would this fact have protected her from unwanted harassment and assault by crew members? Or would it have made her an easier target for assault? Joorayee had no husband to fight for her honour. Would others have intervened on her behalf if necessary? I'd like to think that camaraderie emerged, if only through the shared experience of conditions that none had previously experienced. I'd like to think that slowly, over time, the emigrants learned to trust one another. That smiles replaced the sidelong glances and turned faces. That they were able to forge unity through shared experiences.

~~~~~

The *Kate Kellock* docked in Cape Town on 11 December 1873. Cape Town was a regular stop on the emigration route. Ships needed provisioning. Seamen needed grog. Because it was often stormy around the Cape, the emigrants needed at least the fantasy of dry land. The captain, I imagine, needed a break. And the promise of land and civilization also meant hospitals, magistrates, and prisons.

Once docked, Bevan discharged three members of his crew to hospital. Two more sailors were to be examined by a Dr. Wood, who pronounced that there was nothing much wrong with them and declared that they should just be put to work. John Francis, in particular, Bevan observed, was "addicted to the filthy habit of masturbation, & it is my opinion & that of most of his shipmates that nothing else ails him." And then Bevan hired on two new crew members, W. Hanlon and Paul Nelson, from New York and Norway respectively, "to discharge the duties of the ship as able seamen."

Like Melbourne, the Cape Colony was booming. The discovery of several rich tracts of diamonds, between 1867 and 1871, brought an economic boost to a previously economically depressed colony. The harbour, which had for centuries served as a port of call for passing ships, was now busy with ships filled with adventurers and fortune seekers. And just a week prior to the *Kate Kellock*'s arrival, Cape Town had welcomed the great HMS *Challenger* on its grand tour.

After leaving Cape Town, the *Kate Kellock* didn't reach land again until 28 December, when it docked at Ascension Island, a tiny spot of an island in the middle of the Atlantic, just eighty-eight square kilometres in size. Bevan hadn't necessarily planned a stop at Ascension; St. Helena, farther south and a bit closer to the African continent, was a much more common stop along the West Indies route. But for some reason, Bevan chose to bypass St. Helena. By 26 December 1873, before they got to Ascension Island, however, things were completely out of hand.

On board, the indentured emigrants were restive. They did not trust this ocean. They did not trust the crew members. And they weren't quite sure whether they could trust the doctor. A number of emigrants had already died by this point, over half of them children. Their spirits suspended over a deep ocean and unable to return home, they haunted the ship's labourers, reminding them that there was nothing certain about this oceanic crossing.

I could see Joorayee at her usual spot at the ship's railing, her eyes scanning the horizon, Sahatoo pulling at her legs, desperate for attention. Very early that morning, a woman had laboured in the dark, moaning and gasping until her child—a daughter—was born, and there had been much rejoicing. Just two weeks earlier, another newborn girl—born prematurely—had died soon after birth.

Six women gave birth on the journey between Calcutta and Paramaribo. Depending on how long they'd been at the Calcutta depot, some of them may have become pregnant at the depot. Others, still, became pregnant on board. All these women travelled with uncertainty. All travelled in discomfort. And some laboured in the women's quarters, giving birth far from their own homes and the family networks that might have supported them.

I cannot imagine giving birth alone, among women I barely knew. I am private by nature; I do not easily share either my troubles or my dreams. I carry them inside, ruminate, and stew. But birth is a public event. There's no way to hide it. Women, even those who labour in relative silence, need the support of others. Birth is not something that is easily accomplished alone. Birth on a ship, among strangers and far from any hint of land, from anything that looked remotely familiar, must have been a frightening prospect.

Child mortality rates were high. According to the immigration records, almost every mother who travelled from Calcutta to Paramaribo on the *Kate Kellock*—including my great-great-grandmother—experienced the death of a child, either on the journey itself or after her arrival in Suriname. Several mothers died within the first months or year of their arrival, leaving children orphaned in a new land. Given these statistics, Joorayee and Sahatoo enjoyed considerable luck merely by surviving.

Joorayee, drinking in the fresh air, was uneasy. The atmosphere was unsettled; something was brewing. What would all of this mean for her child and herself?

Things came to a head the very next day. "I, George H.A. Bevan (Master) & the undersigned Officer, Petty Officer, and members of the Crew do hereby assert and agree," Bevan wrote at 3 p.m. on 27 December, "that we consider & believe our lives & safety, as also that of the ship generally to be in jeopardy, while Dr. Bepin Behary Dutt continues in charge of the Coolie Emigrants, and while several of the Coolies are allowed to be at liberty and also agree that it is the most … desirable & prudent course to make for the island of Ascension to obtain proper advice and assistance."

There are numerous accounts of the incidents that took place aboard the *Kate Kellock* in late December 1873. Newspaper reports were decidedly sketchy, offering only a hint of something awry. But there are several other versions. The captain left a detailed narrative in his log books, pointing to the possibility of an emigrant uprising and takeover of the ship. Edmund Fremantle, a British Navy officer conveniently in port at Ascension Island when the *Kate Kellock* arrived, and brought in to oversee an inquiry into the situation, wrote about the events in his memoirs. He agreed with Bevan's account but also offered some intriguing distinctions: among other things, he stated that the emigrants "had heard that their throats would be cut and that they would be thrown overboard." The ship's doctor, Bepin Behary Dutt, meanwhile, offered very different testimony, saying that he had heard from the emigrants that crew members were taunting them. And contemporary scholar Rajinder Bhagwanbali, relying on Dutch colonial records, places the blame directly on ship officer John Evans, who had previously been disciplined for sexually harassing some of the women emigrants. All accounts agree on one point: the ship's surgeon general, Dr. Dutt, was the central figure around which the stories revolved.

There's not a lot to tell about Dr. Dutt. The *Medical Registers* of 1872 and 1873 indicated that he was awarded a licentiate of the Royal College of Physicians in Edinburgh and a similar certification from the Royal College of Surgeons of Edinburgh, both in 1869, and listed his place of residence as Calcutta. Twenty years later, the February 1894 issue of the *Indian Magazine and Review* included him in a list of "Indian Gentlemen in the West," a group of almost sixty Bengali Hindus studying and working in a range of areas, from medicine and the law to history, philosophy, and engineering. Fremantle, writing about Dutt in his memoir, indicated that Dutt had a "Scotch wife," and Bevan noted that they had a child and that both wife and child were travelling on the *Kate Kellock*. Thus, although Dutt was born in India, he appears to have been well integrated into British society.

A chameleon with the skin and voice of an emigrant but the breeding, education, and social status of an Englishman, Dutt was the only person aboard the *Kate Kellock* able to mediate between two distinct worlds: Europe and colonial India. Given his background, he occupied a uniquely powerful position aboard the ship, and it's evident that he was able to leverage this power, either in the service of an emigrant mutiny or in the service of supporting the emigrants, depending on which version of the story you want to believe.

Clearly Dutt was a successful man of intellect, ambition, and means. What's not clear is how he understood his dual roles and how the emigrants understood him. Emigrant oral histories indicated that emigration agents were not necessarily trustworthy; indeed, they were often duplicitous. For colonial authorities, Dutt was also an intriguing character. They would likely have welcomed his role on board; after all, an Indian doctor could make the emigrants feel at ease, thus making for a smoother oceanic crossing. He could also be of assistance to the ship's crew, facilitating encounters with Indian languages, customs, and spiritual belief systems. As a western-trained doctor, he would also have moved easily among the crew, working with Bevan as well as with other crew members. But there were complex racial and colonial politics at play, and those very qualities that made Dutt an ideal surgeon superintendent in colonial eyes also made him an outsider to the mostly European-based crew.

While the crew included—at various points—seamen from England, Scotland, Wales, Ireland, France, Portugal, Norway, and Austria as well as from farther afield, including Canada (Prince Edward Island and Nova Scotia), the US, the West Indies, and even Canton, it doesn't, apart from Dutt, appear to have included anyone from British India. In other words, Dutt was the only person able to mediate between emigrants and crew, and as the tensions rose aboard the ship, it was evident, at least to the other crew members, that Dutt's allegiances were not to the ship, but to the emigrants. They saw him not as a doctor, but rather as something more analogous to a Hindu emigrant: a brown-skinned, foreign-language-speaking man who worshipped not a single god, but several. Whatever the case might have been, Dutt was a polarizing figure who seems to have been fully aware of his power. In the log book, Bevan indicated that Dutt was an obstinate and difficult man. Fremantle echoed this, calling Dutt "most litigious." But, Fremantle continued, he was "certainly more clever than the captain."

In any event, Fremantle ultimately took the side of the captain, and had Dutt and his wife and child removed from the ship. The *Kate Kellock* continued on its voyage, but not without further complications. Witness to the real possibility of emigrant uprising, the crew was, according to Bevan, apparently loath to continue the journey without extra guards. But Bevan, acting as mediator, followed Fremantle's directives: he raised the British flag, told the emigrants through an unnamed interpreter that they would always be safe under that flag, and assured his crew that all would be well. According to Bevan, trust was restored between both passengers and crew, and three weeks later, by the time the ship arrived in Paramaribo, all was well.

The *Kate Kellock* nosed into the Suriname River on 18 January 1874. It laid anchor just outside Fort Nieuw Amsterdam, at the point where the river divided into two: to the left, the Commewijne River snaked into the dense South American rainforest, passing dozens of plantations producing sugar, coffee, and cotton. To the right, the Suriname River flowed past Fort Zeelandia and the colonial city of Paramaribo, with its long row of white mansions.

The emigrants and crew aboard the *Kate Kellock* had been sailing for three months. That night, the last night before the ship's formal arrival in Paramaribo, all was still. It was the beginning of the dry season. The thick equatorial dark descended on the ship, with cool breezes blowing across its bow. What was Joorayee thinking? I wondered. Voyaging along the north coast of South America, she'd likely been able to see land for a while, and she would have known, as the ship turned into the Suriname River, that they were getting close. With mudbanks and mangroves on either side of the river, and evidence of habitation nearby, Joorayee would have known that arrival in this new place that she and her son would call home was imminent. The next morning, the *Kate Kellock* docked along Paramaribo's muddy shoreline, and Joorayee Radha, twenty-five, dark brown, Hindu, and exactly 1.513 metres tall, along with her son and the rest of the human cargo, descended the walkway. Then they walked down the dusty Waterkant, toward the immigration depot for medical examination, before being dispersed to the various plantations to which they were indentured.

What was life like for my great-great-grandmother? I thought, as I shook the waves out of my still wobbling sea legs, and walked the gangplank along with her to the shore. Fully 20 percent of those who sailed with Joorayee and Sahatoo died within the first year of their departure from Calcutta, all the details recorded carefully in the log books and immigration records. One, a thirty-five-year-old

BABA EN MAI

5 JUNI 1873   MONUMENT VAN DE HINDOSTAANSE IMMIGRATIE   5 JUNI 1993

"waar het my goed gaat, daar is myn vaderland"

ONTHULD OP ZATERDAG 04 JUNI 1994 DOOR DE
STICHTING HINDOSTAANSE IMMIGRATIE

woman named Joya Bhugmunnia, had died just as the ship laid anchor outside Fort Nieuw Amsterdam in the evening before its arrival in Paramaribo. Name. Date. Location. Age. Cause. Everything was listed, every detail recorded.

In colonial photos, the emigrants stand close together, a ragged group posed for a class photo, serious dark faces looking straight ahead. Which women were brown? Which were dark brown? Which were married? Which were not? Which one is my great-great-grandmother? It's like a curious game of Guess Who?

~~~~~

On 18 June 1878, the *Kate Kellock*, carrying wheat, flour, teak, and twenty-six crew members, was wrecked off the coast of Chile while on its way from San Francisco to London. The captain, one Charles Ricker, was found guilty of "grave acts of misconduct" (which included leaving the direction of the failing ship to the second mate and going off to pray with his wife), but he was not deemed responsible for the ultimate wreck of the ship, which was "due entirely to the extreme severity of the weather, and to the ship having been pooped when the first officer was in command." No lives were lost.

7. The Baba and Mai monument, commissioned by the Hindustani
    Immigration Foundation and designed by Krishnapersad Khedoe,
    was unveiled in 1994. Placed at the location of the former immigration
    depot, Baba and Mai honours the first indentured immigrants to arrive
    from British India in 1873. In 2015, a reproduction of this statue was
    placed at Suriname Ghat—or Suriname Jetty—in Kolkata, where
    thousands of British Indian indentured labourers stepped aboard
    the ships that would take them to Suriname. *Photo credit: Sonja Boon.*

Six months later, by the end of 1878, the first five-year indenture contracts were coming to an end in Suriname. According to the governor of Suriname, over 450 labourers who had completed their contracts took to the seas once more, returning to the "land of their birth" on the English ship *Philosopher*. My great-great-grandmother was not among this number. In January 1880, almost exactly six years after her arrival in Paramaribo, Joorayee Radha was granted leave to stay in the colony of Suriname. Her immigration record stated that she'd entered into a relationship with a man named U-A-Sai. Now a legal resident, she was no longer of interest to authorities. As far as the immigration records are concerned, Joorayee's life ended after she gained permanent residency. And so, for all intents and purposes, she disappeared.

~~~~~

Joorayee's new partner, a Chinese merchant named U-A-Sai, popped up all over the place, from newspaper announcements to immigration and emigration records, and advertisements. But the story that emerged from all these fragments was baffling.

On 1 July 1863, when the formerly enslaved in Suriname celebrated their new freedom, a man named U Asai sailed into port in Georgetown, Guyana. Dutch colonial immigration records, meanwhile, recorded the arrival in Suriname of a man with the same name in 1868. He was registered as a Chinese immigrant coming from Guyana, and assigned to a five-year contract at Hampton Court, a sugar plantation near the Guyanese border. A year later, in 1869, however, he left his contract unfulfilled, the record listing him as *weggelopen*, or walked away. But three years later, in 1872, the *Surinaamsche courant en Gouvernements advertentie blad* announced his intention to marry Elisabeth Pompadour Daal, then a nineteen-year-old Creole woman formerly enslaved at Hecht en Sterk, a coffee plantation in the Commewijne region, far from Hampton Court.

U-A-Sai must have arrived in Paramaribo around the same time as Joorayee Radha and her son. In any event, at some point he established himself as a merchant and goldsmith in the heart of Paramaribo. Later, he would give his name and profession—and apparently, also his gambling addiction—to Joorayee's son, Sahatoo. Advertisements appeared in local newspapers throughout the 1890s, from a small, fanciful announcement inviting customers to pick up something beautiful, magical, and musical for a special someone in their lives, to large half-page ads welcoming customers to a veritable department store of consumer delights, including corsets, undershirts, umbrellas, shoes, hats, textiles, housewares, and more. In addition, U-A-Sai advertised his expertise in gold- and silversmithing and watch repair.

Joorayee Radha died on 8 June 1900. After this, things changed dramatically for the family. That same month, a newspaper advertisement announced the auction of all the goods in U-A-Sai's property, and reminded those who had left watches and clocks for repair to pick them up. A year later, the property itself was auctioned off. Already a master of reinvention, U-A-Sai appears to have reinvented himself one more time. With a new wife, a formerly indentured Javanese woman named Bok Sinah, he boarded a ship to Amsterdam, later travelling back to Java. According to family lore, this departure was not without its drama: U-A-Sai had invited his stepson and heir to leave with him, but upon Sahatoo's refusal, became so angry that he disinherited him and left with both his new wife and his riches.

Sahatoo U-A-Sai, then about twenty-eight years old, began advertising his own business as a watchmaker and goldsmith. He'd been married for five years by this point and was already twice a father. Later, he was appointed the country's official watchmaker, a role that saw him responsible for all the official clocks in the capital.

But Sahatoo's eldest son, Henry Eugene, didn't continue the family business. He took a very different path, growing up to become a noted musician, a well-known violinist who taught in his studio on the Watermolenstraat and performed frequently in Paramaribo. Mozart. Schubert. Wieniawski. Sarasate. Later, he'd perform, too, with my grandfather's choir. That violinist great-uncle, I learned, a man I never met, had also studied at the Royal Conservatory in The Hague. Music was rooted deep in my family history, travelling down not just one, but both branches of my mother's family tree.

But I still had many questions. How did a Hindu woman from the very north of India end up in a relationship with a Chinese man who had previously announced his intention to marry a formerly enslaved woman named after one of the most politically powerful women in eighteenth-century Europe? What language did they speak together? How did they live? And why didn't they have any children? Joorayee would have been thirty when her contract ended, still within her prime child-bearing years. And yet, apart from the children she had on the plantation, one of whom died and the other of whom seems to have disappeared, she had no more children. All of her attention—and U-A-Sai's—seemed to focus on Sahatoo, the toddler who crossed the ocean with her. Was this just a relationship of convenience that gave my great-great-grandmother economic security and protection while offering U-A-Sai a son, worker, and heir—and free domestic labour? Whatever agreement they must have made, Joorayee would have known that at the very least, she'd been able to secure her son's fortune and future.

And what, then, of Sahatoo himself? How did this man, born in India to a Hindu mother and raised in a Chinese household in Suriname, become a member of the Dutch Reformed Church? And further, how did the Dutch Reformed Sahatoo, an illiterate man who had lived his whole life surrounded by multiple languages and cultures, end up marrying a Catholic woman, Maria Mathilda Ameerbie, a keen reader who always had a book under her arm and, according to family recollections, was known to have on her bookshelf not only the works of Emile Zola but also Dutch translations of Swedish literature?

~~~~~

Sometime around 1935, my Catholic grandmother with her Chinese name and her Hindu indentured ancestors met my grandfather, the child of a German man and his Creole concubine and the descendant of enslaved Africans, and fell in love. My great-grandmother refused to attend the wedding, and the rest, as they say, is history. Chinese. Creole. Hindustani. European. By the time my mother was born, we were a globe within a single family. Out of violence, poverty, enslavement, hope, dreams, and fear, the oceans had brought us together.

8. My grandmother, Henriette Mathilde U-A-Sai, as a toddler. Photographer unknown. *Family photo.*

14

UNFOLDINGS

W HAT DOES IT MEAN TO BE MIXED, to carry the histories of five continents in my body, on my skin, in family memories? Where does someone like me fit into this world that likes to categorize things? I'd started my project in 2012 intending to answer these questions. I wonder, though, if I actually started this journey much longer ago. Could it be that all my adult travels—from small-town Alberta to Victoria to Toronto to Indiana to Manchester to The Hague to Vancouver to St. John's—were part of this grand quest for home? A child of the world, I once thought, can make music anywhere. But that child also needs a home, a place she can return to, a place where she belongs. That child needs harmonies she can call her own.

When my children were small, I read them P.D. Eastman's *Are You My Mother?*, a picture book that follows a determined young baby bird in search of his mother. Along the way, the bird meets a kitten, a hen, a dog, a cow, a car, a boat, a plane, and a power shovel. Each time, he asks the same question: "Are you my mother?" Was I that bird on an endless quest for belonging? *Are you my mother?* I'd asked Toronto, Manchester, The Hague, Vancouver, St. John's. None of them had replied. How would Paramaribo respond?

Back in Suriname for the second time in two years, I'd just spent two summer weeks poring over colonial records of slavery and indenture. I'd taken a second tour through abandoned plantation regions. And I'd walked and walked around the colonial heart of Paramaribo, trying to understand this city and my place in it. I'd taken hundreds of photos.

On the day before my departure, I'd set out before nine. I'd walked past the presidential palace and Fort Zeelandia, and then stopped for some quiet moments in the deep stillness of the Catholic basilica. I'd walked to the Nieuwe Oranjetuin cemetery to pay my last respects to Frederika Rosette. And then, following in the footsteps of my musical ancestors, I'd made my way to the Musicus Helstone monument and down the Watermolenstraat. Later, I'd lingered in the noisy shopping district, imprinting its colour and bustling energy into my body. This was my final chance to feel this place in my bones, to know it on my skin. By the time I turned onto the Keizerstraat for one last look at the mosque and synagogue, it was nearing midday, and the sun was bearing down. There was almost nobody around anymore. If I'd been smart, I would have been back at my air-conditioned apartment, cooling my overheated body. But I knew I needed to make the most of my time.

I saw the house on the Grote Combéweg on my way back to the apartment. Well over a century old, it stood in the middle of a parking lot, seemingly imprisoned in a glittering sprawl of chrome and metal. It was a large structure with a wide verandah, yellow paint peeling from the sides. A few windows were boarded up; the corrugated roof was rusty.

There was nothing at all spectacular about the house; in a city like St. John's, I'd probably pass it right by. For almost two weeks, I *had* passed it by. But on this particular morning, I found myself pausing.

I pulled out my camera—

"No!" The man appeared suddenly in front of me, gesticulating wildly. "You can't take pictures!"

I wanted to pretend I didn't know what he meant. I wanted to claim ignorance, protest my innocence. Instead, flustered and with my heart pounding, I did the only thing I could think of doing.

"Here," I said, thrusting my camera at him. "You can delete them if you like."

"This is my grandparents' house," he said, his voice loud. "It's over 150 years old."

I grasped for words, my mouth opening and closing, feeling a strange mix of bewilderment, mortification, shame—

"It's beautiful," I finally managed.

It wasn't enough, but I was still reeling from this sudden encounter, still trying to figure out how to fix things. The house *was* beautiful. There was a melancholy to it; it wore its ragged heart on its sleeve, and I imagined I could see it breathing.

~~~~~

There's a long and ugly history of what I like to call gawkery; that is, of people coming from wealthy European countries and taking things for their own entertainment—photographs, artifacts, stories—without any consideration for the disruption and devastation they might leave behind. Was I, with my camera, my eager eyes, and my American money, any different?

Over the years, I've picked up my own trinkets during my travels, collecting small mementoes to remind me of where I've been. A tiny figurine acquired during a family trip to Japan and Korea. An even tinier pair of penguins, from the first holiday I took with Búi. A rotund red granite hippo from the British Museum. Shells gathered from the ocean floor in Barbados. A carved dolphin from the Johnson GeoCentre in St. John's. In Suriname, I'd focused on textiles, gathering a rich collection of colourful cottons. And I'd taken so many pictures. All these things acted as touchstones, carrying within them the emotional experience of travel. Together, they formed my own miniature cabinet of curiosities, an eclectic collection of things gathered from away and through which I'd come to define myself.

I know what it is to be affected by gawkery. I know what happens when your home becomes a museum, when the place where you live seems to be there for tourists and not for you. I know what happens when their view of who you are challenges your view of yourself. As a first-year university student living in Victoria, I quickly grew tired of endless tourists that crowded the city's downtown streets in the summer. My friends and I developed a special elbows-out strategy that allowed us to slalom smoothly past camera-toting visitors gawping along Government Street, even as we exploited those same tourists for money by busking outside Munro's Books. In Amsterdam, I'd laughed at the tourists pointing eagerly at marzipan penises and the sex museum. In St. John's, I still smile at visitors gasping in the wind.

I've also been a tourist myself; I've been that person stalled on a sidewalk, my eyes mesmerized by the sights in front of me. I've been the person with a camera stuck to my eye. I've fetishized Dutchness with the best of them: I can't even begin to count the number of photos I have of windmills, canals, and wooden shoes. I've crammed my schedule full of museums and dragged my kids to living history villages. I've tried to memorize landscapes. And, absent my husband and kids, I had tried to do all of this in Suriname too.

Not all stories, Eve Tuck and K. Wayne Yang argue, have a right to be told. And they are right. Just because someone tells you something doesn't necessarily mean that it's yours to share. Just because you've lived something doesn't mean that the story is your own. Just because you see something doesn't mean it's yours to claim.

I haven't always been able to reconcile my own desire to claim the past with my ethical responsibilities. Where do we get this need to collect, to build ourselves up through and with the minutiae we claim from the lives of others? Eighteenth-century men of letters prided themselves on their eclectic interests, designing and developing elaborate cabinets of curiosity that brought together samples of all their interests. Egyptian mummies. Indigenous beadwork. Greek pottery. Roman coins. Medieval relics. But was it ever okay for explorers and adventurers to pillage the world for their own interests? Was I even supposed to be able to look upon Egyptian mummies or ancient bog people? Did I have a right to fish through their stories?

The politics of gawkery are deeply embedded in our cultural histories. It hasn't only been about beautiful cities, galleries, museums, and landscapes. It hasn't just been about T-shirts, trinkets, and photographs. In the nineteenth century, human beings were put on display, their bodily differences turned into a spectacle for eager viewers. The bearded lady. The girl with five arms. The dwarf. The giant and the giantess. These were the staples of American freak shows throughout the nineteenth century, all of them making their livings as objects of fascination, horror, desire, and disgust.

Europeans, meanwhile, revelling in the display of empire, put Indigenous and African peoples on display. Of these, the most famous was perhaps Sara Baartman, a Khoikhoi woman from what is now South Africa who was brought to Europe in the early nineteenth century. Displayed as the Hottentot Venus in Britain before being sold to an animal trainer in France, she was later subject to invasive examinations by a group of French natural scientists. After her death in 1815, her body was dissected, with notes published by a leading anatomist. Specimens of her body were preserved and displayed at a Paris museum until 1974. It would be another quarter century before her remains were finally repatriated to South Africa.

The Netherlands has its own history of human museums. In the late nineteenth century, a colonial exhibition took place on what is now the Museumplein, the big grassy area in the middle of Amsterdam's cultural heart. On one side, the Stedelijk Museum of modern art and the Van Gogh Museum, and on the other, the grand and gracious Rijksmuseum, whose collection is far too large to possibly make sense of in a single day, and the glorious Concertgebouw. Years ago, when I was a student in The Hague, a group of giggling schoolgirls came up to me, looking for an audience. Jockeying against one another, they sang me a song and told me jokes for a guilder, their upturned faces smiling with delight.

In many ways, the Museumplein of today is a place of wonder that celebrates the capacity of the human spirit to imagine and dream beyond our physical worlds. But in 1883, two years before van Gogh painted *The Potato Eaters*, what is now the Museumplein was the site of a different spectacle for a different audience. Then, it was home to a colonial exhibition that celebrated Dutch histories of empire. At its heart was a miniature colonial world, a human zoo peopled by sample populations from Suriname: Maroon, Creole, Carib, and Arawak people, a group of twenty-eight carefully chosen and flown to the Netherlands for the entertainment of the Dutch. For six months they were displayed like trained seals, and every day, audiences would pay extra to see these "human races that had never before been seen in the Netherlands" in their "natural" habitat.

Did they know why they'd been chosen? Had they known what to expect? One Surinamese man told his family he was going to Holland to tell the Dutch king, William III, about the miserable quality of life in Suriname. Indeed, this is apparently what he'd been promised when he was recruited. Until recently, his descendants had no idea he'd been put on display, exploited for the pleasure of the Dutch. They didn't know that the portrait they owned, a drawing made during the exhibition itself, was part of a French book about colonial peoples—*Les habitants de Surinam*, by Roland Napoleon Bonaparte, a distant relative of Napoleon—and that their ancestor's body had been subjected to anthropometric measurement.

~~~~~~

What the agitated man on the Grote Combéweg couldn't have known was that even as I was taking a photo, I was also leaving a piece of myself—a bit of my *bakra* soul—behind. Suriname had lodged itself in me. I wanted to hold on to it. I wanted to sear it into my body and into my memories. But did I have the right to take Suriname's history, its past, and its stories, and claim them as my own? That's what his impassioned response asked me to consider. What responsibilities did I have to this place I'd only just begun to know?

The politics of travel are complicated. Why do we travel? Who gets to travel? Whose journeys are forced? And whose journeys are chosen? I've travelled across the globe, but I've never been hurried onto a ship in the dark. I've never been traded for copper pots and cotton. I've never had to flee a country, nor have I ever had to justify myself at borders. All my journeys have been consciously chosen.

Until recently, I hadn't spent much time thinking about what travel meant. Even as I knew that these constant migrations—mine and those of my family—had fundamentally shaped my identity, I hadn't spent enough time considering how my presence—and the very act of travel itself—had affected the lives of those whose homes and histories I'd visited. I hadn't considered the marks that I, as a tourist, temporary resident, settler, researcher, and descendant, left behind me. What might my own actions have wrought?

No! The man's vocal resistance to my photography laid it all bare. I couldn't hide. I was in Paramaribo, and like the most insensitive of tourists, I was gawking. I couldn't help myself. But for me, it was different. *Right?* I belonged. I had a right to be there. I wasn't like those fools in the fancy hotel down the road. I wasn't that white woman tourist with her mosquito-bitten legs and burnt shoulders. I had a local family. I had a history. I tried to rationalize all of this to myself. But still. There I was. Intruding on this man's life, his space.

Generally I had tried to avoid taking pictures of people in Suriname; I recognized their right to privacy and I thought I had been careful. Still, I knew I had overstepped a boundary. This man saw me as a trespasser. My photography. My research. My visit. But this was his life, his family home, his story. I was treading on long and often painful histories and I wasn't always sure where the boundaries were. How could I know which stories were mine and which ones were not? Did I have a right to claim a part of it through my camera lens?

"It was my grandparents' house," the man said again, pride in his voice.

And then, a pause.

"It's okay," he said.

He handed me back my camera and loped away, disappearing between the cars. I stood there for a moment, waiting as my heartbeat slowed. I had been desperate to capture this place; desperate to lay claim to it. But it had taken me much too long to figure out that the plantation pasts that I so eagerly sought still marked Paramaribo's cityscape in the present. *Combé. Rainville. Tourtonne. Ma Retraite. Morgenstond. Mon Plaisir.* Every city neighbourhood was named after the plantations that had once stood there. I'd been walking plantation lands with every step that I took, my feet following in the footsteps not only of the European elite who had turned swamps into profit, but also of the enslaved and indentured who had toiled for them, and before them, the Indigenous people who had been pushed away from prime coastal lands. I'd searched for my stories in the archives and in the rural regions outside the city, but they'd been right there with me the whole time.

I wanted to call after the man, to tell him that we shared a history. That my Dutch might sound different, that I might not be able to speak Sranan, and that my skin was much lighter than his. But our stories linked; they intersected. I wanted him to know. There were things we had in common.

I'm not a tourist, I wanted to say. *I'm like you. This street. This city. This country. They're mine too.* I would have liked this man to embrace me, to welcome me. But he hadn't recognized me at all.

~~~~~

If I had learned anything as I walked these streets, it was that colonialism had both created and ravaged this place. Suriname, as a concept, as a reality, as a country with a rich and diverse heritage, would not have been possible without colonialism. The flavours, the sounds, the colours, the language, the customs. None of this would have existed. *I* would not have existed. But Suriname has also been destroyed by colonialism. In Paramaribo I walked on lands saturated with violence, through the centuries of blood that seep into the ground around Fort Zeelandia. I walked the road between the murky waters of the Suriname River and the grand houses of the Waterkant, following in the footsteps of ancestors bought, sold, and traded as labour, their names carefully recorded in slave, emancipation, and immigration records. I thought about corruption, power, and the underground economy and how these continue to affect the lives of everyone who calls this place home. I heard my aunt's voice: *We have oil. We have gold. This country should be rich.* And I wondered about the legacy of an independence process that had gone completely awry.

Suriname is a broko pranasi. My uncle's voice intruded on my thoughts. But it is so much more. Dereliction. Abandonment. Destruction. *Yes.* Also glory. Beauty. Mystery. Promise. History. The sweetness of fruit nurtured in the depths of a tropical jungle.

It's complicated and messy. It's rotten at the core. But taken together, we—this place and all of us who carry a piece of it in our hearts—are a story still unfolding.

~~~~~

I left the next morning. The plane began its ascent, and as dawn broke, I looked over the great Surinamese rivers, their wide, chocolatey veins running from deep in the Guyana Shield. An hour or so later, we stopped in Aruba to pick up passengers. From the air, Aruba, my cousin Elvira's home for over a decade, was tiny, a pancake of an island surrounded by ocean. On one end, an army of resorts rose near a bright sandy beach, and on the other, a single mountain rose like a curious haystack in the middle of a wheat field.

New passengers boarded, jostling for overhead bins and seats. A noisy youth soccer team from the Bahamas, flush with energy from their recent tournament, and in front of me, a gregarious missionary. His church, his health, his wife, their pet monkey, the Jonestown massacre. The words bubbled around him. There was so much to process, so much still to sort out.

The plane rose again over the Caribbean Sea. Outside, the clouds painted the continent of Africa onto a translucent ocean, deep, blue, and still. My thoughts turned back to a long-lost summer in Barbados, to a royal wedding, a riptide, and a jellyfish sting. I thought of my toddler toes scrabbling in Surinamese sand and the sticky sweetness of a mango ripe from the tree. I thought of my grandfather's choir, of my great-uncle's violin lessons, and of Fürstenau duets. My great-great-grandmother on the *Kate Kellock*, leaving her family behind. Her son, spinning their story into gold. Frederika Rosette in palest pink. And Frederik Noa, the patriarch, the leader, the ark builder, and the bearer of stories.

There's always something melancholic about returning from a trip, and back in St. John's, I unpacked slowly. There was the expected laundry, of course, a pile of clothes scented with the tropics, but true to form, I'd also brought back some treasures. Fabric earrings made by Maroon women. A tiny hand-carved wooden turtle to join the hippo, dolphin, and penguins. Javanese textiles. Spicy tamarind candies. Two jars of homemade guava jam from my aunt. And inside a red jeweller's box, a very special gold brooch.

The kids passed over the brooch, turning their attention instead to the turtle and the jam, but I focused on it anyway, sharing with them a story my uncle had told me just two days earlier, during our final meal together.

"I must have been about ten years old," he began. Opa, he said, had been at a Freemason's dinner but for some reason, they didn't have enough cutlery, so he'd called my great-grandmother for assistance.

As I retold this story, I could see it happening in my mind's eye: the young boy—my uncle—hurrying down the street behind his grandmother, his long brown legs propelling him forward. It was dark already, with that heavy blackness of the tropics. The air was still but damp, moisture clinging in the atmosphere after the afternoon's downpour. Woman and boy moved quietly down the sandy road, watching for puddles. Behind a fence, a dog barked, startling them, and then, as one, every dog in the neighbourhood joined in, a canine chorus howling and barking. *Run!* the barking said. *Be off with you. This is no place to be at night!* But woman and boy continued, their footfalls soft on the sand.

Suddenly the woman stopped and pulled back, drawing the boy close to her, shielding him from the road. He looked up, a question in his eyes.

"*Masra*," she said—Master—for this is what she always called her eldest grandson. "*Masra*, let them pass."

The boy looked out into the darkness, but he couldn't see anything.

~~~~~

"The past is always with us," my uncle Deryck told me as he sought to explain this story. "The spirits, the ghosts, they journey with us; they are always alongside us. This is how it is here."

This is what I tried to tell my sons.

What had my great-grandmother sensed that night almost seventy years ago? A flicker of light? A sudden shift in the air? An inexplicable feeling that they were not alone? My uncle, as a child, had sensed nothing at all. But for my great-grandmother, things were different. The spirits were present, and they needed to be respected.

We were eating *pom* when my uncle told this story. My aunt Hanny, knowing how much I liked it, had cooked one up for our final meal together—well, she'd cooked up eight actually; the rest were in the freezer—and I was savouring every mouthful and remembering the taxi-bus driver's smile as he offered up his wife's cooking.

The evening was quiet, the birds settling down after a burst of song that followed the afternoon downpour. A gentle breeze floated through the house. Just an hour earlier, we'd been enjoying a relaxing drink on the front porch, when the rain and wind sent us scurrying for cover. The sheer force and volume of tropical downpours, that thick white curtain of rain, always amazed me. Drains couldn't keep up, and the streets overflowed, emerging only bit by bit in the hours that followed. Some streets would still have large puddles the next morning.

"The past is always with us," my uncle repeated. "The spirits are always present."

Nothing happened by chance, he assured me. There was always a reason. Thunder. Lightning. All of this had meaning.

I thought back to comments made by a tour guide. We'd been driving through the Commewijne district. One of the oldest plantation regions in Suriname, it's located just across the river from the capital city of Paramaribo. Today, many of the communities retain the names of the former plantations, and so we passed Peperpot, with its nature park and new housing developments, and then other former plantations, among them Lust en Rust, Marienburg, Ellen, Zorgvliet, Alkmaar, before we drove into a desolate, empty area.

"This is Nijd en Spijt," the tour guide announced. "And this plantation was owned and managed by a woman named Susanna du Plessis, who was said to be a very violent slave owner."

Susanna du Plessis, who lived during the eighteenth century, holds a prime spot in Surinamese histories of slavery. Stories and songs about her abound, many depicting a woman of uncommon evil. In one story, du Plessis, jealous of her husband's attention to an enslaved woman, sliced off that woman's breast and then cooked it up into a stew to feed to him. In another, frustrated by the crying of an enslaved baby, du Plessis grabbed it from its mother's arms and drowned it. "Now," she reportedly said, "it won't cry anymore."

"We don't know if all the stories are true," our guide continued, "but there are some signs that they must be. You will notice that in contrast to Peperpot, nobody lives here in Nijd en Spijt. Nobody wants to develop anything here."

The stories about Susanna du Plessis began circulating during her lifetime, but it's hard to know precisely how much truth there is to them. Was she a vicious, soulless woman prone to excessive violence as she exercised her will and power over those she held as property? Or was she, a woman who knew her own mind and assured her own fortune and independence, just too much for her society to handle? Was she a combination of both? Did stories about her grow ever more grotesque as she gained power?

The tour guide swept her arms over the empty landscape.

"And there's more," she said. "This area has been struck not once but twice by lightning." She shrugged. While an empty landscape might be explained away, lightning couldn't be. The lightning, she said, was a sign—proof positive—that there had been trouble in this place.

At the time, I suspected this was the tourist version, high drama meant to entice us into the story. But thinking back, I wondered. What did the lightning mean?

~~~~~

Masra, let them pass. My great-grandmother's words had sounded a note of caution. The spirits were not always benevolent. You had to learn to live with them, to watch out for them, to listen for them. And you had to protect yourself from them as well.

My uncle pulled out a small red jeweller's box.

"We wanted to give you something special, on this, your last meal with us before you go home. And we wanted it to mean something in relation to all of your work."

He cradled the box in his palm.

"So your aunt chose something from her own jewellery collection."

"You've gone searching so far and so deep into your past," my aunt said, joining in the conversation. "You have disturbed so many stories, walked through history with so many spirits. You, too, need protection."

They handed me the box. Inside, nestled on a white cushion, was a gold pin from which dangled two dark beads.

"These are *ogri ai kralen*," my uncle said, "*ograi krara* in Creole."

"These beads will protect you from the evil eye," my aunt said. "Now, you will be safe."

As I looked down at this gift, an intimate and generous gesture from family members so interested in the stories I was exploring, another memory stirred. In my own jewellery box, at home, I had a similar pin. A tiny gold safety pin with a tiny black bead. It was a birth present from a family friend, I recalled my mother telling me. I'd been carrying protection with me since the day I was born and I hadn't even known it.

I wondered about the spirits and their role in my research. I wondered how their presence had influenced what I had learned. I thought back to my archival work—to the week where the document elevator had suddenly broken down, rendering all the historical documents inaccessible; to the nineteenth-century paper that crumbled into dust as soon as I tried to touch it; to inexplicable dead ends: files that ended just at the moment when I needed them most, documents listed in the finding aids but impossible to find, blotches of ink hiding crucial words.

But I could also think of instances where it seemed like the archival red carpet had been laid out for me, where stories came together as if by magic, opening up new possibilities.

This talk of spirits was disconcerting. I wasn't entirely sure what to make of it. I have prided myself on being a rational being. I love data and facts and figures. Dates. Numbers. Times. I love the texture of ageing paper and the look of ink on paper. These are tangible, concrete, real.

But there were so many things that I couldn't explain, happenings that seemed to fall well outside my rational understanding. What could I make of a great-grandmother who integrated her African *winti* belief with her deep and abiding Protestantism? How could I make sense of an uncle who sensed, from a distance of 7,500 kilometres—across an ocean, a continent, and several time zones—that there was something deeply wrong with his sister, right at the moment that she'd been diagnosed with tuberculosis? What could I make of an aunt's friend, who dreamed one Sunday night that there would be police officers in my grandmother's house on Monday afternoon. My aunt had scoffed at her, but that dream had foreshadowed reality. And how did I make sense of Oma herself, who in the days surrounding her death appeared before her daughters in visions?

~~~~~

In St. John's, as I sifted through my notebooks and my thoughts, I pondered the vagaries of archival research. In the beginning of any project, archival materials make little sense. They're jumbled up, out of order. There are pieces missing. And then, over time, a hint of a pattern starts to emerge. Only after that—only after I've read, sorted, catalogued, and organized, only after I've taken all of this into my body and lived with it for a while—can I begin to find meaning.

In some ways, archival research is a lot like music-making. A pianist friend of mine once told me that she saw the musical score as the point where the composer and the performer meet. The score, she said, is a place of conversation and dialogue; it's where composer, musician, and music get to know one another. There's a sense of give and take—the score is a space of play. How will the music unfold? What kinds of tonal landscapes will we explore? And how will we negotiate the pauses, the silences, the spaces between the notes? It's much the same in the archives. I meet the past in the archival materials, but we need to get comfortable with one another. I need to listen for its voice, to attune myself to its breathing: its thoughts, dreams, and desires. I have to figure out what the documents mean and how they fit together.

In the archives, each fragment is like a musical note, a phrase, a score marking. Each one is a window into the intentions of the past. Arrange them one way to reveal a symphony, another to find a quartet. Some archival stories are dissonant; they bellow, raucous and noisy. Others are lullabies, so fragile and so ephemeral that they can disintegrate in a gentle breeze. But such stories can emerge only through careful puzzling, thinking, and dreaming. History isn't clear and transparent. There are many possible routes, and many possible stories.

Almost every research journey has what might be called an "archival sweet spot," a moment when things start to come into focus. After what sometimes feels like endless puzzling, the pieces arrange themselves a certain way and suddenly you can see clear through them. There's the story you've been looking for, right in front of you. The chorus of angels sings Handel's Hallelujah and the world rejoices.

But at other times, there are almost no stories at all. Sometimes the music comes to a sudden, shuddering halt. And sometimes it loses energy and slowly peters out until there's nothing left.

~~~~~

There is much that remains unsaid in the archives. I thought back to my colleague's comments: "There are no neutral positions." Archives are never neutral. They can tell certain stories. Others, however, are silenced. This is something that all of us who work with the past must confront. There is so much that we can never know. And yet, as my uncle said, everything has meaning.

Even silence.

Perhaps that's my most important responsibility, both as a musician and as a researcher: how I deal with silence. In music, rests and pauses are alive; they are as important—and sometimes more important—than the notes that surround them. Music makes no sense without silence. Nor, in the final analysis, does history.

Like Joorayee aboard the *Kate Kellock*, I found myself at sea during my archival journeying. I was unmoored. There were no landmarks to tell me which direction I should turn. As this project progressed, I seemed to be writing endless coordinates, but I didn't understand them. And just as there was no music in Joorayee's immigration record, there was no song in Sarah plantation's slave registers.

The past is always with us, my uncle had said. But I couldn't find the notes, the harmonies, the music, the voices, the story. Maybe, I think now, that was the point. The stories I'd been looking for couldn't all be told in a rational voice. They weren't always obvious, clear, defined, or verifiable. Instead, they are partial, hints and whispers, flutters of memory, history, and story that live in the silent spaces between the cracks.

What could the *ograi krara* teach me? Perhaps there were secrets that only the spirits were meant to know.

EPILOGUE

<hr/>

Signal Hill, St. John's, April 2017

⌒ THE WIND LASHED OUT, chewing at our faces. Through
squinted eyes, we could see the outline of an iceberg but nothing
more. I pointed my camera into the void and hoped for the best.
It's hard to photograph snow. Later, I fiddled with shadow settings
until I captured it, rising ghostlike from the ice. The photos were
stark and eerie.

It had been a wild start to spring. March had gone out like a
lion, roaring all the way, with high winds and storm surges bringing arctic ice to our shores. The coves were all blocked in, chunks of
ice reaching far into the distance. Underneath, the ocean was still
alive, and we could see the ice carpet breathing and sighing, rising
and falling, undulating.

We weren't the only ones out that morning; there were several
of us braving wind and sleet, crawling out of our houses after a day
of heavy rain to shake out our bones. The wind was still cold. The
sleet was painful. But if we didn't get out then, we might never get
out at all. There was a blizzard in the forecast, with another on its

heels. Thirty to fifty centimetres of snow, the weather reporter said with enthusiasm, and more to come.

Spring hadn't yet made its arrival. It was hiding out. Waiting. The bluster had to get out of winter first. Wait for Sheilagh's Brush, they said, referencing the annual storm that's supposed to mark the end of the snow season. Nothing was certain until after St. Patrick's Day. We thought we'd got away with it this year; surely the late March windstorm that had torn the shingles off our roof was the big one? We were wrong. But then, we're so often wrong about the weather. The weather had plans for us; it just hadn't shared them.

All around St. John's, folks were getting squirrelly. For weeks, Vancouverites had been parading photos of cherry blossoms across social media. My sister, on Vancouver Island, had gone to the garden centre before the end of March. It was warm and sunny in Toronto. Even in rainy Europe, spring had sprung. I consoled myself with the reminder that spring brought allergies, but it didn't help.

A trio of young people walked past us, their shoulders hunched, their faces inscrutable behind hoods tied so tightly that only the glint of their eyes was visible, their hands jammed into jeans pockets.

The wind tore at our hair, our ears, and our faces, its icy fingers pulling us forward. It was foggy, and we couldn't even see Cape Spear. Far below us, the ice left a leopard print in the harbour, with only a narrow line to show where ships had come and gone. This landscape was surreal, lunar almost, stark and barren.

"Tóbin would love this," I said to my husband, thinking about our younger son, a sensualist who always pauses to look at raindrops on spiderwebs.

"He'd complain about the cold."

Yes, he would have. But the ice would have fascinated him. All the shapes. The swelling and surging. The water below burbling up and over, lifting the large pans of it. These waters were alive and powerful.

"History," writes the Zimbabwean-born writer Panashe Chigumadzi, "is like water—it lives between us, and comes to us in waves. At times, still and unobtrusive, and, at other times turbulent and threatening. Even at its most innocuous, water poses hidden dangers, enclosing contested histories, and so we are always living in the tension between water's tranquillity and its tumult."

I have learned, over my years in St. John's, to listen to the ocean. The foghorn lulls me to sleep at night. Crashing waves accompany my thoughts. The rhythms of the sea have imprinted themselves on my psyche. But I am not a creature of water. I watch the ocean from the shore. I have not made my life in the ocean, just near it. And yet, like the lonely icebergs that follow currents west from the glaciers of Greenland to the waters of northern Canada before gliding along the coasts of Labrador and past Newfoundland's many bays every spring, my body and my history, too, are carried by the currents. I listen for the songs of my ancestors in the rolling rhythm of the North Atlantic surf, in the tinkling harmonies of beach stones tumbling along the shore. In this endless flux and flow of oceanic memories and migrations, my family persists, the DNA of a thousand voices united across time.

Something's happened in the eleven years since we arrived on this rocky island. We're still not from here, but we're not quite from away anymore either.

"Imagine," Oma said, way back in December 1992, looking with pride and wonder at the gaggle of cousins laughing and carrying on in my aunt Sheila's living room as we gathered to celebrate my aunt's birthday, "you're all from the same family."

And as if none of us had ever thought about this before, we all paused and looked around. Oma was right. There we were, my cousins and I, looking for all the world as if we'd tumbled out of a box of Crayola multicultural markers. Sienna. Mahogany. Tan. Golden beige. Terra cotta. Beige. Tawny. Bronze.

Imagine, I think, as I recall that family Christmas over twenty-five years ago. *This is my family.* There is awe. There is fear. There is confusion. There is regret. There is hope. There is resistance. There is desire. There is wonder. And all of this is mixed up inside.

~~~~~

I have stood on the shores of the Atlantic, looking out from the rocky cliffs of Newfoundland, the sandy beaches of Vlissingen and Middelburg, and the mud flats of Suriname. I have buried myself in archives in St. John's, The Hague, and Paramaribo, following threads through the records of slaving ships, emigrant vessels, immigration records, newspapers articles, slave registers, cemeteries, musical scores, and photographs. I've wandered through family lore, and through my own memories. And I have communed with the spirits.

I used to think that I came from a family without origins. But perhaps I've been looking at it the wrong way. It's not that I have *no* origins but that I am the inheritor of a story with multiple origins. There is no logical starting point; I have no single home to return to. Rather, the threads of my pasts span the globe, reaching across history and geography, through languages and skins and music and memories, in an intricate counterpoint of melody, rhythm, harmony—and even silence. I thought that the challenge would be to untangle them. But I was wrong. Instead, it's been to find beauty and wonder in the complex patterns that have resulted.

Where are you from?

There is no simple answer to that question, and perhaps it was naïve of me to believe there would be. Maybe origins are a mirage. Maybe belonging is a fiction, something each of us creates for ourselves. And maybe, then, home is the journey itself.

Acknowledgements

FROM CONCEPTION THROUGH TO COMPLETION, *What the Oceans Remember* would not have been possible without the contributions of many, many individuals.

To Natalie Beausoleil, for valuing the artistic, the tactile, the creative, the colourful, and the beautiful. Thank you for introducing me to the work of Gloria Wekker way back on that stormy Valentine's Day in 2008, and for all the conversations we've shared in the intervening years. To Carol Lynne D'Arcangelis, for your enthusiasm for this project, before I'd even fully conceptualized it, and for your sometimes uncomfortable but always important questions and observations about colonialism, empire, and the complexities of belonging. To Jelma van Amersfoort for our more than two decades of music and conversations and friendship (and for the occasional Dutch language query). To my lunching ladies: Amanda Bittner, Marica Cassis, and Jennifer Selby. Where would I be without the three of you? Our journeys have become so interwoven over many years of laughing, raging, listening, working, and ranting together. Thank you for creating the necessary conditions of generosity, kindness, and love. To my colleagues: Jocelyn Thorpe, Nancy Earle, Vicki Hallett, Jennifer Dyer, Rob Finley, Neil Kennedy, Elizabeth Yeoman, Fiona Polack, Rita Manchanda, Sam McLean, and Joan Butler, and to my current and former graduate students, in particular, Lesley Butler, Deirdre Connolly, Daze Jefferies, and Gina Snooks, for all the conversations about autoethnography, slavery, indenture, critical race theory, embodiment, memory, colonialism, feminist post-humanisms, life writing, arts-based research, writing, and more. Thank you.

To the archivists and staff at the National Archives of Suriname, the National Archives of the Netherlands, the National Archives of the United Kingdom, the Zeeuws Archief, and the Maritime History Archive at Memorial University, thank you for your friendly welcome, your helpfulness, and your endless patience as I inevitably ordered more than I could possibly read. My deepest thanks for caring for these documents so that they will be available for years to come.

To Will Pooley, Helen Rogers, and Alison Twells, thank you for coordinating the #storypast Twitter reading group, and for sharing your research and writing experiments through blogging. Special thanks to Will for organizing the fantastic Creative Histories conference in Bristol in 2017. What an absolute delight it was to think through creative ways of writing history (together with the flamingoes at the zoo!); I have so valued this community of creative thinkers, researchers, and writers.

To the Creative Writing Program, School of Continuing Studies, at the University of Toronto, and in particular to my instructors—Michelle Berry, Christy Ann Conlin, Christine Fischer Guy, Allyson Latta, and Ken McGoogan—and to the program director, Lee Gowan: thank you for your thoughtful critiques and observations, and also, for your encouragement. I have loved learning with and from you.

More specific thanks to Allyson Latta, mentor and editor, who very patiently took a somewhat tentative creative writer and nudged her through short essays and into the longer and even more exacting work of a book-length memoir: thank you for teaching me not only about writing and storytelling, but also about my own resistances, and thank you for continually encouraging me to let go of the security of an entirely intellectual lens for something more intimate and personal. This book would not have been what it is today without your critical eye.

To my online writing group, Michelle Contant, Jane Drake, Pam Dillon, and Sandy Lue, only one of whom I've ever met in person: I've learned so much from each of you. My thanks to Michelle for showing me the beauty of a simple sentence, Pam for teaching me what it means to write with vulnerability and intimacy, Jane for leading me into the magic of a child's perspective, and Sandy for telling stories in photos.

To Siobhan McMenemy, senior editor at Wilfrid Laurier University Press: thank you for your enthusiasm and wholehearted commitment to this project before it was even completed, and for your always patient responses to my endless questions. My thanks, too, to Rob Kohlmeier, managing editor; Clare Hitchens, sales and marketing coordinator; Marian Toledo Candelaria, marketing assistant; Marcia Gallego, copy editor; and Lime Design for all of your work with this manuscript. Finally, to the two anonymous reviewers of this manuscript whose enthusiastic embrace of this book buoyed me, and whose suggestions clarified and strengthened the final product: my deepest thanks for believing in this work.

To all my Heinemann relatives in Suriname and the Netherlands: Tante Hanny and Oom Deryck, Tante Sheila and Oom Sonny, Tante Liska and Oom Ber, Tante Hilda, and Tante Riet and Oom Gott. Thank you for always welcoming me into your homes, for long evenings of conversation, for museum visits, for questions and queries, for *koek*, *vla*, and *kaas*, and for your continued and completely unconditional support for all my creative and scholarly endeavours. My deepest thanks to my cousin Elvira for first inviting me to join the collaborative family tree project. And, of course, to my parents, who encouraged me to read, bought me my first flute, and taught me to question further.

To Búi, Stefan, and Tóbin: as always, you are more present in this text (and indeed in all my thinking and feeling) than you will ever know. Thank you for all that you are and for being there, always and unconditionally.

This book is one outcome from a larger research project supported by an Insight Development Grant from the Social Sciences and Humanities Research Council of Canada, and I am grateful to SSHRC for its support. I have shared insights from this research at a range of venues in both Canada and abroad, including Talking Bodies (University of Chester, 2015, 2017), Imagining the Guyanas (London, 2016), Women's and Gender Studies et Recherches Féministes (Calgary, 2016), Creative Histories (Bristol, 2017), Silenced Voices Speak (St. John's, 2018), Locating Nations/Locating Citizens (Toronto, 2015), Gender and Performance Symposium (St. John's, 2016), Canadian Historical Assocation (Calgary, 2016), National Women's Studies Association (Montreal, 2016), and the International Auto/Biography Association (Banff, 2014).

A short excerpt in Chapter 1 was published in an earlier form in *Autoethnography and Feminist Theory at the Water's Edge: Unsettled Islands*, a collaborative book I co-authored with Lesley Butler and Daze Jefferies (Palgrave, 2018). That excerpt has since been rearranged and restructured. A short excerpt in Chapter 14 was first published in "Creative Histories: Vulnerability, Emotions, and the Undoing of the Self," a blog post I wrote for *Storying the Past* (https://storyingthepast.wordpress.com/2017/10/06/creative-histories-vulnerability-emotions-and-the-undoing-of-the-self-by-sonja-boon/) in October 2017. An excerpt from Chapter 14 also appears in my book chapter "Telling Stories with Gold," forthcoming in *Imagining the Guyanas*, edited by Lawrence Aje, Thomas Lacroix, and Judith Misrahi-Barak (PoCoPages: Horizons Anglophones, Presses universitaires de la Méditerranée). "Telling Stories with Gold" considers the theoretical and historical relevance of gold to family histories of migration, looking in particular at colonial intimacies; here, I use a short excerpt from that chapter to contextually locate my journey back to Suriname.

Finally, I owe my greatest debt of gratitude to my ancestors, without whom this story could never have been told. This one is for you.

Notes

DURING THE SEVENTEENTH and eighteenth centuries, the Dutch established a vast trade network that spanned the globe, from Japan to the Americas (den Heijer 2003; Goslinga 1985; Huigen, Kolfin, and de Jong 2010; Postma 1990). Already by the mid-seventeenth century, the Vereenigde Oostindische Compagnie (VOC)—the Dutch East India Company—had set up trading posts from Japan and Indonesia to the Cape of Good Hope. The Geoctroyeerde Westindische Compagnie (WIC)—the Dutch West India Company—meanwhile, established in 1621, transported thousands of enslaved Africans to the Americas. Both the VOC and the WIC had an official administrative presence in Middelburg, material evidence of which is still present in the city's architecture. Many seventeenth-century storehouses have now been transformed into houses and apartments.

The Middelburgsche Commercie Compagnie (MCC), established in 1720, was a regional upstart. Organized by Middelburg merchants to challenge the WIC's trade monopoly, it moved directly into the slave trade once free trade was established. The province of Zeeland then took the leading role in the Atlantic slave trade, transporting fully 77 percent of enslaved Africans between 1730 and 1802 (Postma 2003, 132). The MCC was the largest of several Zeeland-based operations. According to recent economic research, economic spinoffs from the slave trade accounted for 10 percent of Middelburg's local economy, and almost 35 percent of that of neighbouring Vlissingen (de Kok 2016). The archives of the MCC, housed in the Zeeuws Archief in Middelburg, offer invaluable insight into the inner workings of the slave trade during the eighteenth century.

I. TUMBLING STONES

MY JOURNEY into Newfoundland identity and history began in February 2008, when I picked up Linda Cullum, Carmelita McGrath, and Marilyn Porter's edited collection, *Weather's Edge: Women in Newfoundland and Labrador* (Killick Press, 2006) at the St. John's airport before flying back to Vancouver after my interview. Since then, I have read much more, including Sean Cadigan's *Newfoundland and Labrador: A History* (University of Toronto Press, 2009); Pam Hall's *Towards an Encyclopedia of Local Knowledge: Excerpts from Chapters I and II* (ISER Books, 2017); Susan M. Manning's 2018 essay, "Contrasting Colonisations: (Re)storying Newfoundland/Ktaqmkuk as Place" (*Settler Colonial Studies*); and Linda Cullum and Marilyn Porter's edited collection, *Creating This Place: Women, Family, and Class in St. John's, 1900–1950* (McGill-Queen's University Press, 2014).

I was introduced to the work of Gloria Wekker during that same first visit to Newfoundland and have since drawn on it extensively, particularly in my teaching. Wekker's 2006 book, *The Politics of Passion: Women's Sexual Culture in the Afro-Surinamese Diaspora* (Columbia University Press), has been invaluable for thinking not only about the erotic politics of ethnography, but also about sexual cultures more broadly speaking. Her most recent book, *White Innocence: Paradoxes of Colonialism and Race* (Duke University

Press, 2016), which considers colonialism's deep embeddedness in contemporary Dutch society, challenges readers to consider the ongoing legacies of colonial violence in other national contexts—including Canada—as well.

Classical music—in the form of historically informed performance, an approach to musical performance that considers closely the context and conditions in which music was originally composed and performed—was my entrypoint into archival research. It was through searching for manuscripts of eighteenth-century flute sonatas by long-forgotten composers that I discovered the magic of working in the archives.

2. THE FACTS

FOR ALMOST AS LONG AS I CAN REMEMBER, I've been asked to explain my heritage, and over time, I've become a chameleon, moving between identities as these are ascribed to me. The complexities of mixed-race identity have been examined in a number of venues. My first "aha!" moment came when watching Anne Marie Nakagawa's 2005 film, *Between: Living in the Hyphen* (National Film Board), where I recognized my own experiences in the stories shared by the seven people Nakagawa interviewed. I've also taken much from Lawrence Hill's *Blood: The Stuff of Life* (Anansi, 2013) and *Black Berry, Sweet Juice: On Being Black and White in Canada* (HarperCollins, 2010), as well as from the work of Minelle Mahtani, including her book *Mixed Race Amnesia: Resisting the Romanticization of Multiraciality* (UBC Press, 2014); Kamal Al-Solaylee, *Brown: What Being Brown in the World Today Means (to Everyone)* (HarperCollins, 2016); and more recently, David Chariandy's short memoir, *What I've Been Meaning to Tell You* (Penguin Random House, 2018), and Chelene Knight's, *Dear Current Occupant* (BookThug, 2018).

My colleague's "No position is neutral" (p. 27) echoes ideas Dionne Brand explores in her 1998 poetry collection, *No Language Is Neutral* (McClelland & Stewart), and, indeed, in many of her literary works.

3. VAN GOGH'S NOSE

ONLINE ARCHIVES have profoundly changed the nature of research, making it possible for interested researchers to conduct much research from the comfort of their own homes. Particularly useful for this project have been the following: the Open Archives (openarch.nl), "a portal and aggregator of open historical data" that brings together data from Dutch and Belgian archives; Delpher (delpher.nl), a database of digitized books, magazines, and newspapers from the Netherlands and its former colonies, from the seventeenth to the twentieth century, produced by the Royal Library of the Netherlands; and the fantastic visual archives of the Rijksmuseum (https://www.rijksmuseum.nl/en/rijksstudio) and the Nationaal Museum van Wereldculturen (collectie.wereldculturen.nl). Vincent van Gogh's comments about *The Potato Eaters* (p. 30) come from a letter he wrote to his brother on 2 May 1895. The original letter can be found here: http://www.vangoghletters.org/vg/letters/let499/letter.html.

4. LA VIE EN ROSE

THE ITALICIZED ENTRIES in this chapter come from materials pertaining to the 1778 journey of the MCC ship the *Vigilantie*, in particular the journal and the collection of invoices for provisioning the ship, all held at the Zeeuws Archief in Middelburg, the Netherlands. While in 2014 I was able to access hard copies of the MCC's slaving voyages, this is no longer possible. Instead, in order to protect these UNESCO world heritage documents, all materials have been digitized. Those who are interested in examining the journal can find it here: https://proxy.archieven.nl/o/2FE4D 1772CBD476BA7DB0279988F3AA0. The Zeeuws Archief has also created a website that allows visitors to follow the journey of a single slave ship, *De Eenigheid*, which travelled the triangular route from Vlissingen to the African coast and then to the Americas before returning to the Netherlands, between 1761 and 1763. The English version of this journey can be followed here: https://eenigheid .slavenhandelmcc.nl/?lang=en.

The Middle Passage itself, that haunted, liminal space between continents, is the focus of a number of works, including Marcus Rediker's *The Slave Ship: A Human History* (Viking, 2007), Stephanie Smallwood's *Saltwater Slavery: A Middle Passage from African to American Diaspora* (Harvard University Press, 2007), and most recently, Sowande' M. Mustakeem's *Slavery at Sea: Terror, Sex, and Sickness in the Middle Passage* (University of Illinois Press, 2016).

The "books upon a shelf" quote (p. 49) comes from page 32 of the original edition of John Newton's *Thoughts upon the African Slave Trade* (Buckland and Johnson, 1788). A digitized copy of Newton's pamphlet can be found here: http://www.cowperand newtonmuseum.org.uk/wp-content/uploads/2012/01/thought suponafrioonewt.pdf. In a 2016 article, Gerhard de Kok estimates that, in the late eighteenth century, the economic impact of the trade in enslaved Africans was substantial in Middelburg and Vlissingen.

The history of slavery is long, messy, ugly, and complex, and so, too, are the realities of post-slavery societies. I have drawn on the work of a number of scholars and writers. I note in particular the following: Saidiya Hartman's article "Venus in Two Acts" (2008), as well as her memoir, *Lose Your Mother: A Journey along the Atlantic Slave Route* (Farrar, Straus & Giroux, 2007); Christina Sharpe's *In the Wake: On Blackness and Being* (Duke University Press, 2016);

and Katherine McKittrick's *Demonic Grounds: Black Women and the Cartographies of Struggle* (University of Minnesota Press, 2006). In the realm of the history of slavery in the Dutch Caribbean, I have learned much from the work of Leo Balai, Ruud Beeldsnijder, Natalie Zemon Davis, Pieter Emmer, Cornelis Goslinga, Okke ten Hove, Wim Hoogbergen, Humphrey Lamur, Kwame Nimako and Glenn Willemsen, Gert Oostindie, Johannes Postma, and Alex van Stipriaan. Cynthia McLeod's novels, *The Cost of Sugar* (Waterfront Press, 2010) and *The Free Negress Elisabeth* (Arcadia Press, 2008), have also been of interest, as has Ruud Mungroo's novella, *Tata Colin* (Drukkerij Eldorado, 1982).

Prior to being purchased by a group of Liverpool merchants in 1781, the *Zong* was part of the fleet of the Middelburgsche Commercie Compagnie, where, as the *Zorg*—or *Care*—it undertook three separate slaving voyages. During its first voyage, in 1777, it transported enslaved Africans to Suriname and another Dutch colony, Sint Eustatius. I first read about the *Zong* massacre in John Newton's pamphlet, but have also been strongly influenced by literary works in this area, namely Fred d'Aguiar's *Feeding the Ghosts* (Ecco Press, 1999) and M. NourbeSe Philip's *Zong!* (Wesleyan University Press, 2008). A story that I did not include, but which is also important to the history of slavery in Suriname, is the loss of the *Leusden*, another massacre that saw the murder of 664 enslaved Africans at the mouth of the Suriname River in 1738. This is captured in Leo Balai's *Het slavenschip* Leusden: *Slavenschepen en de West-Indische Compagnie, 1720–1738* (Walburg Pers, 2011).

Finally, I cannot underestimate the conceptual importance of Dionne Brand's *A Map to the Door of No Return: Notes on Belonging* (Vintage Canada, 2001) and M. NourbeSe Philip's poetry collection *She Tries Her Tongue: Her Silence Softly Breaks* (Ragweed Press, 1989).

5. OPA'S BOOKS

IT WAS THE WORK of historian Robert Darnton that first asked me to think about how it is that we write and think about the past. His book *The Great Cat Massacre and Other Episodes in French Cultural History*, first published in 1984 (reprinted 1999), was a revelation to me at the time, a fascinating look at what he calls "areas of opacity" (4). As he writes, "the most promising moment in research can be the most puzzling. When we run into something that seems unthinkable to us, we may have hit upon a valid point of entry into an alien point of view" (260).

In this chapter, I also rely on historical newspapers. In addition to being good sources for genealogical research, historical newspapers offer fascinating insights into how people lived. Of particular interest to me have been advertisements. For this book, I have relied most heavily on delpher.nl. I have also drawn on the National Library of Australia's Trove database (https://trove.nla.gov.au/?q=).

6. LINEAGE

THE ONLINE ARCHIVES of the National Archives of the Netherlands in The Hague were my first entry into Dutch histories of slavery and indenture. Easily accessible from home are materials relating to slavery and emancipation, manumission, and indenture. Interested researchers can search by name (enslaved, enslaver, indenturee), plantation, and ship, among others. However, I also worked with physical materials at the National Archives of the Netherlands. In this chapter I drew in particular on the documents for Sarah plantation as found in the records of the Algemene Rekenkamer, or, in English, the General Accounting Chamber.

The watercolour paintings of Sarah plantation (p. 86) are part of the online image collection of the Dutch National Museum of World Cultures (collectie.wereldculturen.nl) and can be found under the following titles: "Plantagehuis met oprijlaan en tuin" (1867), Inventarisnummer TM-3348-6, and "Het hospital op plantage Sarah," Inventarisnummer TM-H-3357. The work of architect Philip Dikland and KDV Architects has proven invaluable to learning the longer histories of Surinamese plantation ownership, and I drew extensively on Dikland's notes (2004, rev. 2010) about Sarah plantation. Some of the history of John Bent (pp. 86–87) comes from University College London's Legacies of British Slave-ownership database.

As the work of Julius S. Scott (2018) has shown, deep communication networks connected the enslaved not only across plantations, but also across the Caribbean and, indeed, across the Atlantic. Through these networks, the enslaved came to know about current news and events, and also about uprisings, resistance, and political debates about freedom. Kwame Nimako and Glenn Willemsen, writing in 2011, observe also that freedom meant different things to different people. "Slavery gave rise to parallel histories and intertwined belonging," they write. "These parallel histories and intertwined belonging in turn gave rise to different understandings and notions of freedom and emancipation. For the enslaver and the nations that enslaved others, freedom frequently implied the freedom to enslave others; for the enslaved, freedom frequently meant finding a place that they could call home without being hunted and dehumanized and humiliated" (186). Jean-Jacques Rousseau's words, quoted on page 94, are from the beginning of his 1762 book, *The Social Contract*. Jean-Paul Sartre's comments are in his 1943 book, *Being and Nothingness*.

Indigenous critical and creative work and activism have emphasized resilience, rebellion, refusal, and resurgence. I want to note here the scholarly and literary work of Leanne Betasamosake Simpson, including her two story and song collections, *Islands of Decolonial Love* (ARP, 2013) and *This Accident of Being Lost* (House of Anansi, 2017), as well as her recent book, *As We Have Always Done: Indigenous Freedom Through Radical Resistance* (University of Minnesota Press, 2017). I have also drawn much from the work of Eve Tuck, in particular her essays with C. Ree (2013) and K. Wayne Yang (2012, 2014a, 2014b). Billy Ray Belcourt's poetry collection, *This Wound Is a World* (Frontenac House, 2017), is revelatory.

7. DUE SOUTH

I CONSULTED numerous books and articles about the history of Suriname, among them Edward Dew, *The Difficult Flowering of Surinam: Ethnicity and Politics in a Plural Society* (Martinus Nijhoff, 1978) and *The Trouble in Suriname, 1975–1993* (Praeger, 1994); André Loor, *André Loor vertelt ... Suriname, 1850–1950* (VACO, 2013); and Hans Buddingh', *De geschiedenis van Suriname* (Nieuw Amsterdam/NRC Boeken, 2012). I also read John Gimlette's travel memoir, *Wild Coast: Travels on South America's Untamed Edge* (Alfred A. Knopf, 2011), and Andrew Westoll's *The Riverbones: Stumbling after Eden in the Jungles of Suriname* (McClelland & Stewart, 2008).

Anti-miscegenation laws were part of the American landscape for a long time, and the effects of such laws continue to echo today, even beyond American borders. Some relevant works include Lawrence Hill, *Black Berry, Sweet Juice: On Being Black and White in Canada* (HarperCollins, 2001); Minelle Mahtani, *Mixed Race Amnesia: Resisting the Romanticization of Multiraciality* (UBC Press, 2014); and Constance Backhouse, *Colour-Coded: A Legal History of Racism in Canada, 1900–1950* (University of Toronto Press, 1999). We might also consider longer tanglings with the artifices of racial categories. In *Carnal Knowledge and Imperial Power: Race in the Intimate in Colonial Rule* (University of California Press, 2010), for example, Ann Laura Stoler looks at how colonial authorities sought—and failed—to manage sexual intimacy in Indonesia. This became even more urgent as it became clear that the children resulting from such intimacies confounded, indeed wholly undermined, the boundaries the authorities sought so desperately to police. Other work that examines interracial colonial intimacies includes Adele Perry's *Colonial Relations: The Douglas-Connolly Family and the Nineteenth-Century Imperial World* (Cambridge University Press, 2015) and Cecilia Morgan's 2008 essay, "Creating Interracial Intimacies: British North America, Canada, and the Transatlantic World, 1830–1914."

On page 115, I draw on Dionne Brand's *A Map to the Door of No Return: Notes on Belonging* (Vintage Canada, 2001), pp. 7–8.

9. ROOSJE

THE STORIES of Frederika Rosette Dessé and Elisabeth Samson, among many others, reveal the profound contradictions at the heart of understandings of gender, race, and class in colonial outposts. Such complexities are also captured in Mattie Boom's 2014 book, *The First Photograph from Suriname: A Portrait of the Nineteenth-Century Elite in the West Indies* (Rijksmuseum, 2014), which explores the story behind the 1845 portrait of Johannes Ellis, the son of an enslaved Ghanaian woman and a powerful Dutchman, and Maria Louisa de Hart, the daughter of a manumitted slave and a Jewish man from Amsterdam. Such mixture was not uncommon. As Boom observes, "the mixing of cultures in Suriname was as old as the colony itself" (6).

I've drawn information about nineteenth-century Paramaribo social and cultural life from digitized copies of early newspapers, available at delpher.nl. Advertisements, in particular, offer fascinating—and sometimes uncomfortably revelatory—glimpses into the lives of the elite during this period. The quote on page 137 about "extra fine muslin" comes from the 3 March 1825 issue of the *Geprivilegeerde Surinaamsche Courant*; the quote about fortepianos (p. 138) comes from the 29 May 1821 issue of the *Surinaamsche Courant*. Also interesting were the novels of Cynthia McLeod, in particular, *The Free Negress Elisabeth* (Arcadia, 2008).

On page 142, I include a quote about Suriname as an artificial construction. This comes from page 249 of a book chapter by Maurits Hassankhan, Martha Ligeon, and Peer Scheepers.

The rehabilitation of the Nieuwe Oranjetuin cemetery began in the summer of 2016, just a few weeks after I returned to Canada following my second trip to Suriname. Photos from this project are available on the Surinamese Built Heritage Society's Facebook page (https://www.facebook.com/pg/Stichting-Gebouwd-Erfgoed -Suriname-SGES-330838463666204/photos/?ref=page_internal).

For musical scores, I have relied on materials collected in the Petrucci Music Library (imlsp.org), which includes a wide range of materials that are no longer under copyright.

10. SLAVENREGISTERS

FIRST-PERSON NARRATIVES OF SLAVERY, including Mary Prince's *History of Mary Prince* (University of Michigan Press, 1997), which I reference on pages 148–49, contributed to its eventual abolition. So, too, did fiction contribute to abolitionist struggles. Harriet Beecher Stowe's *Uncle Tom's Cabin* (1852), a book my mother gave me as a child but which I didn't read until I was well into adulthood, was particularly influential to Dutch abolitionist efforts. However, as Kwame Nimako and Glenn Willemsen (2011) have observed, the Dutch did not have a strong abolitionist movement. Contemporary writers have also been interested in revisiting slave narratives. The most famous of these, Lawrence Hill's *The Book of Negroes* (HarperCollins, 2007), follows the story of the fictional Aminata Diallo. Also important in this regard is Afua Cooper's *The Hanging of Angélique: The Untold Story of Canadian Slavery and the*

Burning of Old Montreal (Harper Perennial, 2006), which follows the trial of Marie-Joseph Angélique, an enslaved woman charged, tortured, convicted, and killed for allegedly setting fire to Montreal.

Questions of reparations have been at the forefront of much contemporary scholarship and political debate. The quote from Guy Emerson Mount (p. 151) comes from a recent essay by John W. Miller, "My Ancestor Owned 41 Slaves: What Do I Owe Their Descendants?" (*America Magazine*, 2018). These questions are echoed in scholarly literature. Saidiya Hartman's comments about reparations (p. 151) can be found on page 4 of her essay "Venus in Two Acts" (*Small Axe*, 2008). I would also point interested readers to Ana Lucia Araujo's *Reparations for Slavery and the Slave Trade: A Transnational and Comparative History* (Bloomsbury, 2017).

Reproduction has always been a matter of politics, reproduction under enslavement, even more so. The reproductive lives and experiences of enslaved women, which I reference on pages 111 and 161, have been the subject of numerous studies in recent years. In the decades preceding the abolition of the slave trade, enslavers implemented a range of polices to ensure the ongoing economic viability of their plantations. Such policies included revised approaches to the corporal punishment of enslaved pregnant women, reduced workloads, improved maternity and delivery care, increased—and healthier—food rations, and even rewards such as money, textiles, and medals (Emmer and van den Boogaart 1998, Morgan 2004, Paton 2017, Turner 2011). As Jennifer L. Morgan has observed, "reproduction became part of [an] owner's mathematics" (115).

In a quantitative study of family size on Surinamese plantations published in 2009, the Dutch historian Alex van Stipriaan notes that, on average, mothers enslaved on Surinamese plantations had four children each. However, fully one-quarter of all enslaved women did not have children at all. The research of Sasha Turner and Jennifer L. Morgan suggests that for some enslaved women, fertility control was an active form of resistance to the realities of chattel slavery; it is possible that enslaved women who did not have children were not necessarily unable to have children, but actively choosing not to, either by avoiding sexual relations or, more likely, by using commonly known abortifacients such as the peacock flower (Schiebinger 2007). It is possible, then, that some women were childless by choice. Other enslaved women, however, appear to have been able to "bargain" with their wombs, using their reproductive capacities in conjunction with pronatalist plantation policies to better their own situations. But, as Diana Paton (2017) has observed, pronatalist policies ricocheted through communities in complex ways; while they may have made life easier for enslaved women who had children, they made life much more challenging for those who did not. I can never know how any of this played itself out in the minds and hearts of my ancestors. What I do know is this: in a time when the average number of children born to enslaved women was four, my ancestors—Eva and Frederika—each had six and seven. Of those thirteen children, two—Frederika's first child, Annette, and Eva's fourth child, a son named Marlon 2—were manumitted. There were not many manumissions at Sarah plantation; two in the same family thus stand out.

The Surinamese slave registers give extensive detail on purchases, sales, and manumissions. In this chapter, I draw on the slave registers in the National Archives of Suriname in Paramaribo, and in particular on the records for Sarah plantation. In the slave registers, one can also trace the activities of Jan Houthakker, which I reference on pages 156–57. His story is also captured in the Dutch website slavernijenjij.nl.

The fictionalized, imagined negotiations in this chapter (pp. 152–55) were developed through the log books and account books I consulted at the Zeeuws Archief in Middelburg, the Netherlands, in particular the account books for the *Welmeenende*'s first voyage in 1769–70 and the *Vigilantie*'s 1778–79 voyage.

The quote from John Newton (p. 156) can be found on pages 38 and 39 of *Thoughts upon the African Slave Trade* (italics in original). The extended quote about the contradictions of plantation life for the enslaved (p. 164) comes from page 109 of Gert Oostindie's book chapter "Slavenleven" (1993; translation mine).

I reference the work of St. John's–based visual artist Pam Hall on pages 164–66. Hall's *Building a Village* collaborative art project took place in 2013 and was exhibited at The Rooms, Newfoundland and Labrador's provincial art gallery, in 2014. More information about the project can be found in the exhibition guide, *Pam Hall: Housework(s)* (Eagan et al. 2014) and in an accompanying video, available on Vimeo: https://vimeo.com/95736487.

II. BROKO PRANASI

THE QUOTE, on page 175 of this chapter, about the relationship between John Bent and Mackillop, Dent, and Young comes from the National Archives of Suriname, Slavenregister Inv. nr. 42, Folio 5064. Information about Hugh Wright's purchase of Bent's Hope (p. 184) comes from page 130 of volume IX, third series of the British and Foreign Anti-Slavery Society's *Anti-Slavery Reporter* (1 June 1861). The nostalgic commentaries about Suriname's fabled past (pp. 176–77) come from two separate sources. The first is an anonymous article, "Matappica en Warappa," published in *De West: Nieuwsblad uit Suriname* on 24 December 1909. The second is from page 29 of *Hoe de tijden veranderen: Herinneringen van een oude planter*—or, in English, *How Times Change: Memories of a Former Planter*—a memoir by E.J. Bartelink published in 1916. The translation is mine. I aso consulted a number of Surinamese *Almanacs*, which were published annually during the nineteenth century.

Brian Dillon's *Ruins* (Whitechapel Gallery; MIT Press, 2011) gave me much to consider. As he observes, ruination "points toward the future ... or rather uses the ruined resources of the past to imagine, or reimagine, the future.... According to this way of thinking and working, the ruin is a site not of melancholy or mourning but of radical potential—its fragmentary unfinished nature is an invitation to fulfill the as yet unexplored temporality that it contains. Ruins ... are freighted with possibility, even with utopian promise" (18).

12. JOORAYEE

THE HISTORY OF INDENTURE has been well researched. Relevant classic works include Hugh Tinker's *A New System of Slavery: The Export of Indian Labour Overseas, 1830–1920* (Oxford University Press, 1974) and K.O. Laurence's *A Question of Labour: Indentured Immigration into Trinidad and British Guiana, 1875–1917* (Ian Randle Publishers, 1994). More recent literature includes *Coolie Woman: The Odyssey of Indenture* (University of Chicago Press, 2014), in which Gaiutra Bahadur traces her great-grandmother's journey from India to Guyana as one of thousands of "coolie" labourers, as well as Suriname-specific literature, including Margriet Fokken's *Beyond Being* Koelies *and* Kantráki*: Constructing Hindostani Identities in Suriname in the Era of Indenture, 1873–1921* (Verloren, 2018), Mousumi Majumder's *Kahe Gaile Bides, Why Did You Go Overseas?* (Mango Press, 2010), several books by Radjinder Bhagwanbali, and the work of Rosemarijn Hoefte, including the book *In Place of Slavery: A Social History of British Indian and Javanese Labourers in Suriname* (University of Florida Press, 1998). Beyond oral histories gathered many years after the fact, first-person memoirs of the indenture journey are rare. In this chapter, I reference a memoir written by Munshi Rahman Khan, a man who arrived in Suriname in 1798 (Prakash, Sinha-Kerkhoff, Bal, and Singh 2006).

The quotes outlining a new Surinamese immigration scheme, as planned by the Surinamese Immigration Society (pp. 196–98), come from the records of the Nederlands Handel-Maatschappij held in the National Archives of the Netherlands (Nederlands Handel-Maatschappij, 1824–1964, Catalogue number 2.20.01, inventory number 12887; translation mine). The quote from the *Report on the Colonial Emigration from the Bengal Presidency* (p. 208) is found in "The Great Escape," an unpublished paper by Pieter Emmer. The story of Matai Chatarpali, which I include on page 209 of this chapter, is from the Scheepslijst Avon, held at the National Archives of Suriname (Agent Generaal Immigratie Departement 1853–1946, inventory number 1181, and also accessible through the online collections of the National Archives of the Netherlands in The Hague; translation mine). Gender-based violence was a reality of colonial plantation life. Bhagwanbali, Laurence, and Look Lai all detail the extensive gender-based violence to which indentured women were subjected; Look Lai indicates that special legislation was brought in to respond to this. Emmer's notion of a "colonial escape hatch" (p. 211) comes from the unpublished paper referenced above.

Between 1873 and 1916, over 34,000 British Indians came to Suriname as indentured labourers. While some returned to India, many stayed, and today, the Hindustani community forms over 25 percent of the Surinamese population. There are numerous inconsistencies in the immigration records; these may be the result of poor record keeping by those who originally entered the data into the logs or of communication problems between colonial officials and indentured labourers. They may also result from the challenges associated with contemporary transcription of these records. Of the 34,000 indentured labourers, only two—Joorayee Radha and her son, Sahatoo—appear to have come from the village of Aburpore. This seems highly unlikely and suggests that an error was made at some point. In addition to this, the city of

Faizabad appears in various forms, including Tyzabad and, more commonly, Fyzabad.

The quote by Lauret Edith Savoy (p. 204) comes from page 108 of her book *Trace: Memory, History, Race, and the American Landscape* (Counterpoint, 2015).

The publication, over the past number of years, of a number of fictional works that look at the intergenerational legacies of indenture suggests that others, too, are grappling with what it might mean to be a descendant of indentured labourers. I note here Peggy Mohan's *Jahajin* (HarperCollins India, 2008), Lainy Malkani's *Sugar Sugar: Bitter Sweet Tales of Indian Migrant Workers* (Hope Road, 2017), and Safdar Zaidi's *De suiker die niet zoet was* (Uitgeverij U2pi, 2005).

A note on language: in Dutch, the common term for indentured labourers from British India, most of whom came from the northern provinces, and/or for their descendants, is *Hindoestaans*, or in English, Hindustani. This is the term that I have chosen to use in this book. When indenture agreements were negotiated, India was under British colonial rule. Therefore, I identify India as British India.

13. OCEANS

AS SOMEONE WHO GREW UP in a landlocked province, I didn't spend much time thinking about oceans. Indeed, it is only since my move to the island of Newfoundland—and to island thinking—that I have begun to engage with what Cecilia Chen, Janine MacLeod, and Astrida Neimanis term "thinking with water" (2013). Thinking with water has been remarkably generative, in part because it allows a move beyond fixity, borders, and boundaries. This, in turn, enables a much richer theorization of mixture. As Renisa Mawani has observed of oceans, "[c]urrents do not have a readily identifiable beginning, a fixed or static center, or a clear end. Animated by multiple movements and countermovements, they join distant coordinates, in both space and time. Through their lively physical properties, currents speak compellingly to the limitations of other transnational and imperial frames, including webs. Currents exist in several registers at once. They follow multiple trajectories, exhibit changing dimensions, and thus offer alternative metaphors and additional ways to chart the discrepant mobilities of colonial and imperial worlds" (2018, 21). Mawani's *Across Oceans of Law: The* Komagata Maru *and Jurisdiction in the Time of Empire* (Duke University Press, 2018), Elspeth Probyn's *Eating the Ocean* (Duke University Press, 2016), Karin Amimoto Ingersoll's *Waves of Knowing* (Duke University Press, 2016), and a range of works by Astrida Neimanis (among them *Bodies of Water: Posthuman Feminist Phenomenology* and *Thinking with Water*, co-authored with Cecilia Chen and Janine MacLeod) have been particularly influential to my thinking through colonial migrations, intimacies, and belongings. They also offered me ways into thinking about "the oceanic" more broadly speaking. The quote about water and the imagination (p. 222), comes from page 6 of Dionne Brand's *A Map to the Door of No Return: Notes to Belonging* (Vintage Canada, 2001).

The more I learned more about the *Kate Kellock*, the more I found myself wanting to know about Charles Kellock as a person. The description of Charles Kellock's country manor (p. 218) comes from page 46 of *Kelly's Directory of Cheshire* (Kelly's Directories, Ltd., 1902). The quote about the wreck of the *Kate Kellock* (p. 235) comes from the "Wreck Report for the 'Kate Kellock' 1878," p. 4. This document is held online at the Southampton Archives in the United Kingdom (https://plimsoll.southampton.gov.uk/SOTON_Documents/Plimsoll/14314.pdf).

I have drawn on a range of materials held at the Maritime History Archive, Memorial University, including the C.W. Kellock Collection, the crew agreements and ships' logs for the *Kate Kellock*'s 1865–66, 1867–69, 1872–73, 1875–76, and 1877 journeys, and the *Lalla Rookh*'s various journeys. My great-great-grandmother Joorayee Radha arrived in Suriname aboard the *Kate Kellock* on its 1873–74 journey. These records are held in the National Archives of the United Kingdom.

The foiled mutiny aboard the *Kate Kellock* in December 1873 (pp. 229–32) is discussed in a range of sources. These include the log books for the *Kate Kellock*'s 1873–74 journey (National Archives, UK); Edmund Fremantle's memoir, *The Navy as I Have Known It, 1848–1899* (Cassell & Co., 1904); an account included in a doctoral thesis by Anil Persaud; and a brief mention in the work of Radjinder Bhagwanbali. Bevan's commentary (pp. 229–30) comes from the log books of the journey; Fremantle's comments (pp. 231, 232) can be found on page 241 of his memoir. A note about spelling: Dr. Bepin Behary Dutt's name appears in a few different spellings across the archival and scholarly materials. I have chosen to use the version that seems to be the most common.

It is worth considering this foiled mutiny in light of Renisa Mawani's work on the 1914 passage of the *Komagata Maru* from Hong Kong to Vancouver. Mawani observes that "the transoceanic passage was a perilous transition zone where Indian passengers were transformed from 'migrants' to 'revolutionaries' that escaped law's reach" (2018, 23). Race, class, gender—and the perceived lawlessness of a vast ocean—all played a role in this transformation, and it is likely that a similar combination of elements was at play in relation to the *Kate Kellock*'s 1873–74 journey.

Early photographs of the Paramaribo immigration depot, which I reference on page 235 of this chapter, can be found in the online collections of the Rijksmuseum (https://www.rijksmuseum.nl/en/rijksstudio).

I have relied almost wholly on newspaper advertisements and notices to construct what I know of the U-A-Sai branch of the family; in addition to this, I have drawn on a sixteen-page typewritten oral history penned by a family member.

14. UNFOLDINGS

MY CONSIDERATION OF GAWKERY is premised on critical and creative literature on the social construction of the "freak," much of which has come from critical disability studies. Of particular relevance here is the work of Rosemarie Garland Thomson, notably *Freakery: Cultural Spectacles of the Extraordinary Body* (NYU Press, 1996) and *Staring: How We Look* (Oxford University Press, 2009). Also vital are Eli Clare's rich autoethnographic works, *Exile and Pride: Disability, Queerness, and Liberation* (Duke University Press, 2015) and *Brilliant Imperfection: Grappling with Cure* (Duke University Press, 2017). Lezlie Frye's essay "Fingered" (2012) offers a brilliant take on redirecting an otherwise hostile gaze.

There have been several books written about Sara Baartman. I will cite here just one: Clifton Crais and Pamela Scully's *Sara Baartman and the Hottentot Venus: A Ghost Story and a Biography* (Princeton University Press, 2010). There are also two relevant documentaries: *The Life and Times of Sara Baartman: "The Hottentot Venus"* (Maseko 1998) and *The Return of Sara Baartman* (Maseko and Smith 2003).

The story and quote about the International Colonial and Export Trade Exhibition (pp. 246–47) come from an essay that Stevo Akkerman wrote originally for the Dutch newspaper *Het Parool*, but which was reprinted in the Surinamese magazine *Parbode*, and a later article he wrote for the Surinamese genealogy magazine *Wi Rutu*.

Questions about the ethics of doing family history research have shadowed me throughout this project. The work of Eve Tuck and K. Wayne Yang has been invaluable to me in this regard. The quote in this chapter comes from pages 233–34 of their essay "R-Words: Refusing Research" (2014).

THE QUOTE by Panashe Chigumadzi (p. 261) comes from "The Story of Life in a Single Photograph" (2018).

Bibliography

Archival Materials

NATIONAL ARCHIVES OF SURINAME, PARAMARIBO, SURINAME

Slavenregisters, 1830–1852, Inventory numbers 24, 25, 28, 32, 33, 40–42.

Agent Generaal (Immigratie Departement), 1853–1946, Inventory numbers 66A & 66B, 616A+B, 618, 667–669, 1181–1191.

NATIONAL ARCHIVES OF THE NETHERLANDS, THE HAGUE, THE NETHERLANDS

Algemene Rekenkamer CB (Comptabel Beheer), Catalogue reference 2.02.09.08, Inventory numbers 224–228.

Nederlandsche Handel-Maatschappij (NHM), Catalogue reference 2.20.01, Inventory numbers 12887, 13209, 13214, 13222, 13234–36, 15543.

MARITIME HISTORY ARCHIVE, MEMORIAL UNIVERSITY OF NEWFOUNDLAND, ST. JOHN'S, CANADA

C.W. Kellock and Co. Collection MHA 00000237.

Board of Trade, KATE KELLOCK 51456, 1866, 1869, 1873, 1876, 1877.

Board of Trade, LALLA ROOKH 17794, 1867, 1868, 1869, 1871.

ZEEUWS ARCHIEF, MIDDELBURG, THE NETHERLANDS

Middelburgsche Commercie Compagnie, Catalogue number MCC 20.2, Inventory numbers 1125–1129 (Snauw de Vigilantie), 1405–1410 (Fregat Zee Mercuur), 1142 (Fregat Vis), 1302–1304 (Snauw Welmeenende), 1393 (Snauw Zang Godin).

NATIONAL ARCHIVES OF THE UNITED KINGDOM,
KEW, UNITED KINGDOM

Registry of Shipping and Seamen: Agreements and Crew Lists, Series II,
    BT 99/1016, 51456, Kate Kellock, 1874.

ONLINE ARCHIVES

Coret Genealogie. Open Archives, openarch.nl.

Koninklijk Bibliotheek et al. Delpher: Boeken, Kranten, Tijdschriften, delpher.nl.

National Archives of the Netherlands, Indexes, https://www.nationaalarchief.nl/
    onderzoeken/collectie.

    "Suriname: Contractarbeiders uit India (Hindostanen)"

    "Suriname en Nederlandse Antillen: Vrijverklaarde slaven (Emancipatie 1863)"

    "Suriname: Slavenregisters"

    "Suriname: Vrijgelaten slaven en hun eigenaren (manumissies)"

National Museum of World Cultures, the Netherlands. Online Collection
    Database. collectie.wereldculturen.nl.

National Library of Australia. Trove. https://trove.nla.gov.au/?q=.

Rijksmuseum. Rijksstudio. https://www.rijksmuseum.nl/en/rijksstudio.

Southhampton Archives, Maritime Digital Archive. https://www.southampton.
    gov.uk/arts-heritage/southampton-archives/plimsoll.aspx.

University College, London. Legacies of British Slave-ownership. https://www
    .ucl.ac.uk/lbs//.

Van Gogh Museum and Huygens ING. Vincent van Gogh: The Letters. http://
    vangoghletters.org/vg/.

Books and Articles

Akkerman, Stevo. "Een woeste en onwillige bende: de geschiedenis achter de Koloniale Tentoonstelling 1883 te Amsterdam." *Wi Rutu* 10, no. 1 (2010): 7–13.

Akkerman, Stevo. "Op den laagste trap van ontwikkeling." *Parbode*, 15 May 2009.

Al-Solaylee, Kamal. *Brown: What Being Brown in the World Today Means (to Everyone).* Toronto: HarperCollins, 2016.

Ankum-Houwink, J.C. "Chinese kontraktarbeiders in Suriname in de 19e eeuw." *OSO: Tijdschrift voor Surinamistiek* 5, no. 2 (1985): 181–86.

Araujo, Ana Lucia. *Reparations for Slavery and the Slave Trade: A Transnational and Comparative History.* London: Bloomsbury, 2017.

Backhouse, Constance. *Colour-Coded: A Legal History of Racism in Canada, 1900–1950.* Toronto: University of Toronto Press, 1999.

Bahadur, Gaiutra. *Coolie Woman: The Odyssey of Indenture.* Chicago: University of Chicago Press, 2014.

Bal, Ellen, and Kathinka Sinja-Kerkhoff. "Hindostaanse Surinamers en India: gedeeldverleden, gedeeldeidentiteit?" *OSO: Tijdschrift voor Surinamistiek* 22, no. 2 (2003): 214–34.

Balai, Leo. *Het slavenschip "Leusden": slavenschepen en de West Indische Compagnie, 1720–1738.* Zutphen, the Netherlands: Walburg Pers, 2011.

Balai, Leo. *Slavenschip Leusden: moord aan de monding van de Marowijnerivier.* Zutphen, the Netherlands: Walburg Pers, 2013.

Bartelink, E.J. *Hoe de tijden veranderen: Herinneringen van een oude planter.* Paramaribo, Suriname: H. van Ommeren, 1916.

Beeldsnijder, Ruud. "'Om werk van jullie te hebben': Plantageslaven in Suriname, 1730–1750." Doctoral thesis, Universiteit Utrecht, the Netherlands, 1994.

Belcourt, Billy Ray. *This Wound Is a World: Poems.* Calgary, AB: Frontenac House, 2017.

Bersselaar, Dimitri, and Henry Ketelaars. *De komst van contractarbeiders uit Azië: Hindoestanen et Javanen in Suriname.* Leiden, the Netherlands: Minderheden Studies, Rijksuniversiteit Leiden, 1991.

Bhagwanbali, Rajinder. "Contracten voor Suriname: Arbeidsmigratie vanuit Brits Indië onder het indentured-labour stelsel, 1873–1916." Doctoral thesis, Katholieke Universiteit Nijmegen, the Netherlands, 1996.

Bhagwanbali, Radjinder. *De nieuwe awatar van slavernij: Hindoestaanse migranten onder het indentured labour systeem naar Suriname, 1873–1916.* The Hague, the Netherlands: Amrit, 2010.

Bhagwanbali, Radjinder. *Tetary, de koppige: het verzet van Hindoestanen tegen het Indentured Labour System in Suriname, 1873–1916.* The Hague, the Netherlands: Amrit, 2011.

Bijnaar, Aspha, ed. *Kind aan de ketting: Opgroeien in Slavernij toen en nu.* Amsterdam, the Netherlands: KIT Publishers, 2009.

Bijnaar, Aspha. "Kinderlijke Ontschuld: Beelden van Slavernij in Suriname." In *Kind aan de ketting: Opgroeien in Slavernij toen en nu,* edited by Aspha Bijnaar, 36–49. Amsterdam, the Netherlands: KIT Publishers, 2009.

Boom, Mattie. *The First Photograph from Suriname: A Portrait of the Nineteenth-Century Elite in the West Indies.* Amsterdam, the Netherlands: Rijksmuseum, 2014.

Botman, Maayke. "Cultuuroverdracht in interetnische families 7. Eigen." In *Cultuur en migratie in Nederland: Veranderingen van het alledaagse 1950–2000,* edited by Isabel Hoving, Hester Dibbits, and Marlou Schrover, 197–223. The Hague, the Netherlands: Sdu Uitgevers, 2005.

Brand, Dionne. *A Map to the Door of No Return: Notes to Belonging.* Toronto: Vintage Canada, 2001.

Brand, Dionne. *No Language Is Neutral.* Toronto: McClelland & Stewart, 1998.

British and Foreign Anti-Slavery Society. *The Anti-Slavery Reporter,* Vol. IX, Third Series, 1861.

Brommer, Bea, ed. *Ik ben eigendom van … Slavenhandel en plantageleven.* Woudrichem, the Netherlands: Pictures Publishers, 1993.

Buddingh', Hans. *De geschiedenis van Suriname.* Amsterdam, the Netherlands: Nieuw Amsterdam; NRC Boeken, 2012.

Byrne, Allan. *A Beautiful Sight: Stories from the Port of St. John's.* St. John's, NL: Flanker Press, 2015.

Cadigan, Sean. *Newfoundland and Labrador: A History.* Toronto: University of Toronto Press, 2009.

Chariandy, David. *What I've Been Meaning to Tell You.* Toronto: Penguin Random House Canada, 2018.

Chen, Cecilia, Janine MacLeod, and Astrida Neimanis. *Thinking with Water.* Montreal, QC: McGill-Queen's University Press, 2013.

Chigumadzi, Panashe. "The Story of Life in a Single Photograph." *LitHub*, 30 July 2018. https://lithub.com/the-story-of-a-life-in-a-single-photograph/.

Clare, Eli. *Brilliant Imperfection: Grappling with Cure.* Durham, NC: Duke University Press, 2017.

Clare, Eli. *Exile and Pride: Disability, Queerness, and Liberation.* 3rd ed. Durham, NC: Duke University Press, 2015.

Cooper, Afua. *The Hanging of Angélique: The Untold Story of Canadian Slavery and the Burning of Old Montreal.* Toronto: Harper Perennial, 2006.

Crais, Clifton, and Pamela Scully. *Sara Baartman and the Hottentot Venus: A Ghost Story and a Biography.* Princeton, NJ: Princeton University Press, 2010.

Cullum, Linda K., Carmelita McGrath, and Marilyn Porter, eds. *Weather's Edge: A Compendium.* St. John's, NL: Killick Press, 2006.

Cullum, Linda, and Marilyn Porter, eds. *Creating This Place: Women, Family, and Class in St. John's, 1900–1950.* Montreal, QC, and Kingston, ON: McGill-Queen's University Press, 2014.

D'Aguiar, Fred. *Feeding the Ghosts.* New York: Ecco Press, 1999.

Darnton, Robert. *The Great Cat Massacre and Other Episodes in French Cultural History.* New York: Basic Books, 1999.

Davis, Natalie Zemon. "Judges, Masters, Diviners: Slaves' Experience of Criminal Justice in Colonial Suriname." *Law and History Review* 29, no. 4 (2011): 925–84.

Davis, Natalie Zemon. "Physicians, Healers, and Their Remedies in Colonial Suriname." *Canadian Bulletin of Medical History* 33, no. 1 (2016): 3–34.

Dentz, Fred. Outdschans. *Grafzerk en Suikerwerk: Namen op oude grafstenen in Suriname en Brits Guyana.* Rhenen, the Netherlands: Stichting voor Surinaamse Genealogie, 2006.

Dew, Edward. *The Difficult Flowering of Surinam: Ethnicity and Politics in a Plural Society.* The Hague, the Netherlands: Martinus Nijhoff, 1978.

Dew, Edward. *The Trouble in Suriname, 1975–1993.* Westport, CT: Praeger, 1994.

Dikland, Philip. "Katoenplantage Sarah aan de Coroniaanse kust." *Research.* KDV Architects, 11 August 2018. www.kdvarchitects.com/smartcms/defaultid43.html?contentID=629.

Dillon, Brian. *Ruins.* London and Cambridge, MA: Whitechapel Gallery; MIT Press, 2011.

Eagan, Mireile, Jennifer Dyer, Pam Hall, and Melinda Pinfold. *Pam Hall: Housework(s)*. St. John's, NL: The Rooms Corporation of Newfoundland and Labrador, 2014.

Emmer, Pieter C. "De werving van kontraktarbeiders in India voor tewerkstelling in Suriname, 1872–1916." *OSO: Tijdschrift voor Surinamistiek* 4, no. 2 (1985): 147–57.

Emmer, Pieter C. "Een goede keus? De migratie van vrouwelijke contractarbeiders van Brits-Indië naar Suriname, 1875–1916." *OSO: Tijdschrift voor Surinamistiek* 3, no. 2 (1984): 213–34.

Emmer, Pieter C. "The Great Escape: The Migration of Female Indentured Servants from British India to Suriname (Dutch Guiana), 1873–1916." Unpublished manuscript, undated. KIT-LV collection, University of Leiden Library. Accession number M1998B1552.

Emmer, Pieter C. "Was Migration Beneficial?" In *Migration, Migration History, History: Old Paradigms and New Perspectives*, edited by Jan Lucassen and Leo Lucassen, 111–30. New York: Peter Lang, 1999.

Emmer, Pieter C., and Ernst van den Boogaart. "Plantation Slavery in Suriname in the Last Decade before Emancipation: The Case of *Catharina Sophia*." In *The Dutch in the Atlantic Economy, 1580–1880: Trade, Slavery and Emancipation*, by Pieter Emmer, 203–26. Aldershot, UK: Ashgate, 1998.

Fokken, Margriet. *Beyond Being* Koelies *and* Kantráki*: Constructing Hindostani Identities in Suriname in the Era of Indenture, 1873–1921*. Hilversum, the Netherlands: Verloren, 2018.

Fremantle, Edmund. *The Navy as I Have Known It, 1849–1899*. London: Cassell & Co., 1904.

Frye, Lezlie. "Fingered." In *Sex and Disability*, edited by Robert McRuer and Anna Mollow, 256–62. Durham, NC: Duke University Press, 2012.

Garland Thomson, Rosemarie, ed. *Freakery: Cultural Spectacles of the Extraordinary Body*. New York: New York University Press, 1996.

Garland Thomson, Rosemarie. *Staring: How We Look*. New York: Oxford University Press, 2009.

Gimlette, John. *Wild Coast: Travels on South America's Untamed Edge*. New York: Alfred A. Knopf, 2011.

Gobardhan-Rambocus, Lila, and Maurits S. Hassankhan, eds. *Immigratie en ontwikkeling: Emancipatie van contractanten*. Paramaribo, Suriname: Anton de Kom University, 1993.

Gobardhan-Rambocus, Lila, Maurits S. Hassankhan, and Jerry L. Egger, eds. *De erfenis van de slavernij*. Paramaribo, Suriname: Anton de Kom University, 1995.

Golen, Cees Jan van. *Footsteps and Fingerprints: The Legacy of a Shared History*. Zwolle, the Netherlands: Waanders, 2010.

Goslinga, Cornelis Ch. *The Dutch in the Caribbean and in the Guianas, 1680–1791*. Assen/Maastricht, the Netherlands, and Dover, NH: Van Gorcum, 1985.

Gupta, Charu. "Writing Sex and Sexuality: Archives of Colonial North India." *Journal of Women's History* 23, no. 4 (2011): 12–35.

Hall, Pam. *Towards an Encyclopedia of Local Knowledge: Excerpts from Chapters I and II*. St. John's, NL: ISER, 2017.

Hartman, Saidiya. *Lose Your Mother: A Journey along the Atlantic Slave Route*. New York: Farrar, Straus & Giroux, 2007.

Hartman, Saidiya. "Venus in Two Acts." *Small Axe* 12, no. 2 (2008): 1–14.

Hassankhan, Maurits S. "De immigratie en haar gevolgen voor de Surinaamsche samenleving." In *Immigratie en ontwikkeling: Emancipatie van contractanten*, edited by Lila Gobardhan-Rambocus and Maurits S. Hassankhan, 11–35. Paramaribo, Suriname: Anton de Kom University, 1993.

Hassankhan, Maurits, Martha Ligeon, and Peer Scheepers. "Sociaal-Economische verschillen tussen Creolen, Hindoestanen en Javanen, 130 jaar na afschaffing van de slavernij." In *De erfenis van de slavernij*, edited by Lila Gobardhan-Rambocus, Maurits S. Hassankhan, and Jerry L. Egger, 249–74. Paramaribo, Suriname: Anton de Kom University, 1995.

Heijer, Henk den. "The Dutch West India Company, 1621–1791." In *Riches from Atlantic Commerce: Dutch Transatlantic Trade and Shipping, 1585–1817*, edited by Johannes Postma and Victor Enthoven, 77–112. Leiden, the Netherlands, and Boston, MA: Brill, 2003.

Hill, Lawrence. *Black Berry, Sweet Juice: On Being Black and White in Canada*. Toronto: HarperCollins, 2001.

Hill, Lawrence. *Blood: The Stuff of Life*. Toronto: House of Anansi, 2013.

Hill, Lawrence. *The Book of Negroes*. Toronto: HarperCollins, 2007.

Hoefte, Rosemarijn. "Control and Resistance: Indentured Labor in Suriname." *Nieuwe West-IndischeGids* 61, no. 1/2 (1987): 1–22.

Hoefte, Rosemarijn. "Mama Sranan's Children: Ethnicity and Nation Building in Postcolonial Suriname." *The Journal of Caribbean History* 48, no. 1/2 (2014): 128–48.

Hoefte, Rosemarijn. "A Passage to Suriname? The Migration of Modes of Resistance by Asian Contract Laborers." *International Labor and Working-Class History* 54 (1998): 19–39.

Hoefte, Rosemarijn. *In Place of Slavery: A Social History of British Indian and Javanese Laborers in Suriname*. Gainesville: University of Florida Press, 1998.

Hoefte, Rosemarijn, ed. *Suriname in the Long Twentieth Century: Domination, Contestation, Globalization*. New York: Palgrave Macmillan, 2014.

Hoefte, Rosemarijn, and Peter Meel, eds. *Twentieth-Century Suriname: Continuities and Discontinuities in a New World Society*. Kingston, Jamaica, and Amsterdam, the Netherlands: Ian Randle Publishers; KITLV, 2001.

Hoogbergen, Wim. *Out of Slavery: A Surinamese Roots History*. Münster, Germany: LIT Verlag, 2008.

Hove, Okke ten. "Surinaamseslavernij: Gescheiden verkoop van moeder en kind(eren)." *OSO: Tijdschrift voor Surinamistiek* 15, no. 1 (1996): 41–55.

Hove, Okke ten, and Wim Hoogbergen. "De opheffing van de slavernij in Suriname: Het Archief van de Algemene Rekenkamer in Nederland." *OSO: Tijdschrift voor Surinaamse taalkunde, letterkunde en geschiedenis* 19, no. 2 (2000): 278–87.

Huigen, Siegfried, Elmer Koffin, and Jan de Jong, eds. *Dutch Trading Companies as Knowledge Networks*. Leiden, the Netherlands: Brill, 2010.

Ingersoll, Karin Amimoto. *Waves of Knowing: A Seascape Epistemology*. Durham, NC: Duke University Press, 2016.

Kelly's Directories, Ltd. *Kelly's Directory of Cheshire*. London: Kelly's Directories, 1902.

Kempen, Michiel van. "De fondantlaag van de Romantiek: Vier teksten over slavernij in Suriname." *Spiegel der letteren* 44, no. 1 (2002): 63–83.

Klerk, C.J.M de. *De Immigratie der Hindostanen in Suriname*. Amsterdam, the Netherlands: Urbi et Orbi, 1953.

Knight, Chelene. *Dear Current Occupant*. Toronto: BookThug, 2018.

Kok, Gerhard de. "Cursed Capital: The Economic Impact of the Transatlantic Slave Trade on Walcheren around 1770." *Tijdschrift voor Sociale en Economische Geschiedenis* 13, no. 3 (2016): 1–27.

Lamur, Humphrey E. "The Evolution of Afro-Surinamese National Movements (1955–1995)." *Transforming Anthropology* 10, no. 1 (2001): 17–27.

Lamur, Humphrey E. "The Slave Family in Colonial 19th-Century Suriname." *Journal of Black Studies* 23, no. 3 (1983): 371–81.

Laurence, K.O. *A Question of Labour: Indentured Immigration into Trinidad and British Guiana, 1875–1917.* New York: St. Martin's Press, 1994.

Look Lai, Walton. *Indentured Labour, Caribbean Sugar: Chinese and Indian Migrants to the British West Indies, 1838–1918.* Baltimore, MD: Johns Hopkins University Press, 1993.

Loor, André. *André Loor vertelt … Suriname, 1850–1950.* Paramaribo, Suriname: VACO, 2013.

Mahtani, Minelle. *Mixed Race Amnesia: Resisting the Romanticization of Multiraciality.* Vancouver: UBC Press, 2014.

Majumder, Mousumi, ed. *Kahe Gaile Bides, Why Did You Go Overseas? On Bhojpuri Migration since the 1870s and Contemporary Culture in Uttar Pradesh and Bihar, Suriname and the Netherlands.* Allahabad, India, and Amsterdam, the Netherlands: Mango Books; KIT Publishers, 2010.

Malkani, Lainy. *Sugar Sugar: Bitter Sweet Tales of Indian Migrant Workers.* London: HopeRoad, 2017.

Man A Hing, William L. "Chinese plantage-arbeiders in de negentiende eeuw." *OSO: Tijdschrift voor Surinamistiek* 19, no. 2 (2000): 320–36.

Manning, Susan M. "Contrasting colonisations: (Re)storying Newfoundland/ Ktaqmkuk as place." *Settler Colonial Studies* 8, no. 3 (2018): 314–31.

Maseko, Zola, dir. *The Life and Times of Sara Baartman: "the Hottentot Venus."* 1998; New York: Dominant 7, First Run/Icarus Films. DVD.

Maseko, Zola, and Gail Smith, dir. *The Return of Sara Baartman.* 2003; Johannesburg, South Africa, and Brooklyn, NY: Black Roots Pictures, First Run/Icarus Films. DVD.

Mawani, Renisa. *Across Oceans of Law: The Komagata Maru and Jurisdiction in the Time of Empire.* Durham, NC: Duke University Press, 2018.

McKittrick, Katherine. *Demonic Grounds: Black Women and the Cartographies of Struggle.* Minneapolis: University Minnesota Press, 2006.

McKittrick, Katherine. "Mathematics Black Life." *The Black Scholar* 44, no. 2 (2014): 16–28.

McLeod, Cynthia. *The Cost of Sugar.* Translated by Gerald R. Mettam. Paramaribo, Suriname: Waterfront Press, 2010.

McLeod, Cynthia. *The Free Negress Elisabeth*. Translated by Brian Doyle. London: Arcadia Books, 2008.

McLeod, Cynthia. *Slavernij en de Memorie*. Groet, the Netherlands: Conserve, 2002.

Menke, Jack. "Diversiteit en huidskleur binnen de Surinaamse samenleving." *OSO: Tijdschrift voor Surinamistiek* 24, no. 1 (2005): 82–95.

Miller, John W. "My Ancestor Owned 41 Slaves: What Do I Owe Their Descendants?" *America Magazine*, 28 November 2018, https://www .americamagazine.org/arts-culture/2018/11/28/my-ancestor-owned-41 -slaves-what-do-i-owe-their-descendants.

Mingoen, Hariëtte, and Yvette Kopijn. *Stille Passanten: Levensverhalen van Javaans-Surinaamse ouderen in Nederland*. Amsterdam, the Netherlands: KIT Publishers, 2008.

Mohan, Peggy. *Jahajin*. Noida, India: HarperCollins India, 2008.

Morgan, Cecilia. "Creating Interracial Intimacies: British North America, Canada, and the Transatlantic World, 1830–1914." *Journal of the Canadian Historical Association* 19, no. 2 (2008): 76–105.

Morgan, Jennifer L. *Laboring Women: Reproduction and Gender in New World Slavery*. Philadelphia: University of Pennsylvania Press, 2004.

Mungroo, Ruud. *Tata Colin*. Paramaribo, Suriname: Drukkerij Eldorado, 1982.

Mustakeem, Sowande' M. *Slavery at Sea: Terror, Sex, and Sickness in the Middle Passage*. Urbana: University of Illinois Press, 2016.

Nakagawa, Anne Marie, dir. *Between: Living in the Hyphen*. National Film Board of Canada, 2005.

National Indian Association. *Indian Magazine and Review*. Archibald Constable and Co., 1894.

Neimanis, Astrida. *Bodies of Water: Posthuman Feminist Phenomenology*. London: Bloomsbury Academic, 2017.

Newton, John. *Thoughts upon the African Slave Trade*. London: Buckland; Johnson, 1788.

Nimako, Kwame, and Glenn Willemsen. *The Dutch Atlantic: Slavery, Abolition and Emancipation*. London: Pluto Press, 2011.

Nishino, Ryota. "Dialogues with Shadows: Reflections on Identity, History and Travel." *Life Writing* 12, no. 1 (2015): 95–105.

Oostindie, Gert, ed. *Dutch Colonialism, Migration and Cultural Heritage*. Leiden, the Netherlands: Brill, 2008.

Oostindie, Gert J. *Facing Up to the Past: Perspectives on the Commemoration of Slavery from Africa, the Americas and Europe*. Kingston, Jamaica: Ian Randle Publishers, 2001.

Oostindie, Gert. "History Brought Home: Postcolonial Migrations and the Dutch Rediscovery of Slavery." In *Migration, Trade, and Slavery in an Expanding World: Essays in Honor of Pieter Emmer*, edited by Wim Klooster, 305–27. Leiden, the Netherlands: Brill, 2009.

Oostindie, Gert. "Migration and Its Legacies in the Dutch Colonial World." In *Dutch Colonialism, Migration and Cultural Heritage*, edited by Gert Oostindie, 1–22. Leiden, the Netherlands: Brill, 2008.

Oostindie, Gert J. *Paradise Overseas: The Dutch Caribbean and Its Transatlantic Legacies*. Oxford, UK: Macmillan Caribbean, 2005.

Oostindie, Gert J. *Postcolonial Netherlands: Sixty-Five Years of Forgetting, Commemorating, Silencing*. Amsterdam, the Netherlands: Amsterdam University Press, 2010.

Oostindie, Gert. "Slavenleven." In *Ik ben eigendom van . . . Slavenhandel en plantageleven*, edited by Bea Brommer, 95–113. Woudrichem, the Netherlands: Pictures Publishers, 1993.

Oostindie, Gert. "The Slippery Path of Commemoration and Heritage Tourism: The Netherlands, Ghana and the Rediscovery of Atlantic Slavery." *New West Indian Guide* 79, no. 1/2 (2005): 55–77.

Oostindie, Gert J. "The Study of Ethnicity in the Dutch Caribbean." *Latin American and Caribbean Ethnic Studies* 1, no. 2 (2006): 215–30.

Oostindie, Gert J., and Rosemarijn Hoefte. "The Netherlands and the Dutch Caribbean: Dilemmas of Decolonisation." In *Europe and the Caribbean*, edited by Paul Sutton, 71–98. London: Macmillan, 1991.

Paton, Diana. "Maternal Struggles and the Politics of Childlessness under Pronatalist Caribbean Slavery." *Slavery & Abolition* 38, no. 2 (2017): 251–68.

Perry, Adele. *Colonial Relations: The Douglas-Connolly Family and the Nineteenth-Century Imperial World*. Cambridge, UK: Cambridge University Press, 2015.

Persaud, Anil. "The Problem of Origin: The Politics of Indigeneity in Post-1830 British Guiana." PhD Thesis, Jwaharlal Nehru University, India, 2007.

Phaf-Rheinberger, Ineke. "Creole Tori, the Waterkant and the Ethics of a Nation: Cynthia McLeod and Astrid Roemer on Suriname." *Matatu – Journal for African Culture and Society* 27, no. 1 (2003): 399–416.

Philip, Marlene NourbeSe. *A Genealogy of Resistance: And Other Essays.* Toronto: Mercury Press, 1997.

Philip, Marlene NourbeSe. *She Tries Her Tongue, Her Silence Softly Breaks.* Charlottetown, PE: Ragweed Press, 1989.

Philip, Marlene NourbeSe. *Zong!* Middletown, CT: Wesleyan University Press, 2008.

Porter, Marilyn, and Linda K. Cullum, eds. *Creating This Place: Women, Family, and Class in St. John's, 1900–1950.* Montreal, QC, and Kingston, ON: McGill-Queen's University Press, 2014.

Postma, Johannes Menne. *The Dutch in the Atlantic Slave Trade, 1600–1815.* Cambridge, UK: Cambridge University Press, 1990.

Postmas, Johannes. "A Reassessment of the Dutch Atlantic Slave Trade." In *Riches from Atlantic Commerce: Dutch Transatlantic Trade and Shipping, 1585–1817,* edited by Johannes Postma and Victor Enthoven, 115–38. Leiden, the Netherlands, and Boston, MA: Brill, 2003.

Powel, J.S., and A.Y.M. Young. *Middelburg: De bakermat van de slavernij in Suriname, 1640–1873.* Middelburg, the Netherlands: Leven en Laten Leven, 1993.

Prakash, Jeevan, Kathinka Sinha-Kerkhoff, Ellen Bal, and Alok Deo Singh, eds. *Autobiography of an Indian Indentured Labourer: Munshi Rahman Khan (1874–1972).* Translated by Jeevan Prakash, Kathinka Sinha-Kerkhoff, Ellen Bal, and Alok Deo Singh. Delhi, India: Shipra Publications, 2006.

Prince, Mary. *The History of Mary Prince: A West Indian Slave.* Ann Arbor: University of Michigan Press, 1997.

Probyn, Elspeth. *Eating the Ocean.* Durham, NC: Duke University Press, 2016.

Rediker, Marcus. *The Slave Ship: A Human History.* New York: Viking, 2007.

Reinders Folmer-van Prooijen, C. *Van goederenhandel naar slavenhandel: De Middelburgsche Commercie Compagnie, 1720–1755.* Middelburg, the Netherlands: Koninklijke Zeeuwsch Genootschap der Wetenschappen, 2000.

Renselaar, H.C., and J. Voorhoeve. "Messianism and Nationalism in Surinam." *Bijdragen tot de Taal-, Land- en Volkenkunde / Journal of the Humanities and Social Sciences of Southeast Asia* 18, no. 2 (1962): 193–216.

Sarasvati, Pundita Ramabai. *The High-Caste Hindu Woman*. Philadelphia, PA: Jas. B. Rodgers Printing Co., 1887.

Sarup, Leela Gujadhar, ed. *Colonial Emigration 19th–20th Century: Proceedings*. Vol. 5, *1870–1873*. Kolkata, India: Aldrich International, 2010.

Savoy, Lauret Edith. *Trace: Memory, History, Race, and the American Landscape*. Berkeley, CA: Counterpoint, 2015.

Schiebinger, Londa L. *Plants and Empire: Colonial Bioprospecting in the Atlantic World*. Cambridge, MA: Harvard University Press, 2007.

Scott, Julius S. *The Common Wind: Afro-American Currents in the Age of the Haitian Revolution*. London and New York: Verso, 2018.

Sharpe, Christina. *In the Wake: On Blackness and Being*. Durham, NC: Duke University Press, 2016.

Simpson, Katy. "Who Can Fictionalize Slavery? On Writing across Time and Space." LitHub, 30 March 2016. https://lithub.com/who-can-fictionalize-slavery/.

Simpson, Leanne Betasamosake. *As We Have Always Done: Indigenous Freedom Through Radical Resistance*. Minneapolis and London: University of Minnesota Press, 2017.

Simpson, Leanne Betasamosake. *Islands of Decolonial Love: Stories and Songs*. Winnipeg, MB: ARP, 2013.

Simpson, Leanne Betasamosake. *This Accident of Being Lost: Songs and Stories*. Toronto: House of Anansi, 2017.

Smallwood, Stephanie. *Saltwater Slavery: A Middle Passage from Africa to American Diaspora*. Cambridge, MA: Harvard University Press, 2007.

Stichting, Lalla Rookh, and Aisa Samachar, eds. *"Van Immigrant tot Emigrant": 110 Jaar Hindostaanse Immigratie*. Utrecht, the Netherlands: Stichting Lalla Rookh Nederland, 1983.

Stipriaan, Alex van. "July 1, Emancipation Day in Suriname: A Contested Lieu de Mémoire, 1863–2003." *New West Indian Guide* 78, no. 3/4 (2004): 269–304.

Stipriaan, Alex van. "Stilte! Niet Storen! De slavernij is afgeschaft." *De Negentiende Eeuw: documentatieblad werkgroeop 19e Eeuw* 29, no. 1 (2005): 45–61.

Stipriaan, Alex van. "The Suriname Rat Race: Labour and Technology on Sugar Plantations, 1750–1900." *New West-Indian Guide* 63, no. 1/2 (1989): 94–117.

Stipriaan, Alex van. "Tussen slaaf en peasant: De rol van de kleine landbouw in het Surinaamsche emancipatie process." In *De erfenis van de slavernij*, edited by Lila Gobardhan-Rambocus, Maurits S. Hassankhan, and Jerry L. Egger, 29–55. Paramaribo, Suriname: Anton de Kom Universit Press, 1995.

Stipriaan, Alex van. "Watramama/Mami Wata: Three Centuries of Creolization of a Water Spirit in West Africa, Suriname and Europe." *Matatu – Journal for African Culture and Society* 27, no. 1 (2003): 323–37.

Stipriaan, Alex van. "'Welke de ware reden zijn, dat Plantaadje negers zoo weinig voortelen': Demografische ontwikkelingen op Surinaams plantages gedurend de laatse eeuw van slavernij." In *Kind aan de ketting: Opgroeien in Slavernij toen en nu*, edited by Aspha Bijnaar, 50–64. Amsterdam, the Netherlands: KIT Publishers, 2009.

Stoler, Ann Laura. *Carnal Knowledge and Imperial Power: Race and the Intimate in Colonial Rule*. Berkeley: University of California Press, 2010.

Tinker, Hugh. *A New System of Slavery: The Export of Indian Labour Overseas, 1830–1920*. Oxford, UK: Oxford University Press, 1974.

Tuck, Eve, and C. Ree. "A glossary of haunting." In *Handbook of Autoethnography*, edited by Stacey Holman Jones, Tony E. Adams, and Carolyn Ellis, 639–58. Walnut Creek, CA: Left Coast Press, 2013.

Tuck, Eve, and K. Wayne Yang. "Decolonization Is Not a Metaphor." *Decolonization: Indigeneity, Education & Society* 1, no. 1 (2012): 1–40.

Tuck, Eve, and K. Wayne Yang. "R-Words: Refusing Research." In *Humanizing Research: Decolonizing Qualitative Inquiry with Youth and Communities*, edited by D. Paris and M.T. Winn, 223–47. Thousand Oaks, CA: Sage, 2014.

Tuck, Eve, and K. Wayne Yang. "Unbecoming Claims: Pedagogies of Refusal in Qualitative Research." *Qualitative Inquiry* 20, no. 6 (2014): 811–18, https://doi.org/10.1177/1077800414530265.

Turner, Sasha. "Home-Grown Slaves: Women, Reproduction, and the Abolition of the Slave Trade, Jamaica 1788–1807." *Journal of Women's History* 23, no. 2 (2011): 39–62.

Webster, Jane. "The Zong in the Context of the Eighteenth-Century Slave Trade." *Journal of Legal History* 28, no. 3 (2007): 285–98. https://doi.org/10.1080/01440360701698403.

Wekker, Gloria. "Of Mimic Men and Unruly Women: Family, Sexuality and Gender in Twentieth-Century Suriname." In *Twentieth-Century Suriname: Continuities and Discontinuities in a New World Society*, edited by Rosemarijn Hoefte and Peter Meel, 174–97. Leiden, the Netherlands: Brill, 2001.

Wekker, Gloria. *The Politics of Passion: Women's Sexual Culture in the Afro-Surinamese Diaspora*. New York: Columbia University Press, 2006.

Wekker, Gloria. *White Innocence: Paradoxes of Colonialism and Race*. Durham, NC: Duke University Press, 2016.

Westoll, Andrew. *The Riverbones: Stumbling after Eden in the Jungles of Suriname*. Toronto: McClelland & Stewart, 2008.

Zaiki, Safdar. *De suiker die niet zoet was*. Translated by Mitra Rambaran. Voorburg, the Netherlands: Uitgeverij U2pi, 2005.

Index

abolition, 70, 77, 143, 150, 157–58, 176, 184; abolitionism, 95, 148; anniversary of, 187; compensation for, 91; debates, 95; Mary Prince and, 148–50. *See also* Keti Koti

agency, 213

Albina (Suriname), xiv, 108, 109, 194

Algemene Rekenkamer, 72, 82, 85

Alliance (plantation), 169, 182, 184

Amsterdam, xiii, 10, 31, 36, 40, 59, 65, 113, 186, 198, 237, 244; Concertgebouw, 31, 69; Museumplein, 246; Queen Beatrix, 31. *See also* International Colonial and Export Trade Exhibition (Amsterdam); Van Gogh Museum

Anne of Green Gables, 90

apartheid, 123

archives, 27, 37, 42, 80, 87, 89, 91, 92, 119, 126, 129–30, 132, 136, 149, 150, 166, 172, 178, 193, 197, 200, 213, 248, 271; archival puzzles, 27, 42; archives time, 127; behaviours in, 75–76, 127, 128; deceptions of, 27; digital, 199, 272; emotional investment in, 76; fragility of, 89; fragmentary nature of, 42, 89, 257; gatekeeping in, 75, 127, 128; intimacy of, 26, 76, 256; medieval manuscripts and, 26; and national identity, 127; neutrality and, 257; rhythms of archival work, 46, 125, 256; and seduction, 1; silence and, 2, 4, 257; as spaces of dreams, 26; tactility of archival materials, 26, 212; work patterns in, 76, 125, 128, 187. *See also* Maritime History Archive; National Archives of the Netherlands; National Archives of Suriname; National Archives of the United Kingdom

Ascension Island, 228, 230

Baartman, Sara, 245, 288

bakra, 114, 116–17, 120, 192, 247

Barbados, 18, 35, 101, 113–14, 118, 119, 121, 140, 143, 223, 243, 250

belonging, 6–7, 11, 13, 21, 25, 37, 172, 241, 276; and Canadian mosaic, 21; as fiction, 262; home, 7; origins, 22, 172; possibilities and limitations of, 8; and race, 71; rights to; 172, 192; unrooted, 19

Bent, John, xii, 86–88, 139, 174–75, 276

Bent's Hope (plantation), 170, 173–76, 184, 282
Bevan, George H.A., 222, 224, 226–32
Bouterse, Dési, xv, 103, 108, 140
Brabant (Netherlands), 32–33
Brand, Dionne, 115, 222, 272
broko pranasi, 142, 177–78, 249
brown, 15, 24, 31, 114–15, 117, 119, 135, 138, 201, 206, 232, 235, 251, 276; family history and, 25; identity and, 20, 22, 71, 113, 120; layers of, 116. *See also* mixed race; race

cabinets of curiosity, 244, 245
Cabot, John, 54
Canada, 8, 15, 23, 35, 37, 64, 66, 92, 102, 104, 145, 185, 192, 232; Canada Day, 185–86; citizenship ceremony, 15–16, 19–20; immigration to, xv, 15, 20, 25, 60; mixed-race relationships in, 123; mosaic and melting pot, 20; multiculturalism, 20, 123; outsider within, 25, 114
Cape of Good Hope, 97, 223, 269
cemeteries, 70, 131–33, 144–45, 189, 242, 262; abandoned, 21, 132, 144; historic, 143; living and dead, 132. *See also* Nieuwe Oranjetuin Cemetery (Paramaribo)
Candide (Voltaire), 104
Come From Away, 7, 10. *See also* Mainlander
Commewijne River (Suriname), 78, 170, 233, 236, 253
Compagnie des mines d'or de la guyane hollandaise, 105–6
Contagious Diseases Acts, 222
Corte-Real, Gaspar, 54

Creole, 24, 35, 63, 77, 81, 88, 105, 107, 108, 110, 113, 120, 170, 172, 184, 186, 198, 200, 236, 239, 246, 254
Cumaná (Venezuela), 15
C.W. Kellock & Co., 218

Darnton, Robert, 65, 275
Dessé (family); Anthony, xiii, 89, 91, 133–34, 136, 141, 143, 145; Edmund, 134, 143; Eleonora, 134, 138, 143; Frederika Rosette, 133–35, 140–41, 145, 242, 250, 278; Ethelrid, 134, 143
Dietzel, J.H., xii, 86
Dillon, Brian, 181, 283
Dongen (Netherlands), 32–33
du Plessis, Susanna, 253
Dutch, 118, 123–24, 244; culture, 34, 42; food, 36, 40–42; Golden Age, 96–97; identity, 17, 20, 22, 30–31, 33, 36–37, 63, 192; language, 1, 40–42, 67–68, 102, 108, 113, 183, 205, 239, 249
Dutch Guyana. *See* Suriname
Dutt, Bepin Behary, 225, 230–32

early music, 60, 178–79; nostalgia and, 178. *See also* historically informed performance
East Indian Railway, 202
Eenigheid, de (ship), 273
Eldorado, 104–5
Emmer, Pieter, 211, 284

Faizabad (India), 199, 285
Faroe Islands, 9, 18, 22, 56, 220; genealogy, 21; tradition, 21
flute, 9–10, 11, 33, 60, 70, 91, 138, 139, 160, 221; career, 3; modern and early flutes, 26. *See also* Frederick

the Great; Fürstenau, Anton
Bernhard; Tulou, Jean-Louis
Fort Saskatchewan (Alberta), 20
Fort Willoughby (Suriname). *See* Fort
Zeelandia (Suriname)
Fort Zeelandia (Suriname),
140–42, 233, 242, 249; Cojo,
Mentor, and Present in, 141;
Decembermoorden, 140; history
of, 140. *See also* Tata Colin
Fox, Terry, 54
Frederick the Great, 92, 127; flute
sonatas of, 92; Sans Souci, 93
freedom, 92, 94, 95, 145, 148, 150,
163, 186, 193, 236, 276; and
incarceration, 94; dictionary
definition of, 95–96; sexual,
209; and unfreedom, 94. *See also*
Prince, Mary; Rousseau, Jean-
Jacques; Sartre, Jean-Paul
Fremantle, Edmund, 230–32. *See also*
Kate Kellock (ship)
Fürstenau, Anton Bernhard
(composer), 138–39, 250

gawkery, 243–45, 288
genealogy, 3, 47; limitations of, 47–48,
50
Geoctroyeerde Westindische
Compagnie (Dutch West India
Company), xii, 43, 97, 269
gold, 112, 212, 219, 249; Canadian
mining interests, 104–5; family
histories of, 24, 35, 65, 105–7,
200, 237, 250, 251, 254; mining,
104, 109; myths of empire, 104;
treasure chest, 105–6; violence
and, 108, 109. *See also Candide;*
Compagnie des mines d'or de la
guyane hollandaise; Eldorado;

Heinemann, Theodor Wilhelm;
ogri ai kralen (ograi krara)
Great Britain, 19, 21. *See also*
Manchester (Great Britain)
Grenfell, Sir Wilfred, 54
Guinea Coast (Africa), 144

Haagsche Jantje, 96
Hague, The (Netherlands), xv, 18, 26,
59–61, 63, 64, 66, 67, 71–73, 75,
91, 92, 96, 98, 126, 128, 143, 147,
148, 158, 159, 163, 181, 186, 188,
196, 199, 213, 238, 241, 246, 262,
275; 2e de Riemerstraat, 59–60;
Historical Museum of, 64;
Paleis Noordeinde, 60
Hall, Pam, 164–66
Harmonica Society, 138
Hartman, Saidiya, 151, 273
Heinemann, Leonard Frederik Adolf,
xiv, xv, 73; books, 61, 65–67;
Harmonie choir and, 70–72;
musical inheritance, 60, 188;
musical training, xv
Heinemann, Theodor Wilhelm, xiv,
105, 194. *See also* Compagnie
des mines d'or de la guyane
hollandaise; gold
Helstone, Johannes Nicolaas
(composer), 69–71, 173; Musicus
Helstone monument, 70, 187,
189, 242
Hindustani, 120, 125, 172, 190, 194,
200, 235, 239, 284, 285
historically informed performance,
271. *See also* early music
History of Mary Prince, The, 148, 279.
See also Prince, Mary
Holocaust, 48, 97. *See also*
Sachsenhausen

home, 11, 22, 25, 63, 99, 118, 222, 241, 262; as collage, 19; longing for, 18, 123; meaning of, 6, 7, 18; 123; multiculturalism and, 20; oceans as, 114; plantation as, 163–64, 166–67. *See also* belonging; Hall, Pam; origins

Hooghly River (India), 202, 225–26

Houthakker, Jan, 156–57, 163, 281. *See also* manumission

Howrah (India), 202, 206

icebergs, 259, 261

identity, 6, 21, 33, 37, 42, 99, 134, 139, 247, 270; hybrid, 20; hyphenated, 73; mixed-race, 116–17, 271

immigration, 35, 196; depots, 119, 213, 233, 236; records, 195, 199, 205, 212, 217, 229, 233. *See also* belonging; indenture

indenture, 21, 25, 35, 119, 133, 141, 151, 169, 173, 177, 181, 183–84, 215, 223, 236; British India and, 198, 202–3; caste system and, 205–6, 209–10; as "colonial escape hatch," 211; economics of, 141, 211; emigration agents, 205; gender and, 201, 208–11; gender-based quotas, 209; gender-based violence and, 210; intergenerational legacies of, 212; oral histories of, 211–12; sexual freedom, 209; social mobility, 210. *See also Kate Kellock* (ship); Khan, Munshi Rahman; *Philosopher* (ship); Radha, Joorayee; Surinamese Immigration Society; U-A-Sai (U Asai); U-A-Sai, Sahatoo

Indigenous peoples, 86, 90, 108, 141, 245, 248

inheritance, 32, 64, 73, 99, 127, 157, 166, 189

International Colonial and Export Trade Exhibition (Amsterdam), 246, 288

Jurgon, Annette Juliane, xiii, 160, 162. *See also* manumission; Redout (family)

Kate Kellock (ship), 198, 205, 212, 218–19, 231, 250, 258, 286–87; assaults on board, 226; at Ascension Island, 228; birth aboard, 228–29; Cape Town (South Africa), 227; crew agreements and ship's logs, 216, 218, 223, 224–25; crew behaviour aboard, 226–28; death aboard, 233–34; failed mutiny, 228, 229–32; Melbourne (Australia), 219–20; painting of, 216; Suriname, 224, 233; wreck, 235. *See also* Bevan, George H.A.; Dutt, Bepin Behary; Fremantle, Edmund; Radha, Joorayee; U-A-Sai, Sahatoo

Kellock, Charles W., 218

Keti Koti, 185, 186. *See also* abolition

Khan, Munshi Rahman, 201, 202, 204, 206

Komagata Maru (ship), 185, 286, 287

Ku Klux Klan, 123

language, 1, 61, 62, 67–68, 77, 90, 108, 172, 205, 223, 231, 249; and identity, 18, 67–68, 232; and intimacy, 36, 67, 238

Lausanne (Switzerland), 27, 127

"La vie en rose" (Piaf), 47
Lethbridge (Alberta), 9
Leusden (ship), 274
Lodewijk. *See* Redout (family)

Manchester (Great Britain), xv, 18, 40,
    220, 241; and class politics, 62;
    place of birth, 15, 62; foreignness
    of, 61–62, 63; industrialization,
    62; marriage in, 63
Mainlander, 7, 13. *See also* Come From
    Away
manumission, 134, 138, 147, 156–57,
    160–63, 275, 278, 281. *See also*
    Houthakker, Jan; Jurgon,
    Annette Juliane; Schove, Jacob
Maritime History Archive (St.
    John's), 217–18, 224, 286–87
Maroons, 108, 109, 141, 177, 181, 246,
    251; fabrics, 191–92
Mauritshuis (The Hague), 96
McLeod, Cynthia, 135, 274, 279
Medea (ship), 205
Middelburg (Netherlands), 2–3,
    40, 42, 43, 44, 47, 48, 51, 53, 77,
    128, 148, 150, 154, 175, 181, 262,
    269–70, 273, 281; built heritage,
    40–42; and seduction
Middelburgsche Commercie
    Compagnie (MCC), 2, 42,
    43–44, 269, 274; economic
    impact of, 51; and slave trade,
    2; UNESCO Memory of the
    World, 2. *See also Eenigheid,
    de* (ship); Middelburg
    (Netherlands); *Vigilantie, de*
    (ship); Vlissingen (Netherlands);
    Welmeenende (ship)
Middle Cove Beach (Newfoundland),
    5; beach stones, 5–6, 115;

belonging, 6, 8; capelin, 8;
    community, 8; ice waterfalls, 5
Mighty Sparrow, 101, 113
mixed race, 25, 123, 136, 194, 271, 277
Mughalsarai (India), 202–3
Mormon, Marsha, 170
multiculturalism, 20–21; family
    history and, 186; in Suriname,
    123
Museumplein (Amsterdam), 246
music, 3, 61, 69, 70, 71, 73, 92, 106, 113,
    120, 138–39, 140, 173, 178, 182, 187,
    188–89, 190, 217, 221, 241, 258,
    262; and archives, 26, 68, 126,
    217, 256–57; as calling and career,
    9–10, 24, 60, 61, 64–65; classical,
    63–64; folk, 64; and grief, 9–10;
    as inheritance, 60, 66, 70–71,
    140, 189, 238, 242; masterclass,
    10; relationship with, 9–10,
    69, 70; as voice, 9; water
    music, 6. *See also* early music;
    flute; historically informed
    performance

National Archives of the Netherlands,
    75, 91
National Archives of Suriname,
    125–27
National Archives of the United
    Kingdom, 224
Necker, Suzanne, 26, 189
Nederlandsche Handel-Maatschappij,
    196. *See also* Resolutie, de
    (plantation); Surinamese
    Immigration Society
Netherlands, the, 3, 13, 17, 24, 31, 61,
    63, 73, 113, 185, 193, 246
Newfoundland, 4, 5–6, 13, 21, 51, 54,
    103, 132, 134, 172, 217, 222, 261,

262; identity and, 6–7, 18, 21, 23,
270; Memorial Day and, 185–86;
roots, 6; saltbox, 179, 180. *See also*
Come From Away; Mainlander;
Middle Cove Beach

Newton, John, 49–50, 155, 163, 273–74,
282

Nieuwe Oranjetuin cemetery
(Paramaribo), 131, 133–34, 143,
144, 145, 242, 279. *See also* Dessé
(family)

Nijd en Spijt (Plantation), 253

oceans, 4, 5, 7, 46, 52, 53, 55, 56–57, 101,
102, 114–16, 132, 149, 166, 189,
217, 220, 222, 223, 226, 228, 239,
256, 259, 261, 285–86; Atlantic
Ocean, 57; Indian Ocean, 225;
migrations, 6, 66, 206; mortality
and, 115; oceanic thinking, 286–
87; Pacific Ocean, 9; storms, 8;
unknowability of, 115. *See also*
Brand, Dionne

ogri ai kralen (ograi krara), 254–55

Oma Heinemann, 36, 61, 63, 66, 114,
194, 256, 261–62

Oostindie, Gert, 163, 166

origins, 11, 25, 262 ; belonging,
7; home, 18. *See also*
multiculturalism

Paramaribo (Suriname), 13, 44, 86,
89, 95, 102–3, 105, 108, 112,
117–18, 123, 126, 131, 133, 134,
144, 148, 165, 181, 182, 218, 224,
233, 241, 242, 249; Basilica of
St. Peter and St. Paul, 122, 131,
242; central market, 120–21; as
cosmopolitan space, 137–39;
insider and outsider in, 113, 182,

247–48; religious diversity, 122–
23; UNESCO heritage, 109, 119,
180. *See also* Harmonica Society;
Nieuw Oranjetuin cemetery;
Samson, Elisabeth; Thalia
theatre; Waag, de; Waterkant

Philosopher (ship), 236

Piaf, Edith. *See* "La vie en rose"

plantation, 61, 70, 77–79, 85–86, 149,
155–56, 158, 162, 169, 182, 193, 195,
197, 211, 215, 233, 276; abandoned,
144, 175, 182, 242; canals and
sluices, 169, 173; as home, 166;
as intimate space, 80, 163–65;
labour on, 197–98, 208; as living
archive, 80, 169–70, 173, 175,
248, 253; as sites of memory,
144, 163, 178; and violence, 159,
210. *See also* Bent, John; *broko
pranasi*; Dessé (family); Sarah
(plantation)

pom, 110, 113, 252

Potato Eaters, The (van Gogh), 29–31,
246

prairie, 8, 15, 20, 55, 114, 215, 220;
skyscape, 17, 55–56; weather, 56

Prince, Mary, 148–51

pysanka, 19

race, 71, 108, 135, 136, 194, 246, 277–78;
anti-miscegenation laws, 123;
mixed-race relationships, 24, 91,
123, 209–10. *See also* brown; Ku
Klux Klan; mixed race; Samson,
Elisabeth

Radha, Joorayee, xiii, xiv, 202–4,
212, 213, 227, 258; in the colonial
record, 195, 199–200, 233, 284–85;
death of, xiv, 237; imagined
life of, 203, 204–5, 206–7, 216,

225–26; indenture and, 195, 198, 229; intimate relationships and, 236, 238; isolation and, 200, 201, 207; love and, 201, 206–7; motherhood and, 201, 227, 238; permanent residency, 236. *See also* Faizabad; indenture; *Kate Kellock* (ship); U-A-Sai (U Asai); U-A-Sai, Sahatoo

rebellion, 95, 102, 276

Redout (family); Adolphina Margaretha, xiv, 105, 194; Amsterdam Job, 80, 81, 162; Annette (Annette Juliane Jurgon), xiii, 160, 161, 162, 163, 191, 281; Cornelis, 80, 81, 162; Edward, xii, 80 81, 82, 85, 159; Eva Albertina, xiii, 80, 81, 95, 159, 161, 162–63, 281; Frederik Noa, xii, xiii, 80, 81, 87, 88–89, 94–95, 98, 159, 250; Frederika, xii, 80, 82, 95, 159, 160, 161, 162, 281; Jack Abraham, 80, 81, 169, 162; Janny Rebecca, 80, 162; Joseph Elias, 80, 81, 159, 162, 194; Leander, 80, 82, 160; Lodewijk, 161–63, 191; Madleentje Paulina, xiii, 80, 85, 89–91, 159–60, 162; Marlon 2e (Jacob Schove), xiii, 162–62, 281; Philip Elias, xii, 80, 82, 87, 95, 193; Sultan Timotheus, 80, 81, 162, 193, 194; Wilson Boas, 80, 82, 159, 160. *See also* Jurgon, Annette Juliane; manumission; Schove, Jacob

Resolutie, de (plantation), 78, 196, 199, 211, 214

Reynsdorp (plantation), 170

Rijksmuseum (Amsterdam), 246

Rousseau, Jean-Jacques (political philosopher), 30, 94, 276

Royal Conservatory of Music (The Hague), xv, 60, 67, 70, 238. *See also* Heinemann, Leonard Frederik Adolf; U-A-Sai, Harry

ruin, 177–82, 183, 184. *See also broko pranasi*

Saavedra, Dario (composer), 70–71, 73, 173

Sachsenhausen, 93

Samson, Elisabeth, 134–35, 139, 278

Sarah (plantation), xii, xiii, 77–89, 133, 141, 158–59, 163, 166, 174–75, 193–94, 258, 275–76, 281. *See also* Bent, John; Dessé: Anthony; Redout (family)

Sarnami, 172

Sartre, Jean-Paul (philosopher), 94, 276

Schove, Jacob (Marlon 2e). *See* Redout (family)

Secret Garden, The (Burnett), 90

slavery, 49, 92, 94, 96, 155, 156–57, 159, 160, 173, 185, 195, 208, 242, 274, 275–76; abolition and, 70, 77, 89, 95, 133, 143, 145, 148, 160, 176, 184, 185, 187, 193, 276; abolitionist efforts, 148, 279–80; afterlives of, 63, 150–51, 166, 194, 273–74; kinship and, 202; reparations for, 150–51, 280; reproduction and, 280–81; resistance and rebellion, 98; violence and, 151, 253, 274; witnessing and, 148–50. *See also* Hartman, Saidiya; Houthakker, Jan; Keti Koti; *Uncle Tom's Cabin* (Stowe)

Smallwood, Joseph R., 76

spirits, 67, 132, 228, 252–56, 258, 262

Sranan Tongo, 77, 108, 114, 142, 249

St. John's (Newfoundland and
    Labrador), 5, 8–10, 13, 21, 25, 51,
    54, 56, 102, 121, 131, 138, 164–65,
    188, 190, 193, 215, 216, 218, 241,
    242, 243, 244, 251, 256, 259, 260,
    261, 262

Suriname, 3, 13, 15, 34, 35, 37, 44,
    73, 123, 133, 134, 135, 169, 170,
    190, 208, 209, 210; as idea,
    102, 142; cemeteries in, 144;
    colonialism and, 61, 135, 246,
    249; elections, 103; family
    history and, 118–19, 124, 193,
    195, 200, 208, 215; Hindu
    marriage in, 210; history of, 85,
    86–87, 103–4, 118, 139–41, 177–78,
    179–80, 236; identity, 169,
    184, 189, 190–91, 192, 211, 247;
    insider and outsider in, 113, 172;
    memories of, 201; military coup,
    118; multiculturalism in, 122,
    123, 171; plantations in, 78, 85,
    87, 91, 94, 169, 182, 194, 211, 215,
    253; return to, 99, 130, 172, 209,
    242; sounds of, 71; *Surinamers*,
    116; Surinamese Built Heritage
    Society, 145; Surinamese
    Immigration Society, 196–98;
    tourist gaze, 244; weather in,
    160; women's sexual cultures
    in, 13. *See also broko pranasi*;
    Eldorado; gold; Paramaribo

Suriname Ghat (India), 225

Surinamese Immigration Society,
    196–98

Stuttgart (Germany), 24, 105

Tata Colin, 89, 95, 141, 142, 274

Thalia theatre (Paramaribo), 120, 138,
    140

Thoughts upon the African Slave Trade,
    49–50. *See also* Newton, John

tourism. *See* gawkery

Tuck, Eve, 244, 277, 288

Tulou, Jean-Louis (composer), 138–39

U-A-Sai (U Asai), 201, 236, 238, 287;
    Bok Sinah and, 237; Elisabeth
    Pompadour Daal and, 236;
    gambling, 237; goldsmith,
    200, 237; in Guyana, 236; in
    Suriname, 236–37

U-A-Sai, Harry (Henry Eugene),
    120, 140

U-A-Sai, Henriette Mathilde, 239.
    See also Oma Heinemann

U-A-Sai, Sahatoo, 237, 238

Uncle Tom's Cabin (Stowe), 95, 279

United Kingdom, 62, 219

Vancouver (British Columbia), 7, 8, 18,
    21, 56, 185, 241, 260, 270, 287

van Gogh, Vincent, 29–30, 31–33, 246,
    272. *See also Potato Eaters, The*

Van Gogh Museum, 29, 31, 34, 246

Vermeer, Johannes, 96–97

Victoria (British Columbia), 66, 185,
    241, 244

Vigilantie, de (ship), 44–47, 272, 282

Vlissingen (Netherlands), 51–53, 54,
    263, 269–70, 273; Fisherman's
    Wife (*Vissersvrouw*), 54–57;
    German occupation of, 52–53;
    Napoleon and, 52; slave trade,
    51–52. *See also* Middelburg;

Middelburgsche Commercie Compagnie (MCC)

Waag, de (Weighing House), 138, 139, 140
Warappakreek, 169–70, 173–75, 176, 177, 282
Waterkant (Paramaribo), 109, 119, 180, 192, 233, 249
Wekker, Gloria, 270–71
Welmeenende (ship), 282
White Australia policy, 123
Windsor (Ontario), 15, 17

Witt, Johan and Cornelis de, 64–65
women's studies, 8
Wright, Hugh, 175, 184, 282

Yang, K. Wayne, 244, 288

Zeekust (Suriname), 85–86, 87
Zeeuws Archief (Netherlands), 2, 186, 270, 272–73, 281–82
Zong (ship), 50, 274
Zutphen (Netherlands), 24, 36, 61, 66, 118, 124

Books in the Life Writing Series

Published by Wilfrid Laurier University Press

Haven't Any News: Ruby's Letters from the Fifties edited by Edna Staebler with an Afterword by Marlene Kadar • 1995 / x + 165 pp. / ISBN 0-88920-248-6

"I Want to Join Your Club": Letters from Rural Children, 1900–1920 edited by Norah L. Lewis with a Preface by Neil Sutherland • 1996 / xii + 250 pp. (30 b&w photos) / ISBN 0-88920-260-5

And Peace Never Came by Elisabeth M. Raab with Historical Notes by Marlene Kadar • 1996 / x + 196 pp. (12 b&w photos, map) / ISBN 0-88920-281-8

Dear Editor and Friends: Letters from Rural Women of the North-West, 1900–1920 edited by Norah L. Lewis • 1998 / xvi + 166 pp. (20 b&w photos) / ISBN 0-88920-287-7

The Surprise of My Life: An Autobiography by Claire Drainie Taylor with a Foreword by Marlene Kadar • 1998 / xii + 268 pp. (8 colour photos and 92 b&w photos) / ISBN 0-88920-302-4

Memoirs from Away: A New Found Land Girlhood by Helen M. Buss / Margaret Clarke • 1998 / xvi + 153 pp. / ISBN 0-88920-350-4

The Life and Letters of Annie Leake Tuttle: Working for the Best by Marilyn Färdig Whiteley • 1999 / xviii + 150 pp. / ISBN 0-88920-330-x

Marian Engel's Notebooks: "Ah, mon cahier, écoute" edited by Christl Verduyn • 1999 / viii + 576 pp. / ISBN 0-88920-333-4 cloth / ISBN 0-88920-349-0 paper

Be Good Sweet Maid: The Trials of Dorothy Joudrie by Audrey Andrews • 1999 / vi + 276 pp. / ISBN 0-88920-334-2

Working in Women's Archives: Researching Women's Private Literature and Archival Documents edited by Helen M. Buss and Marlene Kadar • 2001 / vi + 120 pp. / ISBN 0-88920-341-5

Repossessing the World: Reading Memoirs by Contemporary Women by Helen M. Buss • 2002 / xxvi + 206 pp. / ISBN 0-88920-408-x cloth / ISBN 0-88920-410-1 paper

Chasing the Comet: A Scottish–Canadian Life by Patricia Koretchuk • 2002 / xx + 244 pp. / ISBN 0-88920-407-1

The Queen of Peace Room by Magie Dominic • 2002 / xii + 115 pp. / ISBN 0-88920-417-9

China Diary: The Life of Mary Austin Endicott by Shirley Jane Endicott • 2002 / xvi + 251 pp. / ISBN 0-88920-412-8

The Curtain: Witness and Memory in Wartime Holland by Henry G. Schogt • 2003 / xii + 132 pp. / ISBN 0-88920-396-2

Teaching Places by Audrey J. Whitson • 2003 / xiii + 178 pp. / ISBN 0-88920-425-x

Through the Hitler Line by Laurence F. Wilmot, M.C. • 2003 / xvi + 152 pp. / ISBN 0-88920-448-9

Where I Come From by Vijay Agnew • 2003 / xiv + 298 pp. / ISBN 0-88920-414-4

The Water Lily Pond by Han Z. Li • 2004 / x + 254 pp. / ISBN 0-88920-431-4

The Life Writings of Mary Baker McQuesten: Victorian Matriarch edited by Mary J. Anderson • 2004 / xxii + 338 pp. / ISBN 0-88920-437-3

Seven Eggs Today: The Diaries of Mary Armstrong, 1859 and 1869 edited by Jackson W. Armstrong • 2004 / xvi + 228 pp. / ISBN 0-88920-440-3

Love and War in London: A Woman's Diary 1939–1942 by Olivia Cockett; edited by Robert W. Malcolmson • 2005 / xvi + 208 pp. / ISBN 0-88920-458-6

Incorrigible by Velma Demerson • 2004 / vi + 178 pp. / ISBN 0-88920-444-6

Auto/biography in Canada: Critical Directions edited by Julie Rak • 2005 / viii + 264 pp. / ISBN 0-88920-478-0

Tracing the Autobiographical edited by Marlene Kadar, Linda Warley, Jeanne Perreault, and Susanna Egan • 2005 / viii + 280 pp. / ISBN 0-88920-476-4

Must Write: Edna Staebler's Diaries edited by Christl Verduyn • 2005 / viii + 304 pp. / ISBN 0-88920-481-0

Pursuing Giraffe: A 1950s Adventure by Anne Innis Dagg • 2006 / xvi + 284 pp. (photos, 2 maps) / 978-0-88920-463-8

Food That Really Schmecks by Edna Staebler • 2007 / xxiv + 334 pp. / ISBN 978-0-88920-521-5

163256: A Memoir of Resistance by Michael Englishman • 2007 / xvi + 112 pp. (14 b&w photos) / ISBN 978-1-55458-009-5

The Wartime Letters of Leslie and Cecil Frost, 1915–1919 edited by R.B. Fleming • 2007 / xxxvi + 384 pp. (49 b&w photos, 5 maps) / ISBN 978-1-55458-000-2

Johanna Krause Twice Persecuted: Surviving in Nazi Germany and Communist East Germany by Carolyn Gammon and Christiane Hemker • 2007 / x + 170 pp. (58 b&w photos, 2 maps) / ISBN 978-1-55458-006-4

Watermelon Syrup: A Novel by Annie Jacobsen with Jane Finlay-Young and Di Brandt • 2007 / x + 268 pp. / ISBN 978-1-55458-005-7

Broad Is the Way: Stories from Mayerthorpe by Margaret Norquay • 2008 / x + 106 pp. (6 b&w photos) / ISBN 978-1-55458-020-0

Becoming My Mother's Daughter: A Story of Survival and Renewal by Erika Gottlieb • 2008 / x + 178 pp. (36 b&w illus., 17 colour) / ISBN 978-1-55458-030-9

Leaving Fundamentalism: Personal Stories edited by G. Elijah Dann • 2008 / xii + 234 pp. / ISBN 978-1-55458-026-2

Bearing Witness: Living with Ovarian Cancer edited by Kathryn Carter and Lauri Elit • 2009 / viii + 94 pp. / ISBN 978-1-55458-055-2

Dead Woman Pickney: A Memoir of Childhood in Jamaica by Yvonne Shorter Brown • 2010 / viii + 202 pp. / ISBN 978-1-55458-189-4

I Have a Story to Tell You by Seemah C. Berson • 2010 / xx + 288 pp. (24 b&w photos) / ISBN 978-1-55458-219-8

We All Giggled: A Bourgeois Family Memoir by Thomas O. Hueglin • 2010 / xiv + 232 pp. (20 b&w photos) / ISBN 978-1-55458-262-4

Just a Larger Family: Letters of Marie Williamson from the Canadian Home Front, 1940–1944 edited by Mary F. Williamson and Tom Sharp • 2011 / xxiv + 378 pp. (16 b&w photos) / ISBN 978-1-55458-323-2

Burdens of Proof: Faith, Doubt, and Identity in Autobiography by Susanna Egan • 2011 / x + 200 pp. / ISBN 978-1-55458-333-1

Accident of Fate: A Personal Account 1938–1945 by Imre Rochlitz with Joseph Rochlitz • 2011 / xiv + 226 pp. (50 b&w photos, 5 maps) / ISBN 978-1-55458-267-9

The Green Sofa by Natascha Würzbach, translated by Raleigh Whitinger • 2012 / xiv + 240 pp. (5 b&w photos) / ISBN 978-1-55458-334-8

Unheard Of: Memoirs of a Canadian Composer by John Beckwith • 2012 / x + 393 pp. (74 illus., 8 musical examples) / ISBN 978-1-55458-358-4

Borrowed Tongues: Life Writing, Migration, and Translation by Eva C. Karpinski • 2012 / viii + 274 pp. / ISBN 978-1-55458-357-7

Basements and Attics, Closets and Cyberspace: Explorations in Canadian Women's Archives edited by Linda M. Morra and Jessica Schagerl • 2012 / x + 338 pp. / ISBN 978-1-55458-632-5

The Memory of Water by Allen Smutylo • 2013 / x + 262 pp. (65 colour illus.) / ISBN 978-1-55458-842-8

The Unwritten Diary of Israel Unger, Revised Edition by Carolyn Gammon and Israel Unger • 2013 / ix + 230 pp. (b&w illus.) / ISBN 978-1-77112-011-1

Boom! Manufacturing Memoir for the Popular Market by Julie Rak • 2013 / viii + 249 pp. (b&w illus.) / ISBN 978-1-55458-939-5

Motherlode: A Mosaic of Dutch Wartime Experience by Carolyne Van Der Meer • 2014 / xiv + 132 pp. (b&w illus.) / ISBN 978-1-77112-005-0

Not the Whole Story: Challenging the Single Mother Narrative edited by Lea Caragata and Judit Alcalde • 2014 / x + 222 pp. / ISBN 978-1-55458-624-0

Street Angel by Magie Dominc • 2014 / vii + 154 pp. / ISBN 978-1-77112-026-5

In the Unlikeliest of Places: How Nachman Libeskind Survived the Nazis, Gulags, and Soviet Communism by Annette Libeskind Berkovits • 2014 / xiv + 282 pp. (6 colour illus.) / ISBN 978-1-77112-066-1

Kinds of Winter: Four Solo Journeys by Dogteam in Canada's Northwest Territories by Dave Olesen • 2014 / xii + 256 pp. (illus.) / ISBN 978-1-77112-118-7

Working Memory: Women and Work in World War II edited by Marlene Kadar and Jeanne Perreault • 2015 / vii + 243 pp. (illus.) / ISBN 978-1-77112—035-7

Wait Time: A Memoir of Cancer by Kenneth Sherman • 2016 / xiv + 138 pp. / ISBN 978-1-77112-188-0

Canadian Graphic: Picturing Life Narratives edited by Candida Rifkind and Linda Warley • 2016 / viii + 305 pp. (illus.) / ISBN 978-1-77112-179-8

Travels and Identities: Elizabeth and Adam Shortt in Europe, 1911 edited by Peter E. Paul Dembski • 2017 / xxii + 272 pp. (illus.) / ISBN 978-1-77112-225-2

Bird-Bent Grass: A Memoir, in Pieces by Kathleen Venema • 2018 • viii + 346 pp. / ISBN 978-1-77112-290-0

My Basilian Priesthood, 1961–1967 by Michael Quealey • 2019 • viii + 222 pp. / ISBN 978-1-77112-242-9

What the Oceans Remember: Searching for Belonging and Home by Sonja Boon • 2019 • xvi + 320 pp. / ISBN 978-1-77112-423-2

This book is made of paper from well-managed FSC® - certified forests, recycled materials, and other controlled sources.

PERMANENT

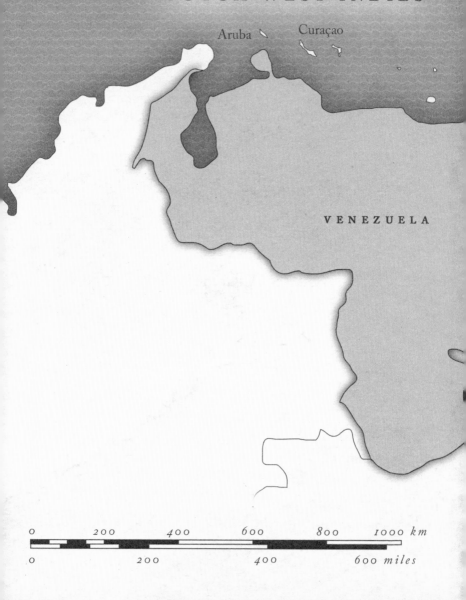

Caribbean Sea

DUTCH WEST INDIES

Aruba   Curaçao

VENEZUELA

| 0 | 200 | 400 | 600 | 800 | 1000 km |

| 0 | 200 | 400 | 600 miles |